DIFFERENCE AND DISABILITY IN THE MEDIEVAL ISLAMIC WORLD

DIFFERENCE AND DISABILITY IN THE MEDIEVAL ISLAMIC WORLD

BLIGHTED BODIES

Kristina L. Richardson

EDINBURGH
University Press

This book is dedicated to Wednesday, 9 May 2007

Edinburgh University Press Ltd
22 George Square, Edinburgh EH8 9LF
www.euppublishing.com

Typeset in 11/13 JaghbUni Regular by
Servis Filmsetting Ltd, Stockport, Cheshire, and
printed and bound in Great Britain by
CPI Group (UK) Ltd, Croydon CR0 4YY

A CIP record for this book is available from the British Library

ISBN 978 0 7486 4507 7 (hardback)
ISBN 978 0 7486 4508 4 (webready PDF)
ISBN 978 0 7486 6491 7 (epub)
ISBN 978 0 7486 6490 0 (Amazon ebook)

Contents

Abbreviations

BEO	*Bulletin d'Etudes Orientales*
BSOAS	*Bulletin of the School of Oriental and African Studies*
EI[2]	*Encyclopaedia of Islam*, 2nd edition
EI[3]	*Encyclopaedia of Islam*, 3rd edition
GAL	*Geschichte der Arabischen Litteratur*
IJMES	*International Journal of Middle East Studies*
JA	*Journal Asiatique*
JESHO	*Journal of the Economic and Social History of the Orient*
JRAS	*Journal of the Royal Asiatic Society*
JSAI	*Jerusalem Studies of Arabic and Islam*
MSR	*Mamlūk Studies Review*
SI	*Studia Islamica*
ZDMG	*Zeitschrift der Deutschen Morgenländischen Gesellschaft*

Figures

Acknowledgements

This book began as a graduate seminar paper on al-Jāḥiẓ's *Kitāb al-Burṣān* for Professor Michael Bonner's course on classical Arabic biographical dictionaries. Set on writing a dissertation on slavery, and convinced that a study of disability would have too few primary sources, I put aside my interest in this text. However, the paper did awaken me to the idea of working on a topic that had not been so thoroughly studied as slavery. Encouraged by Dana Sajdi's fascinating work on a Chester Beatty Library manuscript of an 18th-century Damascene barber's local history, I leafed through the Chester Beatty manuscript catalogue in the hope of finding a singular source on which I could build a similarly interesting study. To my amazement, I stumbled across A. J. Arberry's entry for MS 3838, Ibn Fahd's 950/AD 1543 'treatise on the afflictions suffered by famous scholars'. Only then did I begin to think a study of disability could be a possibility. With the support of the University of Michigan Rackham Graduate School and the International Institute, I arranged a visit to the Chester Beatty Library in the summer of 2005. Dr Elaine Wright, curator of the library's Islamic collections, was of immeasurable assistance during my stay there and granted permission to use a library image as the cover art.

My thesis adviser, Dr Kathryn Babayan, introduced me to al-Badrī's poetry anthology, which quickly led me to the other writers featured in this study. I am immensely grateful for her continued support and mentorship. Support from the National Endowment of the Humanities allowed me to work under the supervision of Dr Monica Green and Dr Emilie Savage-Smith in London in the summer of 2009. These two experts in medieval medical history helpfully introduced me to Latin and Arabic medical literature on *balādhur* and baldness, which has strengthened Chapters 2 and 5. My current intellectual home, Queens College of The City University of New York, graciously granted me a pre-tenure leave and encouraged my participation in the 2010 Faculty Fellowship Publishing Program. There, CUNY colleagues Brijraj Singh, Al Coppola, JoEllen DeLucia, Ramesh Mallipeddi, Karl Steel and Andrea Walkden generously read and commented on various chapters of this work. An ArtSTOR travel grant permitted me to visit archives and museums in Damascus. Julie Singer read

Chapter 2 closely, and usefully suggested ways to reorder the material to emphasise my argument about friendship. Adam Talib offered many keen suggestions and corrections for Chapter 3. Professor Geert Jan van Gelder closely read and helped me revise the introduction. I am extremely grateful for the professionalism and eagle-eyed readings of my copy-editor, Ivor Normand. I would also like to thank the anonymous readers of this manuscript for their helpful suggestions, and my incredibly patient editor at Edinburgh University Press, Ms Nicola Ramsey.

Living and working in New York City has been an incredible cultural experience. With the library, museum and university partnerships, my work is constantly stimulated with new ideas and discussions with learned colleagues. Annick des Roches, the Islamic art collections manager at the Metropolitan Museum of Art, invited me to view specimens and peruse the typed notes on various pieces of artwork at a time when the Islamic wing was closed to the public for renovation. There, I saw 55.121.40 and 1975.360, both of which are featured in this book. I would like to thank Dr Ozgen Felek for her translation of the Ottoman inscription on 55.121.40. And, were it not for my students at Queens College, I would never have looked so closely at representations of disability in visual sources. I thank them for expanding my view.

Especial gratitude goes to my godmother Lillie Virginia Ming, who sadly died just before this book went to press, my mother Ann, who wanted us children and raised us firmly and lovingly, my father Thomas for his patience and intellectual encouragement, my little sister Kelly, who has aided my writing with an endless supply of pens, ink cartridges, paper and notebooks over the years, and my daughter Cecilia Mae Rose is a rose is a rose is a rose.

Introduction

By the 9th/15th century, a distinct, stripped-down visual and literary aesthetic had found expression in Egyptian and Syrian art and literature. The paring down of scenic backgrounds to a wash of colour in paintings, of intricate forms to simplified outlines in visual media, of three-dimensional figures and sets to two-dimensional silhouettes in shadow theatre, and of idiom and formulae to more straightforward language in literature all departed from 8th/14th-century stylistic norms that prized thematic and visual detail, layering and explication. Two exemplary paintings that typify this style receive treatment here for their unique figural representations and later for their relationship to this book's central source-texts.

The earlier of the two is an unknown 8th/14th-century artist's water-colour sketch of men fighting and dying in hand-to-hand combat (Fig. I.1); and the art historian Esin Atıl has noted the 'unusual' simplicity of the painter's technique.[1] In this 14 × 18.3 cm remnant of a larger sketch, ink outlines of male bodies and body parts in profile appear violently posed. Because the blank background offers no sense of scale, situational context or pictorial depth, severed heads and amputated legs seem to float in the scene. One head has the point of a sword lodged in its crown, and a sword runs clean through the thigh of an amputated leg. The bodies are all painted with the same thin brown wash. Aside from one warrior who sports blue-grey forearm guards and a turban, and another man wearing part of a turban, the bodies are nude. The generic, impersonal facial features suggest the artist's disinterest in individual portraiture, which was unusual in 8th/14th-century Arab paintings. Rather, the forms and movements of an anonymous group of men create the greatest impression on the viewer.

A similar style can be observed in an Egyptian or Syrian manuscript of Ibn Zunbul's 1563 *Kitāb qānūn al-dunyá wa-ᶜajāʾibihā min mashriqihā li-maghribihā* (Order of the World and Its Wonders from East to West), which the author illustrated himself. This manuscript technically qualifies as an Ottoman Arab product, since the Ottomans conquered Mamluk Egypt and Syria in 922/1517; but its similarities to works such as the battle

Figure I.1 'Battle Scene'. (Source: Metropolitan Museum of Art, 1975.360, probably Egypt, 8th/14th century. Image copyright © The Metropolitan Museum of Art/Art Resource, New York.)

scene have led Duncan Haldane, for one, to argue for its continuities with Mamluk art and even to feature one of its illustrations in his book *Mamluk Painting*.[2] In most 10th/16th-century *ᶜajāʾib* manuscripts, intricately detailed bodies of monsters and demons, not ordinary human beings, filled the pages. Ibn Zunbul's artistic treatment of these extraordinary bodies is stylised, vivacious and simplified, evoking the minimalist expression of the 8th/14th-century watercolour. A two-folio watercolour in the 1563 piece depicts Solomon and Alexander building walls to sequester the hybrid demons and monsters that live at the end of the world. (Fig. I.2). Such images of monstrous races were common in illustrated *ᶜajāʾib* manuscripts, such as those of al-Qazwīnī's *ᶜAjāʾib*. Persis Berlekamp, in evaluating a 722/1322 copy that is missing several folios, was able to draw on the rather standardised layouts of these works to conjecture that, after a folio describing red-haired inhabitants of Ramni island and blind inhabitants of the islands of Zanzibar, another folio was originally interpolated. She noted: 'One folio apparently missing. It may have had illustrations of the following species: the soft-legged people; winged people with

Figure I.2 Ibn Zunbul, *Kitāb qānūn al-dunyá wa-ʿajāʾibihā min mashriqihāli-maghribihā.* (Source: Library of the Topkapı Sarayı Museum, Istanbul, Revan 1638, Egypt or Syria, 1563, fos. 118v–119r.)

elephant heads; winged people with horse heads; double-faced people; double-headed multi-legged people; and chest-faced people.'[3] Figure I.2 corresponds to this stock image of monstrosity, but is also singular for the simplified human forms that were gaining prominence in visual works. Yājūj, Mājūj (that is, Gog and Magog) and a third figure have elephantine ears, and one of them is shown fully nude with its indeterminate genitals exposed. Of the thirteen other figures behind the wall, one observes: two turbaned men (presumably scholars) without noses or mouths, who each carry a bare-headed bearded male on his shoulders; two yellow-haired supplicants gazing upwards with clasped hands; two individuals with tentacles for legs; two sets of conjoined bodies; a headless person with facial features carved onto the chest; and two other more anonymous-looking figures. As with the Mamluk sketch, the colour palette is muted and dominated by shades of brown. The background of the painting consists entirely of black curlicues and blue-grey dots. This apocalyptic sketch has inspired a range of strongly felt judgements. Richard Ettinghausen, for one, has suggested that it has an 'ornamental aspect', even noting its distinctively 'aggressive directness, revealing at the same time a crude boldness of design and disdain for nonessential detail'.[4] David James, in referring to the corpus of paintings in the manuscript, has judged that '[t]he painter's technical competence did not match his imagination though all [the illustrations] have a simple folkish charm'.[5] Most recently, Rachel Milstein and Bilha Moor praise it as one of only two 'brilliant, although extreme, representatives of their period'.[6] The force of the paintings and, consequently, of the modern judgements appears to stem from the sheer novelty of the artist's aesthetic, not necessarily painterly, technique.

Both of these singular pieces feature stylised, schematic human figures with crude and perfunctory facial features, but otherwise striking physical features, painted against plain or abstract backgrounds. In the 8th/14th-century sketch, the deracinated figures are neither situated in a physical scene nor attributed any sort of social context beyond what one can derive from their physical gestures, postures, garb and accoutrements, essentially from their very bodies. The emphasis lies not in small details, for these are entirely absent, but in the general impression of physicality, such as colour, shape, size and biological sex. One sees in these images no robes decorated with small flowers, no detailed landscapes, no intricate geometrical motifs, no architectural elements, only bodies that are mostly bare in an array of unsettling configurations. Bodies – depicted impersonally, bared unconventionally – are pulled sharply into focus, creating a sense of physical immediacy in the midst of battle chaos and the stirrings of the apocalypse.

What interests me here is not the representation of marked and broken bodies in the 8th/14th and 10th/16th centuries, because such images abounded, but rather the simplified, even crude, method of representing so many different types of bodies. The images project such force precisely because they have been rendered so ordinarily. These two images originated in 8th/14th- and 10th/16th-century Egypt and Syria, as do many of the sources in this study. (The remaining sources come from 10th/16th-century Mecca.) Like the paintings, the sources are distinguished by plainly expressed, but striking, representations of cognitive and physical difference in everyday sources, like personal letters, biographical and autobiographical writings, travel narratives, romantic poetry celebrating male and female beloveds, occasional poetry, polemical tracts, historical chronicles and theological treatises. The stylistic innovation of Mamluk and Ottoman paintings finds a counterpart in the literature of the period.

Blighted Bodies is a critical microhistory of a chain of six male Sunni scholars linked by the social bonds of friendship and academic mentorship in Cairo, Damascus and Mecca who produced writings about bodies marked by 'blights' (*ᶜāhāt*, in Arabic) – a category that included individuals who were cognitively and physically different, disabled and ill.[7] In relation to these six authors, physically marked people in these works figured as selves, lovers, family members, literary subjects and pious authorities, offering insight into the ways in which personal relationships and literary topoi shaped the substance of stories and histories. These men's writings, comprising a sizeable corpus of unpublished manuscripts and edited works, challenged perceptions and boundaries of the community and the category *ahl al-ᶜāhāt* (people of blights). Taken together, these works push the historian to reconsider the centrality of elected affinities in shaping trends in knowledge production, the prominence of physiognomic categories in everyday life and the capacity for anomalous bodies to threaten notions of human decency, Muslim piety and aesthetic beauty.

ᶜĀhāt

In classical Arabic, the term *ᶜāha* denotes a mark that spoils the presumed wholeness of a thing. In Ibn Manẓūr's 7th/13th-century dictionary *Lisān al-ᶜarab*, *ᶜāha* is defined by a single word – *āfa*, which itself means 'blight' or 'damage'. To contextualise the meaning of *ᶜāha*, Ibn Manẓūr cited the following hadith: '[The Prophet Muḥammad] forbade the selling of fruits until they were free of the blight or damage (*al-ᶜāha aw al-āfa*) that afflicts the seed and the fruits and rots them'.[8] In this entire entry, Ibn Manẓūr makes no reference to human or animal bodies, even though, as early as the 5th/11th century, a hagiographer attributed a warning not to interact with 'anyone who has an *ᶜāha* on his body' to Imām al-Shāfiᶜī (d. 204/820).[9]

Adapting modern categories of physical difference to past societies can obscure the particularities of local epistemologies and has clear limitations for the Islamic Middle Period. For one, classical Arabic vocabularies of physical difference are rather specialised and reflect views of body that differ significantly from Western views. The concept of *ᶜāha* does not correspond directly to the meaning of 'disability', a word that conveys a particular perspective on bodies. For one, the focus lies on the body's physical and cognitive limitations, which are determined against the model of a supposedly fully able body.[10] This category of blightedness or being marked encompasses more hybridity than the modern category of 'disability', as people of blights were characterised by physical deviance defined as debility, superability and physiognomic undesirability. (However, in modern standard Arabic, the term *iᶜāqa*, which literally means hindrance, obstacle or retardation, signifies 'disability'.) Disabilities like blindness, deafness and paraplegia; diseases like leprosy and halitosis; temporary ailments like ophthalmia and jaundice; and extraordinary physical features like blue eyes, crossed eyes, flat noses, black skin, baldness, hunched backs, lisps and thin beards all fell under the heading of *ᶜāhāt*. A failure to acknowledge these vocabularies presents other analytical limitations, as linguistic categories often reflect or create cultural categories. One legal historian has gone so far as to claim that 'in classical Islamic sources I could not identify any single general term that would combine all people with disabilities as a group . . . It is only in contemporary literature that we find somewhat generalised terms, such as *ashāb al-ᶜāhāt* or *dhawu al-ᶜāhāt* ("owners" or bearers of impairments, defects).'[11] In fact, both *aṣḥāb al-ᶜāhāt* and *dhawū al-ᶜāhāt* were in currency to refer to what I have termed here 'people of blights', making it possible for scholars to access disability in late medieval and early modern Islamicate history.

Blights formed a central category of identification in the Islamic Middle Ages, as evidenced by the extent to which biographers incorporated physical traits into descriptions of a person's intellect and character. Hilary Kilpatrick has noted that, in *Kitāb al-Aghānī* (The Book of Songs), Abū al-Faraj al-Iṣbahānī (d. 356/967) 'hardly ever refers to the physical appearance of his poets. If he does so, the aspects which interest him are skin colour, partial or complete blindness, lameness and extreme handsomeness.'[12] Furthermore, a person with a noticeable physical difference often incorporated this attribute into his very name, suggesting the body's centrality in subject formation and its prominence in the social imagination. 'The *kunya* [patronymic] reveals intellectual or moral qualities or defects, physical peculiarities . . . A great number of bodily peculiarities and defects are expressed in *alqāb* [nicknames].'[13]

The prose writer Abū ᶜUthmān ᶜAmr b. Baḥr al-Baṣrī (d. 255/868 or 869) acquired the sobriquet al-Jāḥiẓ (lit. 'the goggle-eyed one') because of his protruding eyeballs. He was renowned for his elegant turn of phrase, his keen wit and the breadth of literary subjects he undertook. One of his lesser-studied works transfers this cultural tendency to privilege abnormal physical characteristics as salient identifiers into a way of structuring biographies. His *Kitāb al-burṣān wa'l-ᶜurjān wa'l-ḥūlān wa'l-ᶜumyān* (The Book of the Leprous, the Lame, the Cross-Eyed and the Blind) is an unusual work of anecdotal biography about human and non-human animals that lived with physical blights. (The medical historian Michael Dols has referred to the book as a 'curious compilation'.)[14] In the book's introduction, al-Jāḥiẓ discusses the disfigurements and illnesses that he will use as anecdotal categories. 'I will mention what is said about people lacking beard hair and eyebrows, people with warts, and about hunchbacks, and how body parts (*al-jawāriḥ*) in these illnesses are described and what emerges in poetry, anecdotes, parables and traditions.'[15] Completed sometime between 206/821 and 237/851, *Kitāb al-burṣān* is arranged topically, from roughly the longest section (lepers) to the shortest (handedness), a structure recalling that of the Qur'ān, whose chapters are also arranged by decreasing length. Recognising his own proximity to the subject matter, al-Jāḥiẓ even dedicates a brief section to goggle-eyed people, though he conspicuously does not mention himself there.[16] It is possible that al-Jāḥiẓ wrote other similarly themed works. In his own *Al-Bayān wa'l-tabyīn*, al-Jāḥiẓ refers to works of his titled *Kitāb al-ᶜurjān* (The Book of the Lame) and *Kitāb al-jawāriḥ* (The Book of Body Parts), which he noted mentions 'leprosy (*al-baraṣ*), lameness, left-handedness, hernia, frontal baldness (*al-ṣalᶜ*), hunchbacks, those bald from an illness (*al-qaraᶜ*), and other types of defects of body parts'.[17] Charles Pellat suspects that *Kitāb al-jawāriḥ* is *al-Burṣān* under another title.[18] Pellat also names *Kitāb dhawī al-ᶜāhāt* (The Book of Those with Physical Blights) as one among al-Jāḥiẓ's corpus of more than 200 works, but offers no comment about its relation to *al-Burṣān*.

Modern Historiography

Bodies in Islamicate and Near Eastern scholarship have been approached from various theoretical positions. More broadly conceived studies on the body, like Bedhioufi Hafsi and Malek Chebel's investigations of Muslim bodies in colonial discourses, Fuad Khuri's close readings of Islamic source-texts to understand the contemporary 'Islamic' body, and Traki Zannad-Bouchrara's investigation of bodies and space have tended to be presentist in scope and sociological or anthropological in method.[19] Hafsi and Zannad-Bouchrara are both French-educated Tunisian sociologists who have interrogated the effects of colonial domination on indigenous notions of the social and ritual bodies in Islamic North Africa. Khuri, an anthropologist, draws on Islamic foundational texts to discern body ideology in the contemporary Arab-Islamic world, then reads the body as a system of semiotic signs. His method of using 1st/7th-century texts to decode physical gestures, movements and postures for their universal meanings in a so-called Islamic culture has been critiqued as problematic.[20] Chebel, who is also an anthropologist, examines the anatomical and symbolic dimensions of the body in late 20th-century North Africa. Looking at vocabularies of the body, reproduction, individual body parts, death, body language, superstition and magic, he evokes the ways in which the body was lived, experienced and understood.

General histories on disability are less common, and the only monograph I am aware of, Fareed Haj's *Disability in Antiquity* (1970), is rather dated. This anecdotal survey of disablement caused by disease, armed conflict and corporal punishment summarises much of this history, but advances no arguments about it. In spite of the title, the temporal range is 632 to 1258 CE in the central Islamic lands. More recent encyclopaedic entries on bodies and disabilities frame methodological issues and present historiographical information – work that was not done in the seminal survey publication of Islamicate studies, *The Encyclopaedia of Islam* (1st and 2nd edns).[21] *The Encyclopaedia of the Qur'an* includes entries on specific body parts, illnesses and sense faculties.[22] Separate entries on disabilities and the female body appear in the *Encyclopedia of Women and Islamic Cultures*, and a brief article on disabilities is included in *Medieval Islamic Civilization: An Encyclopedia*.[23] Simply the fact of their inclusion in these works signals an important recognition of these topics as legitimate categories of academic inquiry.

Among historians of Islamicate literatures, only Sadān and Malti-Douglas have taken up the subject of disabled bodies, with Sadān specialising in Abbasid literature about physical defects, and Malti-Douglas concentrating on blindness in the Mamluk period.[24] Art historians have written extensively about figural representation in Islamicate art, though studies of visual representations of disabled people have yet to be completed.[25] Several scholars of the Qur'an and Islamic law have focused their research on the *disabled* body as an analytical category in classical and contemporary legal sources.[26] Ghaly expertly explores a number of theological principles and theological debates in the classical and post-classical eras on bodies and disability. In Islamicate historical studies, research on the body has focused on ritual bodies,[27] gendered bodies,[28] sexual bodies[29] and disabled/marked bodies.[30] Two fields that are under-developed are ethics and archaeology. Leslie Peirce has described what could be a promising opening into the first field: two 10th/16th-century Ottoman Turkish works that link morality to specific body parts and even to certain illnesses.[31] Archaeologists of disease and disability have recovered considerable information about many pre-modern societies, though work on the Middle East could be increased. One intriguing finding was unearthed during an excavation of an Israeli grave near the presumed site of Jesus' baptism. The 3rd/9th-century burial site contained the remains of thirty-four Nubian men and women, many of whose skeletons showed evidence of 'tuberculosis, leprosy and facial disfigurement. Those individuals, attracted to the site, traveled enormous distances in hope of washing away their illness.'[32] Just as the study of disability offers openings into the history of Nubian Christian pilgrimage, healing and sacred spaces, so too does it have the potential to speak to a range of disciplinary questions and historical moments.

Historians of disability in the Middle East have begun incorporating into their own works insights from the debates of theorists and historians of the body and disability. Two major currents of thought that have been integrated into the scholarship are the recognition of the constructedness of conceptions of the body and the positioning of disabled people as historical subjects, not just objects of study. Scholars of the medieval and early modern Middle East have deployed various methods in studying the body as a category of historical and anthropological analysis, and with varying effects have used particular notions of the body to understand histories of disability. In his sweeping history of mental illness, or madness, in Islamicate societies of the 3rd/9th to 10th/16th centuries, Michael Dols recognised that the definitions and boundaries of sanity are culturally constructed. To understand culturally specific ideas about the body, Dols explored the ways in which mental illnesses were treated. As suggested by the title, Dols examined cases of *junūn*, which, though an enormous category, does not include the many degrees and types of mental illness recognised in the Islamicate world. Stephan H. Stephan has produced what could be considered a companion piece to this work in which he explores the vocabularies of mental illness.[33] Dols systematically presents medical, religious and magical cures of mental illness to show how each model presumes a particular attitude to the body. For instance, a medical model of cure presupposes that illness originates within the body, whereas a religious model is based on divine origin and control of bodily processes.

Medieval Historiography

In the introduction of *Kitāb al-Burṣān*, al-Jāḥiẓ preserved the earliest known *ᶜāhāt*-themed Arabic writings, all of which were written by al-Haytham b. ᶜAdī (d. 207/822). The first is a mostly unnarrativised list of noble Muslim men divided into five categories: those who were blind, one-eyed, cross-eyed, blue- or green-eyed (*azraq*) or had protruding teeth.[34] Al-Jāḥiẓ discussed Ibn ᶜAdī twice in his introduction, first affirming that though he has known of Ibn ᶜAdī's piece of writing (*kitāb*) about lepers, the lame, blind, deaf and cross-eyed, he does not want to use these same categories in *Kitāb al-Burṣān*. (It is unclear whether this 'piece of writing' constitutes a longer version of the list of sixty-one men or is an entirely different, perhaps narrativised, work about people of blights.) In the second instance, he reproduced a part of Ibn ᶜAdī's list that has not survived elsewhere – the names of ten lame male *ashrāf* (noble Muslims), adding that '[Ibn ᶜAdī] mentioned no others besides these. However, he did mention the blind, but those he neglected to mention are more than those he did mention.'[35]

This evidence of Ibn ᶜAdī's writing supports a 7th/13th-century writer's claims that Ibn ᶜAdī incurred people's hatred in his lifetime because he revealed their faults and shortcomings (*maᶜāyib*).[36] In spite of a possible backlash from one's contemporaries, other Abbasid writers, like al-Jāḥiẓ, expanded on Ibn ᶜAdī's list of *ashrāf* who were physically blighted. In *Kitāb al-muḥabbar*, Abū Jaᶜfar Muḥammad b. Ḥabīb's (d. 245/860) lists of the physically marked *ashrāf* include some of the same names as Ibn ᶜAdī's, but also contain additional names and incorporate anecdotes and poetry. He also adjusted the categories of physical difference, adding to them leprosy, lameness and thin-beardedness, and omitting blue eyes.[37] Another work of Ibn Ḥabīb's, *Kitāb al-munammaq fī akhbār Quraysh*, follows the same structure and uses the same categories as in *Kitāb al-Muḥabbar*, but its lists and anecdotes focus exclusively on members of the Qurayshi tribe.[38]

Ibn Qutayba (d. 276/889) compiled a list of *ahl al-ᶜāhāt* in his encyclopaedic *Kitāb al-maᶜārif* that begins with the following descriptions of prominent 1st/7th- and 2nd/8th-century Muslim men who possessed multiple *ᶜāhāt*:

> ᶜAṭāʾ b. Abī Rabāḥ [d. 114 or 115/733 or 734] was black, one-eyed, paralysed, flat-nosed and lame. Then he went blind after that. Abān b. ᶜUthmān b. ᶜAffān [d. 105/723 or 724] was deaf – extremely deaf – and had leprosy. His body turned green wherever the leprosy afflicted him, but not on his face. He was hemiplegic, and it was said in Medina, 'May God bestow on you Abān's hemiplegia', as this was his affliction. He was also cross-eyed. Masrūq b. al-Ajdaᶜ [d. 63/682] was hunchbacked and lame because of a wound that he sustained at Qādisiyya. He was also hemiplegic. Al-Aḥnaf b. Qays was one-eyed, and it is said that he either lost his eye in Samarqand or because of a pox. He had a twisted foot and walked on its outer edge. Abū al-Aswad al-Duʾalī [d. 69/688 or 689] was lame, hemiplegic and suffered from halitosis. ᶜAmr b. ᶜAmr b. ᶜUdas [death date unknown], a horseman of the Banū Dārim, had leprosy and halitosis. It is said that his children had mouths like dogs. Al-Aqraᶜ b. Ḥābis [death date unknown] was lame and, due to illness, bald (*aqraᶜ*), and for this reason was called Al-Aqraᶜ. ᶜUbayda al-Salmanī [d. 72/694] was deaf and one-eyed.[39]

Possessing multiple aberrant traits intensified their ugliness, which explains their prominence at the head of the section. After this opening narrative come sections on lepers, the lame, the deaf, hand and nose amputees, those with a mutilated hand, the cross-eyed, the blue-eyed, the bald (*al-ṣal*ᶜ), the thin-bearded, those with protruding teeth, those with bad breath, the one-eyed and the blind. Poetry and anecdotes about the profiled men's physical conditions fill out these sections. In spite of Ibn Qutayba's expansion of categories of blight, the temporal limits of the first century of Islam remain in place. *ᶜĀhāt* remained for many more centuries useful categories for cataloguing the major actors of the early caliphal period. In the case of Abān, son of ᶜUthmān the third Sunni caliph, hemiplegia became his personal disease, a phenomenon reminiscent of diseases in 20th-century America being named after the researcher who discovered it (for example, Parkinson's disease) or renamed after a famous person afflicted with a known illness (for example, Lou Gehrig's disease). Here, the Medinan community appropriated the symbol of Abān's hemiplegia as prideful, and Ibn Qutayba reinforced this 'metaphor of illness' for his 3rd/9th-century audience. The other lists rather function to define physical otherness for the nascent Muslim community, all the while demonstrating that none of these conditions disqualifies a person from being Muslim or precludes full acceptance in the Muslim community. The normative body belongs to an Arab male who has dark (not blue or green) eyes, dark (not light) hair, a hooked (not flat) nose, a full (not thin) beard, and brown (not black) skin, and who stands at medium height. The archetype of male beauty was the Prophet Muḥammad, who is described in Qur'ān 33: 21 as a 'beautiful model' (*uswa ḥasana*).

Ibn Qutayba also wrote about men's and women's *ᶜāhāt* in a chapter on women in *ᶜUyūn al-akhbār*.[40] Poetry, hadith and sayings of the Prophet's companions fill sections on tallness, shortness, beards, eyes (one-eyed, bleary-eyed, cross-eyed and blue-eyed), noses, halitosis, leprosy, lameness and hernia. Ibn Qutayba recorded elsewhere his amazement at the lengths to which people would detail other's physical faults. 'In this *majlis*, a lot of words flowed about the defects of a dark-skinned slave, but I didn't see anyone there who knew the difference between toes that overlap over neighbouring ones and the ankle bone, [or who knew] a club-foot from a deformed foot, or dark lips from a white blotch on the inside of dark lips'.[41] Writing in the same period, the poet and caliph who reigned for a single day, Ibn al-Muᶜtazz (d. 296/908), wrote romantic epigrams about men with ophthalmia and fever.[42]

Mufīd al-ᶜulūm wa-mubīd al-humūm (The Provider of Useful Kinds of Knowledge and Remover of Sorrows), an encyclopaedia compiled circa 551/1156, features information that its author, Jamāl al-Dīn Muḥammad b. Aḥmad al-Qazwīnī, judged to be useful information for an educated reader.[43] The work is organised into books. In 'The Book on Histories', chapter 11 is entitled 'Those with *ᶜāhāt*'; chapter 12 is called '*ᶜĀhāt* of the descendants of the Prophet'; and the title of chapter 13 is 'Also about *ᶜāhāt*, but with some additions'.[44] None of the three chapters features new material. Earlier recorded lists are reproduced.

In *Kitāb al-aᶜlāq al-nafīsa*, an encyclopaedic work on mathematics, geography and history, the Persian author Aḥmad b. ᶜUmar b. Rusta (d. 4th/10th century) lists the names of famous people with *ᶜāhāt*, those who were excessively tall and short, those who had multiple *ᶜāhāt*, lepers, the lame, the deaf, amputees (nose, ear and hand), the cross-eyed, the blue-eyed, the bald (*al-aṣlaᶜ*), one-eyed descendants of the Prophet, the blind, those who were post-term infants and those who were pre-term.[45] Aside from omitting the categories of mutilation, thin-beardedness and halitosis, and adding sections on extreme height, Ibn Rusta's section follows Ibn Qutayba's discussion in *Kitāb al-maᶜārif* rather closely, with only some minor word variations. In the same century, Abū al-Ḥasan b. Aḥmad Sarī al-Raffā (d. 4th/10th century) penned erotic verses celebrating male beloveds with blue eyes, crossed eyes and ophthalmia; and the Buyid vizier Ibn ᶜAbbād (d. 385/995) praised a young lisper with these verses:

> I asked a young fawn: What is your name?
> He answered simpering: ᶜAbbath [for Abbas, a common name].
> I started to lisp myself,
> I asked him: where are the cupth and the plateth?[46]

Al-Baṣā'ir wa'l-dhakhā'ir (Visions and Treasures), an anthology on literary topics by the Buyid writer Abū Ḥayyān al-Tawḥīdī (d. 414/1023), defined a number of physical traits, some of which were considered blights, with incredible precision.

> If his eye protrudes visibly, then he is *jāḥiẓ*. If his eye is small and narrow, then he is *aḥwaṣ*. If his wanders towards his ear, he is *akhzar* . . . If his nose is short and narrow, then he is *adhlaf*. If his eye is green, then he is called *azraq*. If it [the eye] is between white and green, he is called *ashhal*. If they are veiny, he is *ashkal*.[47]

Though al-Tawḥīdī does not mention any historical figures in this section of his book, the inclusion of clear definitions of types of physical difference offers insight into their salience for writers of the period.

Al-Thaᶜālibī's (d. 429/1038) *Kitāb laṭāᵓif al-maᶜārif* (The Book of Curious and Entertaining Information) is another encyclopaedic compilation with a section on *ahl al-ᶜāhāt*. Departing from the organisational schemes of earlier writers, he starts by dividing his list of men with *ᶜāhāt* into social groups: rulers, Qurayshi, poets and legal scholars. Then the list shifts to being organised by physical traits: the one-eyed, one-eyed military commanders, the blind, rulers who were blinded, the very tall, the very short, post-term and pre-term infants and bald caliphs.

In *Talqīḥ fuhūm*, Ibn al-Jawzī (d. 597/1201) based his list of names of notable men and women with physical blights on the works of Ibn Rusta and al-Thaᶜālibī.[48] One major difference is his section on black notables, which includes the Companions of the Prophet, the pious men who came after them, poets, ascetics and female devotees. This section is the only one with such a detailed subcategorisation of people. According to Taqī al-Dīn al-Badrī (d. 894/1489), Shams al-Dīn Muḥammad al-Jazarī al-Shāfiᶜī (d. after 660/1262) included a list of blind notables in his similarly titled work *Tanqīḥ fuhūm al-āthār* (Re-Examination of the Knowledge of Hadith).[49]

With the exception of al-Jāḥiẓ's *Kitāb al-Burṣān*, these pre-8th/14th-century works were largely enumerations of names. The 8th/14th century marked the resurgence of narrativised biographies of *ahl al-ᶜāhāt*. Ṣalāḥ al-Dīn al-Ṣafadī's (d. 764/1363) *Nakt al-himyān ᶜalá nukat al-ᶜumyān* (Emptying the Pockets for Anecdotes about the Blind) consists of 313 biographical entries about prominent blind men, and in it he apologised for not using al-Khaṭīb al-Baghdādī's (d. 463/1071) work about blind men, because he could not find a copy from his local bookseller or in libraries.[50] His much later *Al-Shuᶜūr bi'l-ᶜūr* (Knowledge of the One-Eyed) consists of entries about one-eyed men and women. According to al-Sakhāwī (d. 902/1497), al-Ṣafadī wrote as yet unrecovered histories about weak-sighted and hunchbacked people.[51] He was also a prolific poet whose *Al-Ḥusn al-ṣarīḥ fī miᵓat malīḥ* includes many verses about men who bore *ᶜāhāt* on their bodies. Some of these romantic poems, including ones about a lame man and a man with a wounded cheek, are preserved in al-Badrī's *Ghurrat al-ṣabāḥ* (The Shining Dawn), a work that will be treated in greater detail in Chapter 3.[52]

Methodology

Blighted Bodies takes up this literary history in early 9th/15th-century Cairo, carries it into 9th/15th-century Damascus and culminates in 10th/16th-century Mecca, incorporating throughout the analysis a social, lived dimension to a close reading of texts. It is meant to highlight texts that engage sustainedly with *ahl al-ᶜāhāt* and to contextualise them with the voices of the authors, communities and audiences that created and responded to these texts, and that sometimes in responding managed to alter the texts. Although *ahl al-ᶜāhāt* signifies more than just disabled people, it is through the lens of disability aesthetics that I have chosen to approach this study, because this method invites consideration of blighted bodies, and of other bodies they encounter, and even forces me to consider how my own reactions to these bodies may influence my analysis. '*Aesthetics* studies the way that some bodies make other bodies feel', in Tobin Siebers' succinct encapsulation of the field. Investigating emotion places the individual at the centre of historical inquiry, a method that provides a critical launching point for larger social histories, allowing historians to trace broad social responses back to the aggregation of individual responses. As Siebers notes, 'when bodies produce feelings of pleasure or pain, they also invite judgments about whether they should be accepted or rejected in the human community'.[53] The physical body becomes interchangeable with the social body through a metonymic identification. Aesthetic theory invites us to consider stages of encounters and exchanges that reveal dialectics of influence, rather than a unidirectional flow of power from the top down. The ways in which dominant and subjugated bodies participate in sustaining systems of oppression form the foundation of all theories of difference. What is interesting about combining aesthetic and disability theories is that 'disability is the master trope of human disqualification, not because disability theory is superior to race, class, or sex/gender theory, but because all oppressive systems function by reducing human variation to deviancy and inferiority defined on the mental and physical plane'.[54] Disability theory pares down a host of interactions to discrete bodies and our reactions to them, much as the simplified visual expressions in Mamluk and Ottoman watercolours (and, as we shall see, texts) invited viewers to confront blunt representations of all sorts of bodies.

Chapter Summaries

The chapter structure of this book developed from my methodological choices. If aesthetic theory privileges 'stages of encounters and exchanges' and disability theory focuses on embodied systems of oppression, then a history of writers (some blighted) and of their blighted literary and historical subjects finds its richest representation as an amalgam of interconnected personal exchanges. Aside from the first chapter, each chapter focuses on people and texts connected to people and/or texts featured in earlier chapters. By exploring a chain of men writing on a shared theme, one not only sees how mentors and friends shaped their professional work, but also begins to appreciate the role of emotional bonds in the history of knowledge production. Chapter 1 explores the theme of *ʿāhāt* in religious and juridical sources and examines representations of the bodies of the Prophet Muḥammad. According to Islamic hagiographical writings, Muḥammad possessed a raised disc of skin the size of a pigeon's egg between his shoulder blades that resembled a hump but was described by early Muslim theologians as a singular 'mark of prophethood'. His body is thus *perfectly* marked, as opposed to unblemished, and he is never described in Islamic sources as being among the *ahl al-ᶜāhāt*. Chapter 2 traces the late medieval development of a body aesthetic that invited appreciation of blighted bodies, drawing mainly from the personal letters and poetry of the Cairene hadith specialist and writer Shihāb al-Dīn al-Ḥijāzī (d. 875/1471). His literary production and personal relationships were fraught with the intersections of body aesthetics, Sufism, disability, illness and sexuality. In his early twenties, he survived an overdose on *balādhur*, a potentially fatal drug valued by scholars for its ability to enhance memorisation, though the ordeal marked his body with red boils, forcing him to realign perceptions of his own body and to craft new visions of physical desirability. His friendships and encounters with six other men named Shihāb al-Dīn (collectively known as the Seven *Shihāb*s, meaning the Seven Shooting Stars), especially the famed intellectual Shihāb al-Dīn b. Hajar al-ᶜAsqalānī (d. 852/1449), give texture to al-Ḥijāzī's attempts to make sense of the extreme ostracism he endured after the overdose, feeling sequestered like the demons of the 1563 painting, who, marked in body, are relegated to the end of the world. Chapter 3 reveals how the body is remembered in two anthologies assembled by al-Ḥijāzī's student, the Damascene Taqī al-Dīn al-Badrī (d. 894/1489), who compiled prose materials about the human eye and erotic verses about men with marked bodies. In the second anthology, al-Badrī groups the verses by blight. The reassembly of poems about subjective body parts creates a hybrid corpus of work and a conglomerate human body that is the sum of its individual diseased parts. Al-Badrī is not only assembling a set of poems, but also reassembling a segmented male body that is wholly blighted. The disjointed bodies of the Mamluk battle sketch recall al-Badrī's anthology of blighted body parts. Chapter 4 turns to the relationship of al-Ḥijāzī with another of his Damascene students, Yūsuf b. ᶜAbd al-Hādī (d. 909/1503), who transcribed a list of 2nd/8th- and 3rd/9th-century hadith-transmitters with blighted bodies. This chapter also draws out Ibn ᶜAbd al-Hādī's close relationship with his most famous student, Ibn Ṭūlūn (d. 953/1546), a Damascene historian who wrote a book consoling people who were losing their eyesight. Finally, Chapter 5 gives dimension to the close friendship of Ibn Ṭūlūn with Ibn Fahd (d. 954/1547), a Meccan historian who wrote a book that controversially exposed some of his contemporaries as being bald underneath their turbans. (Ordinarily, a man would only have removed his turban in public to perform ablutions before prayer or to enter public baths. Some of the fighters in the Mamluk battle sketch are depicted without turbans, underscoring the violent upending of norms that combat produces.) His work so angered these men that they seized the book from his home and washed the pages at the local mosque, dissolving the ink. He attempted to undo their shame (and his own) through public debates with the Meccan theologian Ibn Ḥajar al-Haytamī (d. 974/1567), who had been named in the book as bald, about the lawfulness of revealing others' physical blights and by ultimately rewriting the work, omitting the names of these bald men.

Notes

1. Esin Atıl, *Renaissance of Islam: Art of the Mamluks* (Washington, DC: Smithsonian Press, 1981), p. 254, fn. 36. An 8th/14th-century Shirazi illustration of two individuals and a shepherd with his flock shares artistic elements with this work. See *Kitab-i Samak Ayzar*, Bodleian Library, University of Oxford, MS Ousely 380, 1330–40 CE, fo. 387v.
2. Duncan Haldane, *Mamluk Painting* (Warminster: Aris and Phillips, 1978), p. 56.
3. Persis Berlekamp, 'From Iraq to Fars: Tracking Cultural Transformations in the 1322 Qazwīnī ᶜAjāʾib Manuscript', in Anna Contadini (ed.), *Arab Painting: Text and Image in Illustrated Arabic Manuscripts* (Leiden: Brill, 2010), p. 90.
4. Richard Ettinghausen, *Arab Painting* (New York: Rizzoli, 1977), p. 182.
5. David James, 'Arab Painting, 358 A.H./969 A.D.–1112 A.H./1700 A.D.', *Mārg: A Magazine of the Arts* 29.3 (June 1976), p. 46.
6. Rachel Milstein and Bilha Moor, 'Wonders of a Changing World: Late Illustrated *ᶜAjāʾib* Manuscripts (Part I)', *JSAI* 32 (2006), p. 2.
7. One definition of 'blight' is 'an eruption on the human skin consisting of minute reddish pimples', and it has application to an incident that will be analysed in Chapter 2. However, I am using this term in its more general sense of 'any cause of impairment, deterioration or decay'.
8. Muḥammad b. Mukarram Ibn Manẓūr (d. 711/1311 or 1312), *Lisān al-ᶜarab* (Language of the Arabs) (Beirut: Dār Ṣādir, 1956), 13:520. The entries for *ᶜāha* in al-Fīrūzābādī's (d. 815/1412 or 1413) *Al-Qāmūs al-muḥīṭ* (Comprehensive Dictionary) and al-Zabīdī's (d. 1205/1791) dictionary *Tāj al-ᶜarūs* (Crown of the Bride), a commentary on *Al-Qāmūs*, very closely mirror the one in *Lisān al-ᶜarab*. See al-Fīrūzābādī, 2:579 of the 1855 Cairene edition, and al-Zabīdī, 9:401 of the 1888 Egyptian edition.
9. Abū Bakr al-Bayhaqī (d. 458/1065 or 1066), *Manāqib al-Shāfiᶜī* (Excellent Deeds of al-Shāfiᶜī), ed. Aḥmad Saqr (Cairo: Dār al-turāth, 1971), 2:132.
10. Of course, disability scholars take issue with the notion that any body is

perfectly able-bodied or whole, as all bodies operate within specific limitations. Some scholars have linked the social classification of bodies by their cognitive and physical capabilities with the rise of neoliberal capitalism, which values bodies for their productive labour, privileging the able-bodied person as the ultimate citizen. See Robert McRuer's essay 'Capitalism and Disabled Identity: Sharon Kowalski, Interdependency, and Queer Domesticity' in his *Crip Theory: Cultural Signs of Queerness and Disability* (New York: New York University Press, 2006), pp. 77–102.

11. Vardit Rispler-Chaim, *Disability in Islamic Law* (New York: Springer, 2006), p. 3.
12. Hilary Kilpatrick, 'Abū l-Farağ's Profile of Poets: A 4th/10th Century Essay at the History and Sociology of Arabic Literature', *Arabica* 44.1 (1997), p. 105. These categories are not so arbitrary as they appear. Alexander Borg has suggested that, because shape and colour 'differentiate surface qualities in the visual world[, . . . i]t may therefore be symptomatic of a principle of iconicity in the morphological subsystem of Arabic grammar, determining the correlation of form and meaning, that attributes of both shape and color in this language [classical Arabic] are encoded by the same canonic form: the scheme *aCCaC*'. See his 'Towards a History and Typology of Color Categorization in Colloquial Arabic', in Robert E. MacLaury et al. (eds), *Anthropology of Color: Interdisciplinary Multilevel Modeling* (Amsterdam: John Benjamins Publishing, 2007), p. 264.
13. Annemarie Schimmel, *Islamic Names* (Edinburgh: Edinburgh University Press, 1989), pp. 50, 54. For representative examples of such *alqāb*, see M. A.-C. Barbier de Meynard, 'Surnoms et sobriquets dans la littérature arabe', *JA* 9 (March–April 1907), pp. 173–244.
14. Michael Dols, 'The Leper in Islamic Society', *Speculum* 58.4 (October 1983), p. 901.
15. Al-Jāḥiẓ, *Kitāb al-burṣān wa'l-ᶜurjān wa'l-ᶜumyān wa'l-ḥūlān* (The Book of the Leprous, the Lame, the Blind and the Cross-Eyed), ed. Muḥammad Mursī al-Khawlī (Cairo/Beirut: s.n., 1972), p. 9. For an outline of the book's contents, see pp. 570–81 of the 1990 Beirut edition.
16. Ibid. p. 276.
17. Al-Jāḥiẓ, *Al-Bayān wa'l-tabyīn*, ed. ᶜAbd al-Salām Muḥammad Hārūn (Cairo: Maktabat al-khānjī, 1968), 1:94–5.
18. Charles Pellat, 'Nouvel essai d'inventaire de l'oeuvre Ġahizienne', *Arabica* 31 (1984), pp. 129, 137.
19. Hafsi, *Corps et traditions islamiques: divisions ontologiques et ritualités du corps* (Tunis: Noir sur Blanc, 2000); Chebel, *Le corps dans la tradition au Maghreb* (Paris: Presses Universitaires de France, 1984); Khuri, *The Body in Islamic Culture* (London: Saqi Books, 2001); Zannad-Bouchrara, *Symboliques corporelles et espaces musulmans* (Tunis: Cérès, 1984); and Anna Barska, 'Ways of Understanding Body in the Maghreb', *Hemispheres* 21 (2006), pp. 17–29.

20. Madeline Zilfi, 'Review of *The Body in Islamic Culture*', *MESA Bulletin* 39.2 (2005), pp. 206–7.
21. According to a 9 November 2006 email from Everett Rowson, *EI*[3] will include entries on the body, sexuality and disability.
22. See s.v. 'Ears', 'Eyes', 'Face', 'Feet', 'Hand(s)', 'Heart', 'Womb', 'Insanity', 'Plagues' and 'Hearing and Deafness'.
23. *Encyclopedia of Women and Islamic Cultures*, 1st edn, s.v. 'Disabilities, Arab States', 'Body: Female', 'Science, Medicalization and the Female Body'; Meri and Bacharach (eds), *Medieval Islamic Civilization: An Encyclopedia*, 1st edn, s.v. 'Disabilities'.
24. Yūsuf Sadān, *Al-Adab al-ᶜarabī al-hāzil wa nawādir al-thuqalāʾ: al-ᶜāhāt wa 'al-masāwiʾ al-insāniyya wa makānatuhā fī al-adab al-rāqī* (ᶜAkkā: Maktabat wa-Maṭbaᶜat al-Sarūjī, 1983); Fedwa Malti-Douglas, '*Mentalités* and Marginality: Blindness and Mamluk Civilisation', in C. Issawi et al (eds), *The Islamic World from Classical to Modern Times: Essays in Honour of Bernard Lewis* (Princeton: Darwin Press, 1989), pp. 211–37.
25. See, for example, Rachel Milstein, *Miniature Painting in Ottoman Baghdad* (Costa Mesa, CA: Mazda Publishers, 1990); Eva Baer, *The Human Figure in Islamic Art: Inheritances and Islamic Transformations* (Costa Mesa, CA: Mazda Publishers, 2004); Emilie Savage-Smith, 'Anatomical Illustration in Arabic Manuscripts', in Anna Contadini (ed.), *Arab Painting: Text and Image in Illustrated Arabic Manuscripts* (Leiden: E. J. Brill, 2010), pp. 147–60.
26. See Rispler-Chaim, *Disability*; Mohammed Ghaly, *Islam and Disability: Perspectives in Theory and Jurisprudence* (London and New York: Routledge, 2010) and his 'Islam en Handicap: theologische perspectieven', *Theologisch Debat* 2.3 (2005), pp. 20–3; Muḥammad b. Maḥmūd Ḥawwā, *Ḥuqūq dhawī al-iḥtiyājāt al-khāṣṣah fī al-sharīᶜat al-Islāmiyya* (Beirut: Dār Ibn Ḥazm li'l-ṭibāᶜa wa'l-nashr wa'l-tawzīᶜ, 2010).
27. See, for example, Brannon Wheeler, 'Touching the Penis in Islamic Law', *History of Religions* 44.2 (2004), pp. 89–119; Megan Reid, 'Exemplars of Excess: Devotional Piety in Medieval Islam, 1200–1450 CE' (PhD diss., Princeton University, 2005); Shahzad Bashir, 'Shah Isma'il and the Qizilbash: Cannibalism in the Religious History of Early Safavid Iran', *History of Religions* 45.3 (2006), pp. 234–56; Bashir, *Sufi Bodies: Religion and Society in Medieval Islam* (New York: Columbia University Press, 2011); Scott Kugle, 'The Heart of Ritual is the Body: Anatomy of an Islamic Devotional Manual of the Nineteenth Century', *Journal of Ritual Studies* 17.1 (2003), pp. 42–60; Kugle, *Sufis and Saints' Bodies: Mysticism, Corporeality, and Sacred Power in Islam* (Chapel Hill: University of North Carolina Press, 2007).
28. See, for example, Leila Ahmed, 'Arab Culture and Writing Women's Bodies', *Feminist Issues* 9.1 (1989), pp. 41–55; Paula Sanders, 'Gendering the Ungendered Body: Hermaphrodites in Medieval Islamic Law', in Nikki

R. Keddie and Beth Baron (eds), *Women in Middle Eastern History: Shifting Boundaries in Sex and Gender* (New Haven: Yale University Press, 1991), pp. 74–98.

29. See, for example, Abdelwahab Bouhdiba, *Sexuality in Islam*, trans. Alan Sheridan (London: Saqi Books, 1998); Ze'ev Maghen, *Virtues of the Flesh: Passion and Purity in Early Islamic Jurisprudence* (Leiden: E. J. Brill, 2005); and Dror Ze'evi, *Producing Desire: Changing Sexual Discourse in the Ottoman Middle East, 1500–1900* (Berkeley: University of California Press, 2006).
30. See, for example, Michael Dols, *Majnūn: The Madman in Medieval Islamic Society* (New York: Oxford University Press, 1992); Nicholas Mirzoeff, 'Framed: The Deaf in the Harem', in Jennifer Terry and Jacqueline Urla (eds), *Deviant Bodies: Critical Perspectives on Difference in Science and Popular Culture* (Bloomington: Indiana University Press, 1995), pp. 49–77; Firoozeh Kashani-Sabet, 'The Historical Study of Disability in Modern Iran', *Iranian Studies* 43.2 (2010), pp. 167–95; Boaz Shoshan, 'The State and Madness in Medieval Islam', *IJMES* 35 (2003), pp. 329–40; Sara Scalenghe, *The Body Different: Disability in the Middle East, 1500–1800* (Cambridge: Cambridge University Press, forthcoming); M. Miles, 'Signing in the Seraglio: Mutes, Dwarfs and Jestures at the Ottoman Court 1500–1700', *Disability and Society* 15 (2000), pp. 115–34; and J. W. Frembgen, 'Honour, Shame, and Bodily Mutilation: Cutting Off the Nose Among Tribal Societies in Pakistan', *JRAS* 16 (2006), pp. 243–60.
31. Leslie Peirce, *Morality Tales: Law and Gender in the Ottoman Court of Aintab* (Berkeley: University of California Press, 2003), p. 178.
32. Orit Shamir and Alisa Baginski, 'Medieval Mediterranean Textiles, Basketry, and Cordage Newly Excavated in Israel', in Yaacov Lev (ed.), *Towns and Material Culture in the Medieval Middle East* (Leiden: E. J. Brill, 2002), p. 152. Also of interest is Piers Mitchell's publication on syphilis in Mamluk Palestine: 'Pre-Columbian Treponemal Disease from 14th-Century AD Safed, Israel, and Implications for the Medieval Eastern Mediterranean', *American Journal of Physical Anthropology* 121.2 (2003), pp. 117–24.
33. Stephan H. Stephan, 'Lunacy in Palestinian Folklore', *Journal of the Palestine Oriental Society* 5 (1925), pp. 1–16, esp. pp. 2–3.
34. *Azraq* can also mean 'blind', 'ill-omened', or 'deceitful', but because Ibn ᶜAdī had already used blindness as a category, and all the categories were physical features, the definition of 'blue-eyed' makes the most sense here. For discussions of definitions of *azraq*, see al-Thaᶜālibī, *The Laṭāʾif al-maᶜarif of Thaᶜālibī: The Book of Curious and Entertaining Information*, trans. C. E. Bosworth (Edinburgh: Edinburgh University Press, 1968), p. 93, fn. 27, and Geert Jan van Gelder, 'Kitāb al-Burṣān: Al-Jāḥiẓ on Right- and Lefthandedness', in Arnim Heinemann et. al. (eds), *Al-Jāḥiẓ: A Muslim Humanist for Our Time* (Beirut: Orient-Institut/Würzburg: Ergon Verlag,

2009), p. 239, fn. 4. I am also preparing a monograph about blue and green eyes in medieval Islamdom.

35. Al-Jāḥiẓ, *Kitāb al-burṣān* [1968], p. 7.
36. Jamāl al-Dīn Ibn al-Qiftī (d. 646/1248), *Inbāh al-ruwāh ᶜalá anbāh al-nuḥāh*, ed. Muḥammad Abū al-Faḍl (Cairo: Dār al-kutub al-miṣriyya, 1950), 3:365. For more on the works of Ibn ᶜAdī, see Stefan Leder, *Das Korpus al-Haiṯam ibn ᶜAdī (st. 207/822): Herkunft, Überlieferung, Gestalt früher Texte der aḫbār Literatur* (Frankfurt am Main: Klostermann, 1991).
37. Ibn Ḥabīb, *Kitāb al-muḥabbar* (The Book of the Elaborately Ornamented), ed. Ilse Lichtenstadter (Beirut: Manshūrāt al-maktab al-tijārī li'l-ṭibāᶜa wa'l-nashr, 1942), pp. 296–305.
38. Ibn Ḥabīb, *Kitāb al-munammaq fī akhbār Quraysh* (The Book of Embellishment: Reports on the Quraysh), ed. Khvurshid Aḥmad Fariq (Beirut: ᶜAlam al-kitāb, 1985), pp. 404–6.
39. Ibn Qutayba, *Kitāb al-maᶜārif* (The Book of Knowledge) (Cairo: s.n., 1882), p. 194; *Kitāb al-maᶜārif*, ed. Tarwat ᶜUkāsha (Cairo: Dār al-maᶜārif, 1969), pp. 578–9.
40. Ibn Qutayba, *Kitāb ᶜuyūn al-akhbār* (The Book of Choice Anecdotes) (Cairo: Dār al-kutub al-miṣriyya, 1925–30), 4:53–69.
41. (*Mā raᵓytu aḥad^{an} minhum yaᶜrif farq mā bayna l-wakaᶜi wa'l-kawaᶜi wa-lā al-ḥanafa min al-fadaᶜa, wa-lā al-lamā min al-laṭaᶜi.*) Ibn Qutayba, *Ādab al-kātib* (The Qualifications of the Scribe), ed. M. Grünert (Leiden: E. J. Brill, 1900), p. 9.
42. Al-Badrī, *Ghurrat al-ṣabāḥ fī waṣf al-wujūh al-ṣibāḥ*, British Library, London, England, MS 1423 (add. 23,445), 875/1471, fos 156b and 162b.
43. This work has been frequently misattributed to al-Khawārizmī (d. 383/993), though the author makes reference therein to his 6th/12th-century contemporaries. For a discussion of its authorial attribution, see Geert Jan van Gelder, 'Mirror for Princes or Vizor for Viziers: The Twelfth-Century Arabic Popular Encyclopedia *Mufīd al-ᶜulūm* and Its Relationship with the Anonymous Persian *Baḥr al-fawāᵓid*', *BSOAS* 64.3 (2001), pp. 313–15.
44. Jamāl al-Dīn al-Khawārizmī (misattributed), *Kitāb mufīd al-ᶜulūm wa-mubīd al-humūm*, ed. ᶜAbdallāh b. Ibrāhīm al-Anṣārī (Ṣaydā and Beirut: Manshūrat al-maktabat al-ᶜaṣriyya, 1980), pp. 477–81.
45. Aḥmad b. ᶜUmar Ibn Rusta, *Kitāb al-aᶜlāq al-nafīsa* (The Book of Precious Objects), ed. M. J. de Goeje (Leiden: E. J. Brill, 1891), pp. 221–5.
46. Abū al-Ḥasan b. Aḥmad Sarī al-Raffā, *Al-Muḥibb wa'l-maḥbūb wa'l-mashmūm wa'l-mashrūb* (The Lover, the Beloved, the Scent and the Drink), ed. Miṣbāḥ Ghalāwinjī (Damascus: Majmaᶜ al-lughat al-ᶜarabiyya, 1986), 1:91–124. Cited in Thomas Bauer, *Liebe und Liebesdichtung in der arabischen Welt des 9. und 10. Jahrhunderts: eine literatur- und mentalitätsgeschichtliche Studie des arabischen Gazal* (Wiesbaden: Harrassowitz, 1998), pp. 285–7. The Buyid verse is cited in Frédéric Lagrange, 'The Obscenity of the Vizier', in Kathryn Babayan and Afsaneh Najmabadi

(eds), *Islamicate Sexualities: Translations Across Temporal Geographies of Desire* (Cambridge, MA: Harvard University Press, 2008), p. 170.

47. Abū Ḥayyān al-Tawḥīdī, *Al-Baṣāʾir wa'l-dhakhāʾir*, ed. Wadād al-Qāḍī (Beirut: Dār ṣādir, 1988), 6:146.
48. ʿAbd al-Raḥmān Ibn al-Jawzī, *Talqīḥ fuhūm ahl al-athar fī ʿuyūn al-taʾrīkh wa'l-siyar* (The Inculcation of Knowledge of Hadith Specialists: On the Best of History and Biographies) (Cairo: Maktabat al-ādāb, 1975), pp. 446–50.
49. Taqī al-Dīn al-Badrī, *Al-Durr al-maṣūn, al-musammá bi-Siḥr al-ʿuyūn* (The Hidden Pearl, also known as, The Magic of the Eye), ed. Ṣiddīq ʿAbd al-Fattāḥ (Cairo: Dār al-shaʿb, 1998), 1:105.
50. Yūsuf Sadān, 'Risāla fī al-damāma li-Muḥammad b. Ḥamza al-Kūzliḥṣārī al-Īdīnī wa-mā sabaqahā min muwāqif al-udabāʾ min al-ʿāhāt wa'l-qabḥ', *al-Karmil* 9 (1988), p. 14.
51. Franz Rosenthal, *A History of Muslim Historiography* (Leiden: E. J. Brill, 1968), p. 432.
52. Khalīl b. Aybak al-Ṣafadī, *Al-Ḥusn al-ṣarīḥ fī miʾat malīḥ* (The Pure Beauty of 100 Handsome Men), ed. Aḥmad Fawzī Hayb (Damascus: Dār Saʿd al-Dīn, 2003); al-Badrī, *Ghurrat*, fos 153a, 156a, 158a, 158b, 160a.
53. Tobin Siebers, *Disability Aesthetics* (Ann Arbor: University of Michigan Press, 2010), p. 25.
54. Ibid., p. 27.

1

ᶜĀhāt in Islamic Thought

Islam is a praxis-orientated religion, meaning that religious devotion resides in and on the body and is expressed through such bodily acts as ritualised prayer, fasting, dietary restrictions, modest dress and pilgrimage to Mecca. With bodies figuring so centrally in Islamic theology, it is essential for any study of bodies in Islamicate culture to examine how bodies are presented in the Islamic source-texts of Qur'an and hadith, which provide the basic narratives about the body which Muslim theologians and scholars have used in constructing and refining notions of the body and physical difference.

Included among the approximately 6,000 verses of the Qur'an is a variety of verses about different types of blights. It is worth mentioning that, of all the blights, blindness (spiritual and physical) is disproportionately well represented. In addition to forty-eight verses about blindness, there are also seven on muteness, two on lameness, two about leprosy and one mention of blue eyes.[1] The Qur'anic position on the moral state of blighted people may be summarised in the following verse: 'there is no blame on the blind, nor is there blame on the lame, nor is there blame on the sick'. Though people with these physical conditions carry no adverse moral associations, God does not view them as the same as their sighted, walking, healthy counterparts. 'The blind and the seeing', God proclaims, 'are not alike'.[2] They are physically distinct, physically different; and the Qur'an even addresses the unethical responses to such differences in 1st/7th-century Arabian society. One reads, for example, the Qur'anic suggestion for believers to share meals with the blind, as well as the sighted.[3] This particular verse speaks to the tendency among Arabs to avoid eating with the blind, as many found the experience unsavoury, allegedly because the blind would touch food in order to identify it.[4] Difference is duly acknowledged as a condition of humanity in the Qur'an, but the behaviour of believers towards the physically different is regulated, not the behaviour of the marked. It is incumbent on every Muslim to respond ethically to human differences.

In the six canonical Sunni hadith collections, one finds more specific and anecdotal discussions of disability. Marked bodies do appear in Sunni hadith literature, especially as subjects of anecdotes. For instance, certain accommodations are made for participation of physically disabled people in rituals, prayers and other religious obligations. But neither Muḥammad nor his companions ever referred to the ill, disabled or physically marked as a particular class of people; and the term *ᶜāha* only appears in reference to blighted crops. Even so, several later hadith-compilers who reorganised reports by topic did insert chapter headings classifying certain reports as pertaining to *dhawī al-ᶜāhāt*. This consistency in terminology suggests that chapter headings were transmitted from a common source or sources. Qāḍī al-ᶜIyāḍ's *Al-Shifāʾ* (The Cure), al-Nuwayrī's *Nihāyat al-arab* (Wish-Fulfilment), Ibn Ḥabīb al-Ḥalabī's *Al-Najm al-thāqib* (The Piercing Star) and al-Qasṭallānī's *Al-Mawāhib al-laduniyya* (The Mystical Blessings), for instance, are extended works about the Prophet's physical characteristics, moral behaviour and divine mission. In each one's sections on Prophetic miracles (*muᶜjizāt*), the authors included subsections on healing sick and physically blighted people. These miracles are contained in Ibn Mājah's (d. 273/886 or 887) *Sunan*, which is one of the six books of canonical Sunni hadith. Ibn Mājah himself did not use the term *ᶜāhāt*, but these later compilers did. Qāḍī al-ᶜIyāḍ entitled his chapter 'On healing the sick and *dhawī al-ᶜāhāt*', whereas Ibn Ḥabīb named his 'On the speech of the dead and of children and on his healing of *dhawī al-ᶜāhāt*'. Al-Qasṭallānī described his chapter as being about 'healing *dhawī al-ᶜāhāt*; raising the dead; the speech of the raised dead; and the speech of young boys who confirm Muḥammad's prophethood'.[5] Significantly, all three authors use the same phrase to refer to marked people.

These section headings allow the reader to understand how these individual writers constructed the category of the physically blighted. It is particularly easy with al-Qasṭallānī's collection, for in his section on the physically blighted, distinguishing between reports on *dhawī al-ᶜāhāt* and everything else is not difficult. By reading al-Qasṭallānī's list, one finds that demonic possession/mental illness (*junūn*), blindness and injury to eyes and thighs constitute *ᶜāhāt*. With Qāḍī al-ᶜIyāḍ's grouping, the distinction is less distinct, for what is the difference between a sick individual and one with physical blights? Is there an implicit overlap between the two categories, making easy separation of the two a fruitless undertaking? In any case, Qāḍī al-ᶜIyāḍ's list includes the *ᶜāhāt* of al-Qasṭallānī's list, as well as head fractures, dropsy, amputated hands, and injuries to the leg, forearm and throat. Significantly, Muḥammad's corporeality was central to healing episodes involving *dhawī al-ᶜāhāt*. After Muḥammad spat on the afflicted body part, it was healed. In one case, a woman's mute son speaks after drinking water that Muḥammad had used to rinse his mouth and wash his hands. Even indirect contact with the body of the Prophet proved sufficient to cure muteness. The Prophet physically transmitted his *baraka* (spiritual wisdom and blessing transmitted from God) through a bodily fluid to people afflicted with illnesses or blights and thereby cured them.[6] Blighted bodies are always presented to the Prophet as being in need of fixing or curing. Unlike other Muslim petitioners who visit the Prophet seeking advice that would restore their spiritual equilibrium, the spiritual needs of the *ahl al-ᶜāhāt* are apparently fulfilled when their bodies are 'normalised'.

Although hadith literature purportedly places Muḥammad in direct bodily contact with *dhawī al-ᶜāhāt*, perhaps the emphasis on eradicating their blights stoked fears and misgivings about the people of blights in the popular Mamluk and early Ottoman imagination. In *Al-Maqāṣid al-ḥasana* (Excellent Goals), al-Sakhāwī (d. 902/1497), a Shāfiᶜī historian and hadith specialist, scrutinised proverbs and sayings that held dubious hadith status in order to determine their authenticity or weakness. One such hadith reads: 'Fear the people of blights (*Ittaqū dhawī al-ᶜāhāt*)'.[7] Al-Sakhāwī does not know the origins of this saying, but speculates that it could either be a corruption of al-Shāfi'ī's exhortation to 'Beware the fair-haired' or a corruption of the prophetic hadith '(There is) no ᶜadwā (no contagious disease is conveyed without Allāh's permission), . . . nor is there any Hāmah [protection], nor is there any bad omen in the month of Safar, and one should run away from the leper as one runs from a lion'.[8] The physician and theologian Ibn Qayyim al-Jawziyya (d. 751/1350) interpreted the Prophet's command to flee the leper as medically sound advice, as leprosy was transmitted through shared air and physical contact. Therefore, the Prophet could not have been advocating the social isolation of lepers, but was trying to protect non-afflicted individuals.[9] Al-Sakhāwī appears to accept a similar justification of the hadith, arguing that, if the dubious hadith were indeed a distortion of the Prophet's words, then running from lepers in fear is the same as fearing the blighted. This transfer of ideas, he reasons, must have been how the command to fear people with physical blights gained currency as a *bona fide* hadith. Whatever the transmutations that resulted in the diffusion of this false hadith, it is nonetheless significant that the notion had become popularly accepted in Mamluk Cairo as Muḥammad's actual words.

What moral and cultural conditions existed to create a space where such a command could acquire the status of doctrine? Tobin Siebers has traced the hysteria surrounding the coding of the eye as treacherous in various cultures and times, finding that, in times of chaos, people tend to search out

> the slightest discrepancy in the group in the hope of recognising the powers of evil. Immediately a mark or blemish that was considered perfectly natural becomes a sign of the supernatural. It is viewed as being different, even though it does not change appearance. In other words, the community not only remarks but marks the accused.[10]

The criteria for what constitutes a mark or a blemish or an indication of difference are arbitrarily determined and socially constructed, and the process of isolating certain physical characteristics as signs of evil is not particular to Islamicate societies. Even so, there are Islamic traditions that support the association of *ᶜāhāt* with immorality and avoidance, some of which have corollaries in Jewish and Christian thought. Al-Sakhāwī does not mention these sources, which might lend credence to his claim that 'Fear the people of blights' was regarded as a true hadith; but they were likely to have been well known. The devil (*iblīs*) and the antichrist (*dajjāl*) are typically described in hadith and post-formative theological writings as one-eyed, and Iblīs's epithet is 'The One-Eyed'.

Anecdotes about the untrustworthiness of one-eyed people circulated in 10th/16th-century Cairo. The encyclopaedist al-Ibshīhī related that, one day, al-Mughīra ᶜAbd al-Raḥmān b. al-Ḥārith b. Hishām al-Makhzūmī, a one-eyed Companion of the Prophet, was dispensing food to the poor. A fellow Arab was watching him from a distance but did not partake in the feast. When al-Mughīra noticed him, the Arab said: 'Your food looks delicious, but I am afraid of your eye'. When al-Mughīra asked him to explain his feelings, he replied that al-Mughīra and al-Dajjāl have only one eye. An observer commented to the Arab that al-Mughīra lost his eye in battle while defeating the Byzantines, to which he responded: 'Truly, al-Dajjāl would not have lost his eye fighting for the cause of Allah'![11] He finally deduced that al-Mughīra could not be the antichrist. In Muslim eschatology, al-Dajjāl will appear at the end of times to lead obedient Muslims astray. Only Jesus the Messiah will be able to defeat him; and, once he does, a forty-year period of peace will prevail on earth before the Day of Judgement. Al-Dajjāl will be identified by the word 'unbelief' etched into his forehead, by his obesity and by blindness in one of his eyes.[12] Partial blindness has linguistic associations with the concept of deficiency and moral connotations of evil. The Arabic term for 'one-eyed' or 'blind in one eye' (*aᶜwar*) shares a triliteral root with the words *ᶜawār* (blemish) and *ᶜawra* (genitalia, women or women's voices). Shame and deficiency are common to all three words; and, according to Abdelwahab Bouhdiba, this connection probably pre-dated Islam: 'From pre-Islamic times Arab society, like many others, was ill disposed towards the one-eyed, who were supposed to bring misfortune . . . The one-eyed is the half-condemned.'[13] Other undesirable characteristics are frequently ascribed to Iblīs and al-Dajjāl, like black skin and slitted eyes, which altogether may have fed into the popular belief that the hadith which al-Sakhāwī was investigating was indeed sound.

Imām al-Shāfiᶜī and Blighted Bodies

Why would al-Shāfiᶜī (d. 204/820), the eponymous founder of a Sunni school of legal thought, have commanded his followers to beware the fair-haired, and how significant was such an idea to Shāfiᶜī jurisprudence? These questions take on greater urgency in light of the fact that, of the six scholars featured in this book, five are identified as followers of the Shāfiᶜī school. The other two, Ibn ᶜAbd al-Hādī and Ibn Ṭūlūn, were Ḥanbalīs from Damascus. This section's focus is not to suggest that Aḥmad b. Ḥanbal (d. 241/855) never discussed blighted bodies. In fact, he married his cousin Rayḥāna, a smart, one-eyed woman, and rejected her less intelligent, though quite beautiful, sister as a marriage partner.[14] Inner qualities of beauty prevailed over considerations of physical beauty, and this choice confirmed for his followers his deep commitment to a pious lifestyle. However, no biographies or hagiographies mention any comments he ever made about physiognomy or disability.

As for al-Shāfiᶜī, it is known that his interest in theology and law developed later in life. As a young man, archery, medicine (*ṭibb*) and physiognomy (*firāsa*) captured his interest most strongly. His poetry *dīwān* even includes the following homoerotic couplet about physical recovery from illness. It is distinguished by its inversion of the common literary trope of a lover made sick by his love for a whole and healthy beloved and the circularity of illness and sound health.

> When my love fell ill, I visited him.
>   Then I fell ill from being around him.
> So my beloved came to visit me,
>   And his gaze upon me cured me.[15]

Al-Shāfiᶜī's interests infused many aspects of his intellectual life. He even went to Yemen in search of books on physiognomy. No descriptions of his physique have been transmitted, though al-Ghazālī (d. 505/1111) did describe him as physically unattractive.[16] The centrality of theology and medicine to al-Shāfiᶜī is reflected in the maxim 'Knowledge is twofold: knowledge of the body and knowledge of religion', which has been frequently attributed to the Prophet; but, according to al-Dhahabī

(d. 748/1348) and al-Suyūṭī (d. 911/1505), themselves both Shāfiᶜīs, al-Shāfiᶜī actually spoke these words. Ibn Abī Uṣaybīᶜa (d. 668/1269 or 1270) wrote without attribution in his biographical dictionary on physicians that 'knowledge of bodies has become linked with knowledge of religion' (*jaᶜala ᶜilm al-abdān qarīnan li-ᶜilm al-adyān*),[17] which is perhaps a corruption of the aforementioned maxim or even a reference to the specialised study of prophetic medicine (*al-ṭibb al-nabawī*). Also, followers of al-Shāfiᶜī have noted the resemblance between his name and *al-Shāfiᶜ*, which is one of God's names and means 'The Curer'.

Al-Bayhaqī (d. 458/1065 or 1066), one of the earliest compilers of al-Shāfiᶜī's teachings, reported that Ḥarmala b. Yaḥyá (d. 243/857) heard al-Shāfiᶜī urge his followers to

> beware the one-eyed, the cross-eyed, the lame, the hunchback, the fair-haired, the thin-bearded and anyone with a blight (*ᶜāha*) on his body. And anyone who diminishes creation, beware of him, for he is a friend of controversy, and his behaviour is distressing. And he repeated, 'Truly, he is a friend of deception'.[18]

Identifying an entire group of people as deceptive, controversial and distressing marks their characters as fundamentally counter to *shariᶜa* ideals. Some of these conditions could not be altered or reversed, so a one-eyed person, for instance, is condemned for life to being morally compromised and marked as an object of apprehension. Unlike people with moral failings who can change their attitudes and actions to accord with Islamic ideals, blighted people are condemned by their own bodies and have no hope for moral redemption.

To continue with al-Shāfiᶜī's musings on blightedness, he also offered pronouncements and anecdotes about physiognomy and afflictions, including two variations of an anecdote about the fair-haired. In the first story, a man approached al-Shāfiᶜī with some perfume that he had purchased and began to describe it to him. Al-Shāfiᶜī asked him from whom he had bought the perfume, and the man replied: 'From a fair-haired man'. Al-Shāfiᶜī responded: 'Return it to him. Nothing good has ever come to me from a fair-haired man.' His reaction is deeply personal. His own experience has taught him not to expect good from this particular group, and by universalising his experience he acquires the authority to order his followers to steer clear of them. In the second version, al-Shāfiᶜī asked the man if he had bought the perfume from a thin-bearded, fair-haired man, and when the man responded yes, he ordered him to return the perfume.[19] This particular version excludes the personal dimension, though repeating the same sentiments. Full beards were, and are still today, signs of masculinity and virility in the Islamicate world, so much so that sparse facial hair came to be seen as a physical defect. Fair hair may refer to Persian, Slavic or Turkish identity.

Al-Shāfiᶜī's attribution of moral deficiencies and behavioural difficulties to the entire category of *ahl al-ᶜāhāt* represents a sweeping judgement that, on the face of it, contradicts Islamic doctrine that moral failings inhere in no individual. This seeming disconnect between al-Shāfiᶜī's pronouncements and Islamic doctrine does not seem to have affected his theology or jurisprudence. Islam does not admit to the doctrine of 'original sin', and many of Muḥammad's companions were among the *ahl al-ᶜāhāt*, as shown in the Introduction; but certain Qur'anic verses can be interpreted in support of al-Shāfiᶜī's ideas. Qur'an 40: 58 reads: 'And the blind and the seeing are not alike, nor those who believe and do good and the evildoers'; and, if 'the blind and the seeing' refer to the physiologically unsighted and sighted, then al-Shāfiᶜī's interpretation becomes possible. The sighted and unsighted represent polar opposites in terms of physical ability, just as the believer and evildoer represent dichotomous spiritual orientations. Could al-Shāfiᶜī have understood this verse to suggest that moral and physical extremes are related? Neither al-Shāfiᶜī nor his followers and companions offer explanations for the numerous negative judgements he made regarding a variety of physical attributes, but such readings of the Qur'an as this one allow for conclusions such as those at which al-Shāfiᶜī arrived. He believed that different characteristics augured different moral connotations. Perhaps tellingly, Ibn Abī Hātim al-Rāzī conspicuously omitted al-Shāfiᶜī's disciple al-Rabīᶜ b. Sulayman al-Jīzī (d. 256/870) who may have been lame, from his biography. Other biographers tried to associate al-Jīzī with Mālik b. Anas.[20]

The invisible blight of mental illness/demon possession (*junūn*) was also construed as a reflection of one's moral standing. Al-Shāfiᶜī defined *majnūn* as the opposite of rightly guided (*rashīd*).[21] Al-Shāfiᶜī drew links between physiognomic traits and intelligence, once remarking: 'I have only ever seen one smart fat man'.[22] Linking weight to intellect appears to have been a rare connection, as most early Islamic sources were ambiguous about the topic, leading one modern historian to declare that 'it remains open to debate if the quality of corpulence implied in early and classical Islam is a positive or negative attitude'.[23] However, in terms of physical aesthetics, plump women were generally considered desirable.[24]

In the same chapter on physiognomy, al-Shāfiᶜī pronounced that 'there is no good in Abyssinia. When Abyssinians are hungry, they steal. When they have enough to eat, they drink and fornicate.'[25] Such negative opinions about Ethiopians were sufficiently widespread in al-Shāfiᶜī's time that al-Jāḥiẓ, a 3rd/9th-century writer who is thought to have been of African descent (the evidence is inconsistent), penned a work extolling the virtues of Ethiopians.[26] The two men had met each other, but al-Jāḥiẓ gives no indication in this text that al-Shāfiᶜī influenced his choice of topic. If the following exchange did, in fact, take place, then it must have been a very early meeting between these two scholars who had demonstrable interests in physiognomy and physical difference. Al-Jāḥiẓ encountered al-Shāfiᶜī upon entering a mosque in Baghdad and reportedly asked him: 'What can you say about a castrated man?' Al-Shāfiᶜī responded: 'Have you seen him, just as I'm looking at you now, Abū ᶜUthmān (al-Jāḥiẓ)?'[27] In other words, al-Shāfiᶜī had nothing to say because he could not identify a castrated man by casual sight; he could only speak to traits visible through ordinary social interactions.

Al-Ibshīhī, a Cairene writer who studied with and later taught many Shāfiᶜī scholars, echoed a similar sentiment in the eightieth chapter of his encyclopaedia. He terminated a section on 'illnesses like halitosis, lameness, blindness, deafness, ophthalmia and paralysis' with a supplication: 'O God, by your mercy, grace and magnanimity, may you keep us from the evil of blights (*sharr al-ᶜāhāt*)! Amen.'[28] In spite of this dramatic and negative closing, the section itself incorporates anecdotes and poems that showcase humorous and negative associations with blighted people. While the precise route of transmission of al-Ibshīhī's knowledge is not known, he is closely linked with Shāfiᶜī circles of learning. In fact, one of his students was Taqī al-Dīn b. Fahd al-Makkī, the great-grandfather of our historian Jār Allāh who in his 950/1543 treatise on physically marked hadith specialists quoted al-Shāfiᶜī as saying 'Beware the fair-haired, blue-eyed'.[29] This citation in a 10th/16th-century biographical work explicitly demonstrates the transhistorical significance in Muslim contexts of al-Shāfiᶜī's teachings on physiognomy in the Muslim world.

The Prophet Muḥammad's Body

Within Arabic and Persian Islamic literatures, extensive archives of material exist about the bodies of Muslim prophets, particularly Muḥammad. In early modern Persianate and Shiᶜi visual arts, prophets were commonly depicted with their faces and hands exposed, unlike the practice in Arab–Sunni contexts of veiling or blanching out the faces of prophets.[30] The quality and quantity of information about Muḥammad's physical appearance and behaviour far exceed what is available for earlier prophets. The written material is sufficiently vast that the genre is referred to as *shamāʾil* literature. Al-Tirmidhī compiled the first major collection of hadith that dealt specifically with the behaviour and physical characteristics of the

Prophet. The resulting work, *Al-Shamāᵓil al-muḥammadiyya*, includes an entire chapter devoted to the seal of prophethood. The earliest description of Muḥammad is found in this work and has become one of the most authoritative and definitive ones for Muslims. Related by ᶜAlī b. Abī Ṭālib, the Prophet's cousin and son-in-law, it offers little subjective evaluation of Muḥammad's form. ᶜAlī is almost matter-of-factly descriptive in the following narrative:

> The Prophet was neither tall nor short; the fingers and the toes were thick, the head was large, the joints were broad and a long thin line of hair stretched from the chest to the navel. While walking he used to bend forward as if he was descending from a higher level to a lower. I have never known the like of him before or since.[31]

Other companions and contemporaries of the Prophet were more forthcoming in their praise of him. Barāᵓ b. ᶜĀzib (d. 72/691 or 692) said: 'I have never seen anything more beautiful than the Prophet', and Jābir b. Samura (d. 74/693) affirmed that 'he certainly appeared to me to be more beautiful than the moon itself'.[32] Ibn ᶜAbbās (d. 68/688) declared that 'when he conversed it seemed as if light was coming out of the two front teeth'.[33] These descriptions came to represent the ideal male body, one that was perfectly marked with the seal of the prophets. His name was sometimes identified with the perfect, presumably unsexed, human body.

Of the various properties attributed to the name Muḥammad, al-Qasṭallānī mentions one that inscribes the human body in the graphic form of his name. The name in Arabic is written thus: محمد, and al-Qasṭallānī notes that

> Among all that God has honoured is the human being, whose form resembles the writing of this word (Muḥammad). The first م is his head; the ح is his two sides; the م is his navel; and the د is his two legs. And it is said that whoever deserves to enter the hellfires will not, except for the deformed of body, out of respect for (the perfection of) the form of the word (Muḥammad).[34]

Those who are 'deformed of body' are subject to a different set of rules governing their eternal fate. They will not be spared God's wrath and will consequently spend the afterlife suffering in hell if their lives have warranted such a punishment. Ibn Marzūq al-Ṭilimsanī (d. 766/1364) related this tale before him, and others like al-Ḥallāj (d. 309/922) and Ibn ᶜArabī (d. 638/1240) recorded their own versions of the symbolism of Muḥammad's name.[35]

Muᶜtazilī theologians in medieval Baghdad also contemplated the ways in which bodily marks functioned in terms of religious identification. Al-Muᶜāfā al-Jarīrī (d. 390/1000) summarised a theological debate among Muᶜtazilī scholars who disputed whether religious men could legitimately perform miracles or whether all claims to miraculous works after the Prophet's death necessarily came from charlatans and false prophets. Ultimately, they determined that, although the visible blight (*ᶜāha ẓāhira*) of having one blind eye is al-Dajjāl's distinguishing physical sign, half-blindness is not a universal mark of evil. After all, many good-hearted people share this trait with al-Dajjāl. As such, false and true prophets cannot be distinguished by particular physiognomic marks. 'As for prophethood, the true prophet is he who is called to prophethood, and the false one is he who lies about his claims to it. These two types are the same in physiognomy (*khilqa*), form and the human body.'[36] The outer surfaces of the body provide no evidence of the authenticity of one's claims to prophethood, which is a novel reading of the outward (*ẓāhir*) reflecting the (*bāṭin*).

Muḥammad was said to have a singular marking on his body that marked him as a prophet. Though no sources describe it as a blight, hagiographers depict it as something that arose through an angelic intervention that split his body open. Ibn Isḥāq (d. between 150/767 and 153/770), the Prophet's earliest biographer, reported that Muḥammad had his belly split open by two angels, corroborating God's statement in Qur'an 94: 1: 'Have We not opened up your heart and lifted from you the burden that had weighed so heavily upon your back?' Al-Ṭabarī, al-Qasṭallānī and other later authors have also transmitted this story with slight variations. Related in Muḥammad's voice, it unfolds as follows:

> One day while I was in a wide plain in Mecca, two angels appeared to me. One of them fell to the earth, and the other hovered between the earth and sky. One asked the other, 'Is this the one?', to which he replied, 'This is he'. Then the first angel commanded the second one to rip open my belly and take out the heart. The angel cleansed the heart of Satan's influence, then performed the ritual cleansing on both the heart and belly. Next, the first angel commanded the second angel to sew me back up, and the seal (*khātim*) of prophethood appeared between my shoulder blades just after this incident.[37]

Once the cleansing was complete and his torso sewn up, the seal materialised on his body, symbolising the unification or completion of the Abrahamic prophetic tradition. For Muslims, Islam represents a seamless continuation of Judaism and Christianity, not a reactionary belief system against them. In Qur'an 33: 40, Muḥammad is described as the seal of the prophets (*khātim* [or *khātam*] *al-nabiyyīn*); and hadiths and literature on *shamāʾil* (physical and abstract characteristics of Muḥammad) elaborate on this characterisation. In a tradition narrated by ᶜAlī b. Abī Ṭālib, he is the final messenger of God who bears on his body the seal or mark of prophethood (*khātim al-nubuwwa*) – a raised disc of skin the size of a pigeon's egg located between his shoulder blades.[38] The term *khātim* can mean 'stopper' or 'authenticating mark', and there was considerable debate among medieval theologians about how to understand the use of this word in the Qur'an.[39] If we are to interpret this term as a mark of prophethood, then the alignment of prophethood with physically distinguishing characteristics added new dimensions to discussions of physical difference.

Conclusion

The interrelatedness of body aesthetics, piety and physical difference emerged in the Islamic source-texts and in biographical and hagiographical writings about Imām al-Shāfiʿī. In the predominantly Shāfiʿī environments of Mamluk and Ottoman Arab territories, such a focus carried weight in these milieus. Imām al-Shāfiʿī's suggestion that 'anyone with an *ʿāha* on his body' is prone to certain negative behaviours reinforced existing associations between physical difference and moral behaviour in the 2nd/8th and 3rd/9th centuries. Such notions certainly cropped up in religious, literary and historical works of the late Mamluk era. Competing representations of and reactions to physical difference (such as praise for the pious, one-eyed Companion of the Prophet Abū Sufyān and condemnation of the one-eyed antichrist al-Dajjāl) circulated in juridical and religious sources, exposing the capacities of Mamluk subjects for tolerance and anxiety towards a single form of difference. In spite of this dichotomous range of moral associations with blighted people, numerous sources of Shāfiʿī jurisprudence reveal negative depictions of individuals with marked bodies, informing social and theological conceptions of the body and difference in the Arab world.

Notes

1. For blindness, see Qur'an 5: 71; 6: 154; 11: 28; 22: 46; 27: 66; 28: 66; 41: 17, 44; 47: 23 and so on. For muteness, 2: 17–18; 2: 171; 16: 76; 6: 39; 8: 22; 17: 97. For lameness, 24: 61 and 48: 17. For leprosy, 3: 49 and 5: 110. For blue eyes, 20: 102. A more detailed analysis of disability terminology and symbolism in the Qur'an can be found in Maysaa S. Bazna and Tarek A. Hatab, 'Disability in the Qur'an: The Islamic Alternative to Defining, Viewing, and Relating to Disability', *Journal of Religion, Disability and Health* 9.1 (2005), pp. 5–27.
2. Qur'an 48: 17; 35: 19; 40: 58. Sometimes when blindness is evoked in the

Qur'an, a metaphorical, spiritual blindness is meant, so this last verse could alternatively be interpreted as a statement about humans' moral states.

3. Qur'an 24: 61.
4. See Muḥammad b. Aḥmad al-Qurṭubī (d. 671/1273), *Al-Jāmiʿ li-aḥkām al-Qurʾān* (Cairo: Dār al-kitāb al-ʿarabī li-ṭibāʿa wa-nashr, 1967), 12:312–19.
5. Qāḍī al-ʿĪyāḍ (d. 544/1149), *Al-Shifāʾ bi-taʿrīf ḥuqūq al-Muṣṭafá*, ed. ʿAlī Muḥammad al-Bajāwī (Cairo: Maṭbaʿat ʿĪsa al-Bābī al-Ḥalabī, 1977), 1:451; Shihāb al-Dīn Aḥmad b. ʿAbd al-Wahhāb al-Nuwayrī (d. 732/1332), *Nihāyat al-arab fī funūn al-adab* (Cairo: Maṭbaʿat dār al-kutub al-miṣriyya, 1923), 18:331–3; Badr al-Dīn al-Ḥasan Ibn Ḥabīb al-Ḥalabī (d. 779/1377), *Al-Najm al-thāqib fī ashraf al-manāqib*, ed. Muṣṭafā Muḥammad Ḥusayn al-Dhahabī (Cairo: Dār al-Ḥadīth, 1996), p. 100; Aḥmad b. Muḥammad al-Qasṭallānī (d. 923/1517), *Al-Mawāhib al-laduniyya bi'l-minaḥ al-muḥammadiyya*, ed. Ṣāliḥ Aḥmad al-Shāmī (Beirut: Al-Maktab al-islāmī, 1991), 2:577.
6. There have also been reports of the Prophet's *baraka* being transmitted in dreams. In Mecca, a pious woman named al-Muwaffaqa (d. 634/1236 or 1237) was cured of her lameness after dreaming that the Prophet took her hand and made her walk. For her tomb inscription, see Marco Schöller, *The Living and the Dead in Islam: Studies in Arabic Epitaphs* (Wiesbaden: Harrassowitz, 2004), 2:489–90.
7. Muḥammad b. ʿAbd al-Raḥmān al-Sakhāwī, *Al-Maqāṣid al-ḥasana fī bayān kathīr min al-aḥādīth al-mushtahirat al-alsinah* (Egypt: Maktabat al-khānijī, 1956), p. 18.
8. Muḥammad b. Ismāʾīl al-Bukhārī, *Ṣaḥīḥ al-Bukhārī: The Translation of the Meanings of Ṣaḥīḥ al-Bukhārī*, trans. Muḥammad Muḥsin Khān (Beirut: Dār al-ʿarabiyya, 1985), 7:409.
9. Ibn Qayyim al-Jawziyya, *Medicine of the Prophet*, trans. Penelope Johnstone (Cambridge: Islamic Texts Society, 1998), p. 113.
10. Tobin Siebers, *The Mirror of Medusa* (Berkeley and Los Angeles: University of California Press, 1983), p. 21.
11. Shihāb al-Dīn Muḥammad b. Aḥmad al-Ibshīhī (d. 850/1446), *Mustaṭraf fī kull fann mustaẓraf* (The Most Fascinating Topics from Every Elegant Art), ed. Muṣṭafá Muḥammad al-Dhahabī (Cairo: Dār al-ḥadīth, 2000), p. 643. Al-Mughīra is identified as a one-eyed noble in Ibn Ḥabīb, *Kitāb al-Muḥabbar*, p. 303.
12. In many medieval Christian European texts, the antichrist is described as possessing unusual physiognomic traits. See Bernard McGinn, 'Portraying Antichrist in the Middle Ages', in W. Verbeke et al. (eds), *The Use and Abuse of Eschatology in the Middle Ages* (Leuven: Leuven University Press, 1988), pp. 1–13.
13. Bouhdiba, *Sexuality*, p. 62.
14. Christopher Melchert, *Ahmad ibn Hanbal* (Oxford: OneWorld Publications,

2006), p. 5. Because none of the scholars in this study belonged to the Mālikī or Ḥanafī schools, my analysis will focus on the Shāfiʿī and Ḥanbalī schools.

15. Muḥammad b. Idrīs al-Shāfiʿī, *Dīwān al-Imām al-Shāfiʿī*, ed. Imīl Badīʿ Yaʿqūb (Beirut: Dār al-kitāb al-ʿarabī, 1991), p. 115. Al-Badrī cites another version of this poem, the second verse of which reads 'When my beloved was cured, he visited me, / And his gaze upon me cured me'. See his *Ghurrat*, fo. 162b.
16. Carole Hillenbrand, 'Aspects of al-Ghazali's Views on Beauty', in Alma Giese and J. Bürgel (eds), *Gott ist schön und Er liebt die Schönheit: Festschrift für Annemarie Schimmel zum 7. April 1992* (Bern and New York: Peter Lang, 1994), p. 256.
17. Ibn Abī Uṣaybiʿa, *Kitāb ʿuyūn al-anbāʾ fī ṭabaqāt al-aṭibbaʾ* (Choicest News about the Classes of Physicians), ed. Umruʾ al-Qays b. al-Ṭaḥḥān (Egypt: Maṭbaʿat al-wahbiyya, 1882), p. 2. Michael Cooperson translates *ʿilm al-abdān* as 'knowledge of bodily ailments' in *Classical Arabic Biography: The Heirs of the Prophet in the Age of al-Maʾmūn* (New York: Cambridge University Press, 2000), p. 16.
18. Al-Bayhaqī, *Manāqib*, 2:132. Similar versions of this story are recorded in Ibn Abī Ḥātim al-Rāzī (d. 327/938), *Ādāb al-Shāfiʿī* (Manners of al-Shāfiʿī), ed. ʿAbd al-Ghānī ʿAbd al-Khāliq (Beirut: Dār al-kutub al-ʿilmiyya, 1953), pp. 131–2, and Fakhr al-Dīn al-Rāzī (d. 606/1210), *Manāqib al-Shāfiʿī* (Egypt: Al-Maktabat al-ʿalāmiyya, 1862), p. 121. Al-Sakhāwī listed more than thirty authors, including Ibn Ḥajar al-ʿAsqalānī, who penned works in the *manāqib al-Shāfiʿī* genre. See his *Al-Jawāhir waʾl-durar fī tarjama Shaykh al-Islām Ibn Ḥajar* (Beirut: Dār Ibn Ḥazm, 1999), 3:1,258–9. Al-Rūmī, in his own hadith collection, transmitted a variant of the warning against those who diminish creation: 'Every defect is cursed'. See Mihran Afshārī and Mahdī Madāyanī, *Chahārdeh risāleh dar bāb-e futuvvat-o aṣnaf* (Tehran: Chashmah, 2002), p. 89. I am grateful to Kathryn Babayan of the University of Michigan for this last reference.
19. Al-Bayhaqī, *Manāqib*, pp. 132–3.
20. R. Kevin Jacques, 'The Other Rabīʿ: Biographical Traditions and the Development of Early Shāfiʿī Authority', *Islamic Law and Society* 14.2 (2007), pp. 152–3.
21. Dols, *Majnūn*, p. 436.
22. Ibn Abī Ḥātim al-Rāzī, *Ādāb*, p. 132. The editor identifies this man as one Muḥammad b. al-Ḥasan.
23. John Nawas, 'A Profile of the ʿmawālī ulamaʾ', in Monique Bernards and John Nawas (eds), *Patronate and Patronage in Early and Classical Islam* (Leiden: E. J. Brill, 2005), p. 472, fn. 15.
24. Doris Behrens-Abouseif, *Beauty in Arabic Culture* (Princeton: Markus Wiener, 1999), pp. 56–65.
25. Ibn Abī Ḥātim al-Rāzī, *Ādāb*, p. 135.
26. Ethnic tensions may have been exacerbated by the rebellion of African slaves

working the Basran marshlands, which lasted from 259/869 to 265/882. For more on this rebellion, see Alexandre Popovic, *The Revolt of African Slaves in Iraq in the 3rd/9th Century* (Princeton: Markus Wiener, 1998). For a review of medieval and early modern Arabic- and Turkish-language refutations of anti-Ethiopian prejudice, see Baki Tezcan, '*Dispelling the Darkness*: The Politics of "Race" in the Early Seventeenth-Century Ottoman Empire in the Light of the Life and Work of Mullah Ali', *International Journal of Turkish Studies* 13.1 (2007), pp. 85–95. The Iraq War has raised popular interest in the contemporary situation of Africans in Iraq, for which see Theola Labbé, 'A Legacy Hidden in Plain Sight', *Washington Post*, 11 January 2004, p. A01; and Ann M. Simmons, 'Back to Africa, from Iraq', *Los Angeles Times*, 14 January 2004, pp. A1 and A14.

27. Al-Bayhaqī, *Manāqib*, p. 135.
28. Al-Ibshīhī, *Mustaṭraf*, p. 644.
29. Jār Allāh Ibn Fahd al-Makkī, *Al-Nukat al-ẓirāf fī al-mawʾiẓa bi dhawī al-ᶜāhāt min al-ashrāf* (Charming Anecdotes: An Admonition of Descendants of the Prophet with *ᶜĀhāt*), Chester Beatty Library, Dublin, Ireland, AH950/1543 CE, MS 3838, fo. 5a.
30. Wijdan Ali, 'From the Literal to the Spiritual: The Development of the Prophet Muḥammad's Portrayal from 13th-Century Ilkhanid Miniatures to 17th-Century Ottoman Art', *Electronic Journal of Oriental Studies* 4 (2001), pp. 1–24; Raya Y. Shani, 'Noah's Ark and the Ship of Faith in Persian Painting: From the Fourteenth to the Sixteenth-Century', *JSAI* 27 (2002), pp. 127–203; Oleg Grabar and Mika Natif, 'The Story of Portraits of the Prophet Muḥammad', *SI* 96 (2004), pp. 19–38 + 4 plates.
31. Hidayet Hosain, 'Translation of Ash-Shamaʾil of Tirmizi', *Islamic Culture* 7 (July 1933), p. 398.
32. Ibid., pp. 398, 400.
33. Ibid., p. 401.
34. Al-Qasṭallānī, *Al-Mawāhib*, 2:25.
35. Annemarie Schimmel, *And Muhammad Is His Messenger: The Veneration of the Prophet in Islamic Piety* (Chapel Hill: University of North Carolina Press, 1985), p. 115.
36. Muᶜāfá b. Zakariyyā al-Jarīrī, *Al-Jalīs al-ṣāliḥ al-kāfī wa'l-anīs al-nāṣiḥ al-shāfī*, ed. Muḥammad Mursī Khawlī (Beirut: ᶜĀlam al-kutub, 1987), 3:316.
37. Ibn Hishām, *The Life of Muḥammad: A Translation of Isḥāq's Sīrat Rasūl Allāh*, trans. A. Guillaume (Lahore and Karachi: Oxford University Press, 1967), p. 72; al-Qasṭallānī, *Al-Mawāhib*, 1:166.
38. Muḥammad b. ᶜĪsā al-Tirmidhī, *Al-Shamāʾil al-muḥammadiyya*, ed. Muḥammad ᶜAwwāma (Medina: s.n., 2001), p. 88.
39. Chase F. Robinson, 'Neck-Sealing in Early Islam', *JESHO* 48.3 (2005), p. 402, fn. 2; Yohanan Friedmann, 'Finality of Prophethood in Sunnī Islām', *JSAI* 7 (1986), pp. 180ff.

2

Literary Networks in Mamluk Cairo

The English term 'disability' focuses on physical and cognitive performance and productivity – what the body can or cannot do. The equivalent classical Arabic term *ᶜāha* literally means 'blight' or 'damage', and it can refer to objects both inanimate (crops, trees) and animate (human and non-human animals). The category of blightedness certainly encompasses 'disability', but incorporates aesthetics and character. Blights disrupt beauty and can constitute character flaws. Like 'disability' or 'handicap' today, the meaning of blightedness was changing and performing new work in culture throughout the Islamicate Middle Ages. For instance, from the 8th to the 13th centuries, blue eyes were included with such impairments as blindness, deafness and paralysis on Arabic-language lists of people with physical defects; and, as early as the 9th century, Arab poets wrote erotic verses to individuals with such physical blights as blue eyes, crossed eyes and ophthalmia. The earliest negative mention of blue or green eyes in the Islamic period is preserved in Qur'an 20: 102, which reads: 'the day when the trumpet is blown, and on that day We will gather the guilty, blue-eyed [*zurq*ᵃⁿ]'.[1] (This is the lone mention of blue eyes in the Qur'an.) Blue eyes were extraordinary physical traits among Arabs, marking blue-eyed people as physically and, in this context, morally other. The Prophet, for instance, reportedly had deep black eyes. Al-Thaᶜālibī (d. 873/1468), a Mālikī theologian from North Africa, summarised the two most common interpretations of the term *zurq* in the Qur'an. The first explanation, which was also supported by Muḥammad's cousin Ibn ᶜAbbās (d. 68/688), purports that the people to be gathered are those who have black skin and blue eyes, for these traits are ugly. After being assembled, they will then be blinded. A second interpretation is that people with blue complexions are extraordinarily ugly, because their skin is the colour of ashes (*ramād*). 'It is official in the speech of the Arabs that this [ashen] colour is called *azraq*.'[2] Another observer, al-Biqāᶜī (d. 885/1480), indicated in his commentary on this verse that *zurq* referred to people with blue eyes and bodies, meaning that they were once beautiful and then their bodies changed.[3]

In the later Middle Ages and the early modern period, blue eyes still retained their associations with aberration and difference. For instance,

Andreas Tietze translated Muṣṭafā ᶜAlī's description of a man in 1599 Cairo as 'a young lad on horseback his head wrapped, thick-lipped, with churlish feet, with boorish claws, with sores on his cheeks and wounds on his back, mis-shapen and ugly, when he opens his mouth resembling a blue-eyed (?) ogre'.[4] In a litany of terms signifying physical unattractiveness and disgusting mien, the inclusion of blue eyes as a category of ugliness confounded Tietze, who seems to have perceived blue eyes positively, leading him to question his reading or the copyist's accuracy.

In a reversal of norms, Arab writers of the 9th/15th and 10th/16th centuries produced male homoerotic verses to blighted beloveds. One such author, Shihāb al-Dīn al-Ḥijāzī, not only penned romantic poetry for male and female beloveds but was also physically and intellectually transformed and marked by a drug overdose. In his work and life, one finds the emergence of an alternative vision of dignity and desirability that gives new dimension to everyday life, love, courtship and friendship.

Shihāb al-Dīn al-Ḥijāzī

Medieval Arab names incorporate histories of paternal descent, migration, tribal affiliation and religious identification. The full name of this chapter's main subject is Shihāb al-Dīn Aḥmad b. Muḥammad b. ᶜAlī b. Ḥasan b. Ibrāhīm al-Ḥijāzī al-Anṣārī al-Khazrajī al-Saᶜdī al-ᶜUbādī al-Qāhirī al-Shāfiᶜī. His given name is Aḥmad, and his honorific is Shihāb al-Dīn, which means 'shooting star of the faith'. His father's name was Muḥammad, his paternal grandfather was ᶜAlī, and his paternal great-grandfather was named Ḥasan.[5] Al-Ḥijāzī also claimed descent from the Khazrajī tribe, one of the two Medinan clans that welcomed Muḥammad and his followers into the city after they had departed from Mecca. The two tribes later merged and became collectively known as the Anṣār, or helpers. Al-Ḥijāzī's name also indicates that he claimed Cairo as his home and that he was an adherent of the Shāfiᶜī legal school, which was the majority legal group in northern Egypt before the arrival of the Ottomans in 922/1517, after which time the Ḥanafī school came to predominate. So, al-Ḥijāzī's name gives information on formal aspects of his identity that would have been intelligible to anyone with knowledge of Arabic in Mamluk Cairo, but tells little about how he functioned within the specific social and cultural environments there.

The year of al-Ḥijāzī's birth, 790/1388, was an eventful time in Cairo. Chroniclers recorded widespread pestilence, extreme weather patterns and an imperial project to remove poor and disabled people from the streets of Cairo. In Rabīᶜ I/March 1388, high winds blew through Egypt, stirring up so much dirt and sand that women walking in the streets were nearly blinded. Sound ophthalmic health was a rare physical condition in Mamluk Cairo. The soundness of one's body and one's health emerges as salient preoccupations in travel writing and in the chronicles of native Egyptians, reflecting to some degree the visibility of illness and the centrality of human bodies in reconstructing cityscapes for an audience.

A fierce plague also struck Egypt in this month and lasted three full months, claiming close to 300 victims daily.[6] It would have been perceived as a minor miracle that al-Ḥijāzī's mother survived the plague to give birth to her son on 27 Shaᶜbān 790/20 August 1388.[7] Pregnant women and young children were considered particularly susceptible to the ravages of the plague. Al-Maqrīzī attested that, when the plague first struck Cairo in this year, scholars read portions of religious texts in the city's mosques in order to request God's mercy; and, at one such public reading in al-Azhar, the audience was composed entirely of children and orphans.[8]

Plague viruses spread quickly and frequently through the urban centres of the Mamluk sultanate, usually with devastating effect, though the effects were less severe than in rural areas. Still, in cities, the disposal of masses of human remains in a timely manner sometimes proved difficult, thereby posing threats to public health and sanitation. Were a city's water supply to become polluted, the entire urban population would be exposed to the contagion. Even survivors of earlier plague epidemics did not necessarily escape unscathed. Children and the elderly were easy victims, though the virus afflicted all segments of society. Entire families were destroyed or weakened by the plague, and the plague-afflicted person was a ubiquitous figure. Those individuals infected with the plague virus may have suffered from swollen necks, armpits and groins, but were most readily identified by the characteristic pustules that erupted on their bodies and, if they survived, could permanently mar their skin or disfigure body parts. The image of plague affliction was apparently so ubiquitous and recognisable in 8th/14th-century Mamluk lands that al-Ṣafadī, who himself died of the plague in Damascus in 764/1363, wrote at least one epigram about a male beloved who had contracted the plague:

> Plague boils (*damāmil*) broke out on my beloved's leg,
> But far be it for adversity to overshadow his grace.
> So I said to our critics, 'There is nothing new in this, for have you ever seen
> The dawn unaccompanied by the bright gleam of morning?'[9]

These verses capture the mundanity of illness ('there is nothing new in this'), while also suggesting that the process of habituating oneself to the physical effects of disease opens spaces for aestheticising these diseased bodies. And their beauty seems as natural as a sunrise. Just as dawn and morning are inseparable phases of the day, the beauty of the beloved is inseparable from grace and thus impervious to blights.

Blighted Bodies on Display in Mamluk Cairo

The devastations of plague certainly affected the perspectives of individuals dwelling in Mamluk cities and also led to concerted efforts by sultans to eradicate these blighted bodies from public urban spaces. Imperial projects of removing the visible blight of beggars and disabled people from the urban landscape began before al-Ḥijāzī's birth and continued during his lifetime.[10] The first Mamluk sultan to initiate such a project of exclusion was al-Ẓāhir Baybars I, who in 664/1265 or 1266 assembled *ahl al-ᶜāhāt* in the Khān Sabīl and then ordered their transfer to al-Fayyūm, a province approximately 80 km south-west of Cairo, where he had established a separate living area for them. Although the basic needs of *ahl al-ᶜāhāt* were provided for, many of them returned to Cairo shortly after this forced exile.[11] The designation of al-Fayyūm, a Coptic Christian oasis settlement with many monasteries, as a suitable place of exile is never explained. Perhaps Baybars I thought that the Christian monastic population would show greater sympathy to the plight of *ahl al-ᶜāhāt.* Whatever his reasons, more than half a century later, on 16 Dhū al-Qaᶜda 730/31 August 1330, Sultan al-Nāṣir Muḥammad decreed that all lepers (*min al-jadhmāʾ wa'l-burṣān*) living in Cairo and Old Cairo must move to an unspecified location in al-Fayyūm.[12] In Shawwāl 794/September 1392, Sultan al-Ẓāhir Barqūq also ordered all lepers (*al-burṣān wa'l-jadhmāʾ*) to leave Cairo and its surrounding areas under penalty of death. The exile was short-lived, as the lepers were soon invited back to the city.[13] None of the chroniclers speculated on the sultans' reasons for these forced removals, suggesting that their audiences would have known of wider debates about the desirability of *ahl al-ᶜāhāt* as a visible social class. In an interesting turn, in Shawwāl 841/April 1438, Sultan al-Ẓāhir Barsbāy ordered able-bodied mendicants off the streets, leaving only 'chronically ill, blind and blighted people' (*al-zamanī wa'l-ᶜumyān wa-arbāb al-ᶜāhāt*) to beg publicly.[14] Ibn Taghrībirdī explained that the sultan's order was occasioned by the mistreatment of his royal envoy who was distributing alms to the poor. A crowd of alms-seekers encircled him as he sat on his horse, and managed to pull him off it. The sultan forced professional beggars off the streets, leaving only disabled poor to beg in public spaces.[15]

Official reactions to *ahl al-ᶜāhāt* dovetailed with Mamluk chroniclers' general characterisations of disabled people as socially marginal, undesirable, desperately poor people who may manipulate public goodwill by seeking handouts and alms. (This attitude may have led to judges and sultans manipulating the category of mental illness by ascribing it wantonly to those who threatened social order. Boaz Shoshan has discussed the extent to which 'mentally ill' individuals, who were all incidentally embroiled in 'religious scandals', in Cairo were ordered by judges or sultans into hospitals and subjected to harsh curative measures.[16]) Some *ahl al-ᶜāhāt*, on the other hand, emerged publicly of their own agency to seek cures and healing from saints and blessed sites. In Ṣafar 854/March 1450, during the reign of Jaqmaq, a black freedman named Saᶜdallāh or Saᶜdān, who was revered for his piety, publicly cursed the *ustādār*, or royal majordomo, Zayn al-Dīn Yaḥyá b. ᶜAbd al-Razzāq (d. 874/1469), and accused him of seizing his deceased master's property.[17] Zayn al-Dīn sent messengers to arrest Saᶜdān, but they were unable to approach him, either through a magical spell or because of physical force. Realising that he could not subdue his opponent, Zayn al-Dīn returned what he had taken. Upon learning of Saᶜdān's victory, a group of commoners (*al-ᶜawāmm*) to whom he had taught piety hurried to 'visit him and seek his blessing'.[18] His defiance of authority and his virtuous reputation made him a living saint. Al-Sakhāwī described the blessing-seekers as a large mob that included Turks and women and grew to include local princes, officials and jurisprudents. Many of the blessing-seekers were 'chronically ill, blighted and sick people'.[19] Ibn Iyās also recorded this event, but omitted any descriptions of the crowds that thronged Saᶜdān.[20] His charismatic leadership and brave defiance of the Mamluk power structure imbued his claims of piety with an authority that appealed to a major cross-section of Cairenes. If figures of piety held particular attractiveness for people of blights, then histories of cemeteries, shrines and saints' tombs should offer windows onto the religious lives of disabled Muslims in the Middle Ages. The archaeologist Bogdan Zurawski has excavated a 1,300-year-old Nubian church whose walls bear witness to the disabled and ill pilgrims who sought succour there. The image of one visitor, a visually impaired Muslim man who carries a cane and seems to have unsure footing, is painted on a wall. The painting is captioned in Arabic 'Ḍayf ᶜAlī', which means 'ᶜAlī the guest', suggesting that the visitor arrived after the Muslim conquest of Egypt in the 2nd/7th century.[21]

So, it was in this milieu of pestilence, public restrictions on the visibility of disabled people and, consequently, an acute awareness of marked bodies that al-Ḥijāzī lived. He was born in 790/1388 – during the reign of Sultan al-Ẓāhir Barqūq (r. 784–91, 792–801/1382–9, 1390–9) – in the old Fatimid capital of Cairo near the Baybarsiyya madrasa-khānqāh complex. When al-Ḥijāzī was only seven days old, his father carried him to holy sites in the city, seeking blessings for his infant son.[22] What little more is known of his early life has been mostly related by friends and associates. He was born on Yellow Lane (*Al-Darb al-aṣfar*), a side street that linked al-Baybarsiyya to Bayn al-Qaṣrayn Street (*Shāriᶜ Bayn al-Qaṣrayn*), a major thoroughfare reserved for royal processions and public ceremonies. Amirs and royal women who wanted to construct visible religious institutions tended to build on streets feeding into Bayn al-Qaṣrayn Street.[23] In 684/1285, Tidhkārbāy Khātūn, the daughter of Baybars I, built Ribāṭ al-Baghdādiyya, a women's religious convent, on Yellow Lane.[24] This *ribāṭ* dominated the street architecturally until 706/1307 or 1308, when the Mamluk amir Baybars al-Jāshankirī (later known as Baybars II when he became sultan) began construction on the Baybarsiyya compound. It was finally completed in 709/1310 during his year-long reign as sultan. The Baybarsiyya was constructed on Festival Gate Street (*Shāriᶜ Bāb al-ᶜĪd*) on the site of the Fatimid palace of the viziers and consisted of a Sufi lodge, hospice, mausoleum for the founder and a minaret, and it benefited from considerable funding and support.[25] This institution would remain a significant one in the lives of Shihāb al-Dīn and his father, Shams al-Dīn Muḥammad al-Ḥijāzī, a Qur'an-reciter renowned for 'the tenderness of his voice and the beauty of his inflections'.[26] Shihāb al-Dīn later became a Qur'an-reciter at the Baybarsiyya and was recognised as 'one of the notables in Qur'an recitation'.[27] There, he also delved into the Sufi way of life, eventually receiving the Sufi cloak from Shihāb al-Dīn al-Nāṣiḥ (d. 804/1402), a respected Sufi shaykh in Cairo, and learning *dhikr* from al-Ḥāfī.[28] Shihāb al-Dīn b. Ḥajar al-ᶜAsqalānī (773–852/1372–1449), who is most often recognised for his scholarly contributions to Islamic studies and his position as the Shāfiᶜī chief justice of Egypt, was intermittently *nāẓir* (director) and grand shaykh of the Baybarsiyya from 813/1410 until his death thirty-nine years later. At some point during his tenure there, al-Ḥijāzī heard hadith from this master. They cultivated a close teacher–student relationship that developed into a friendship based in part on their shared interests in writing poetry, composing riddles and exchanging personal letters. Teachers and students often described their relationships in terms of love, physical attachment and friendship. Although 'lecturing, reading, writing, reproducing texts, debating, discipleship, and scholarly friendship seem so widespread as to be marginal to the interests of social historians', analysing friendship invites access to how certain ideas were communicated. The history of sentiment possesses the potential to make everyday experience accessible to the historian.[29]

The friendship of these two men endured until Ibn Ḥajar's death in 852/1449 following a two-month illness. On this solemn occasion, al-Ḥijāzī wrote a lengthy, touching eulogy for him, the last of many expressions of love, sympathy and warmth for his friend and teacher.[30] Al-Sakhāwī said that, of the many poets who eulogised Ibn Ḥajar, al-Ḥijāzī presented the best tribute.[31] A crowd of thousands gathered in the rain to watch the funeral cortege carry Ibn Ḥajar's bier through the streets of Cairo to the Qarāfa cemetery, south-east of the city.[32] Various scholars and political dignitaries, including Sultan al-Ẓāhir Jaqmaq (r. 842–57/1438–53), numbered among the elite processioners. After witnessing this event, the poet Shihāb al-Dīn al-Manṣūrī (d. 887/1482) honoured Ibn Ḥajar with this couplet: 'Clouds wept rain on the chief judge, / Demolishing the pillar strengthened by the stone [*ḥajar*]'.[33] Before this final illness, Ibn Ḥajar had suffered other setbacks to his health, about which his friends wrote poems. After he had been cured of ophthalmia (*ramad*), an ocular inflammation thought to be caused by sand blowing into the eye, al-Ḥijāzī wrote two verses for him during his convalescence:

> You are not embarrassed by ophthalmia and you are not afraid
> Of an envious person holding grains of sand.
> May God protect you from the enemy's sand.
> Yes, may He turn you from the evil of the eye.[34]

The date of composition is not mentioned, but Ibn Ḥajar must have suffered from ophthalmia at least twice. The poet al-Shihāb b. Ṣāliḥ also wrote two poems for Ibn Ḥajar about his ophthalmia, and in the second one, he mentions that he is writing about a reoccurrence of the affliction. Ibn Ḥajar's illness must not have progressed to blindness in either or both of his eyes, as al-Sakhāwī described him as a man 'sound of hearing and sight'.[35] Otherwise, he may have been asked to relinquish his post as supervisor, as Amir Baybars al-Jāshankirī stipulated in the pious endowment deed (*waqfiyya*) that 'anyone whose body or clothing contradicted the perfect and sacred Islamic law' could not serve as administrator.[36] Leonor Fernandes interprets this clause as a restriction on people with disabilities or blights, among other groups, from assuming these high positions.[37] This stipulation is also curious given the fact that Baybars deposed al-Nāṣir Muḥammad, a popular sultan whose lameness figured as a large part of his public image. A song of political support for al-Nāṣir Muḥammad included the line 'Bring us the lame one!' – a reference to the Egyptian people's beloved leader. The two men's contest for the sultanate was fierce, especially after it was revealed that al-Nāṣir Muḥammad had plotted to overthrow his rivals in 708/1308, just as Baybars was beginning construction on the Baybarsiyya complex.[38] There is insufficient evidence to conclude that this intense political experience embittered him against placing physically blighted people in positions of power, though the timing of these events is suggestive.

Another possible explanation for the inclusion of such language is the prevalence of disease – particularly ophthalmic disorders – in Egypt. The visibility of blights made it a particularly salient category in late Mamluk Cairo. In keeping with the deed's emphasis on administrators' possessing ideal bodies, an eye doctor (*kaḥḥāl ṭabaʾiʿī*) was resident in the Baybarsiyya.[39] Still, in one respect, the deed's restriction provides evidence that al-Shāfiʿī's denigrating remarks against *ahl al-ʿāhāt* were accepted as authentic legal doctrine, especially as Shāfiʿīs are the only ones who fully accept the leadership of a blind imam; Shiʿis, Ḥanbalīs and Ḥanafīs deem leadership of a blind man reprehensible, and Mālikīs find the situation acceptable, but not preferable to a sighted imam.[40] The endowment deed specifically invokes Islamic law as the moral system that forbids blighted people from participating equally in religious offices – not the Qur'an or sunna.

Although people with certain physical disabilities were prevented from assuming high positions of power at the Baybarsiyya, the institution's charitable care of sick and dependent people resonated with the values of Ibn Ḥajar and his wife Uns Khātūn. They both took time to tend to the unwell. Ibn Ḥajar 'was dedicated to visiting the sick and attending funerals, especially those who depended on him (*man yalūdhu bihi*). And for those who were suffering acutely, he would visit the person bearing a gift'. Al-Sakhāwī attested that one time when he himself was sick, Ibn Ḥajar charitably sent al-Shihāb b. Yaʿqūb, a close friend of his, to look after him.[41] Uns Khātūn also kept company with widows and 'women who depended on leaders and others' (*yaludhna bi'l-ruʾasāʾ wa-ghayrihim*) for material support.[42] Living near al-Ribāṭ al-Baghdādiyya, a religious convent that only accepted unsupported women and female heads of households (divorcées, widows, abandoned wives, single mothers) as residents, Uns Khātūn likely devoted time and energy there. Evidently, caring for sick and dependent people constituted a firm and shared priority in Ibn Ḥajar's household.

Baybars II, a passionately religious man, intended his madrasa to have a Shāfiʿī character. The actual endowment deed (*waqfiyya*) stipulates that a Shāfiʿī and a Ḥanafī imam must be resident at the Baybarsiyya, though the Shāfiʿī imam would receive a higher stipend that could be as much as forty additional dirhams every month.[43] Having dual heads at the Baybarsiyya was a political move to ensure peace between the dominant

Shāfiᶜī school and the increasingly numerous Ḥanafīs, who belonged to the madhhab officially supported by the Mamluk sultanate. 'One of the remarkable aspects of the Mamluk society was the sharp cleavage between the Shafiᶜites and the Hanafites. The cleavage became as serious as the Shiᶜa and the Sunni feuds in the past centuries. From Baybars [II]'s time this feud went on increasing and during the 15th century it reached a climax.'[44] The Egyptian historian Ibn Duqmāq (d. 809/1407) identified the Baybarsiyya as an establishment shared by Shāfiᶜīs and Mālikīs, but al-Maqrīzī (d. 845/1442) designated it a Shāfiᶜī institution.[45] Although the endowment deed authenticates the founder's intended legal character for the institution, the remarks of these contemporary observers suggest that the affiliation changed under different leadership or due to internal or external pressures. However, all the sources agree that the Baybarsiyya catered, at least in part, to a Shāfiᶜī constituency.

Returning to al-Ḥijāzī's education, his father Shams al-Dīn also taught his son prosody and music.[46] Shams al-Dīn al-Ḥijāzī died in 809/1406 when his son was 18 years old; and, according to al-Sakhāwī, Shihāb al-Dīn related so many stories to him about his father's life that he came to feel that he had actually studied with Shams al-Dīn. As al-Sakhāwī expressed this connection, 'he was my shaykh indirectly'.[47] Shihāb al-Dīn's loyalty to his family impressed another of his close friends, who claimed that 'he loved . . . his family and honoured them. He neither talked about them in a backbiting manner (*bi-ghība*) nor with slander nor condescension.'[48]

In addition to al-Ḥijāzī's early education in Sufism, he memorised al-Ḥarīrī's grammatical treatise *Mulḥat al-iᶜrāb* and recited it to his teacher Zayn al-Dīn al-ᶜIrāqī (d. 806/1403) when he was only seven years old.[49] Acquiring such knowledge and performing it publicly constituted a common rite of passage for seven-year-old boys. According to an 8th/14th-century Cairene manual on morals and market inspection, 'when a boy is seven years old the teacher must order him to say his prayers with the congregation'.[50] Even if such feats of memorisation were expected of young boys, al-Ḥijāzī must still have impressed his teacher in legal studies, because, by the time he was 16 years old, al-ᶜIrāqī had qualified him to teach hadith to others. Al-Ḥijāzī also counted Ibn Abī Majid, al-Tanūkhī, Ibn Kuwayk and al-Nūr al-Fawī among his hadith instructors. He also pursued studies of jurisprudence, methodologies of jurisprudence and Arabic with al-Shams al-Suyūṭī, al-Shihāb al-Maghrāwī, al-Nāṣir b. Anas and al-ᶜIzz b. Jamāᶜa (d. 819/1416). Having studied with such scholarly luminaries, it is unsurprising that al-Ḥijāzī gained a reputation as a capable and eager student. Al-Sakhāwī, a biographer and student of al-Ḥijāzī's, praised his prodigious memory and related the following story about his quest to memorise increasingly more.[51]

> He continued to be foremost in intelligence and skilful in memorisation until he started taking anacardium nut (*ḥabb al-balādhur*). He took so much that his health became irregular. He said, 'Thereupon, I was only able to memorise with enormous strain. This happened to me the year after a burning broke out on my body. More than 100 boils (*miʾah dummal*) reddened and stayed on my body, and every little one afflicted me.'[52]

In Mamluk Cairo, Muslim and Jewish scholars partook of *balādhur* to excel in their studies, which centred on memorising and reciting lengthy texts.[53] This episode influenced al-Ḥijāzī so deeply that he related to a friend his personal experience with physical blightedness, and he also composed poetry dedicated to others like himself who had been impaired bodily and disabled socially because of their blights.

Balādhur

According to the medieval medical model of the body, memory loss arises from an excess of coldness or moisture of the brain. To restore memory, one could ingest substances, like *balādhur*, with dry and hot qualities. *Balādhur* is a nut that has been used in the Middle East as a memory-enhancing substance since at least the 3rd/9th century.[54] (It appears that Galen and Hippocrates were unaware of this drug.) Between its outer wall and its pericarp lies an amber-coloured, inky, sticky, pungent sap that when mixed with honey or another sweet substance was used to treat a predominantly cold humour, languor following an illness, forgetfulness and a diminished ability to memorise. Smoking anacardium was even said to cure haemorrhoids.[55] Because the nut itself possessed a hot quality, medieval pharmacologists cautioned young people and others with predominantly hot humours to avoid the drug, since it heats the blood and could lead to tuberculoid and lepromatous leprosy (*baraṣ* and *judhām*), itching (*saḥj*), hearing the voice of the devil (*waswās*), stupidity (*ḥumq*), rotting flesh (*ᶜafn*) and even early death. Today, anacardium is known as 'marking nut' because its sap is used to stain linens and paper, and it can also mark bodies as a tattooing ink. The anacardium extract is so abrasive that it is equally effective in removing tattoos.[56]

The Bundahishn, a 3rd/9th-century Zoroastrian creation myth, mentioned *balātur* in Pahlavi, and a commentary on an Avestan text referenced the contradictory medicinal properties of anacardium nut, warning that 'sometimes in curing by poison [it] kill[s] the man'.[57] The 3rd/9th-century

Persian physician ᶜAlī b. Sahl Rabbān al-Ṭabarī described an electuary of *balādhur* that would relieve stomach pain, memory loss and forgetfulness.[58] The Jewish pharmacist Abū Naṣr al-ᶜAṭṭār al-Isrāʾīlī (d. 658/1260) provided recipes for both a minor and a major *balādhur* electuary, with the latter being attributed to Galen. 'The minor *balādhur* electuary increases memory and drives away forgetfulness and works against paralysis . . . and various other illnesses owing to an excess of cold complexion.'[59] Ibn al-Bayṭār (d. 646/1248) compiled descriptions and commentaries on this plant from a host of 4th/10th- and 5th/11th-century physicians and pharmacologists.[60] By the 11th/17th century, ideas of *balādhur* had not much changed. According to the medical botanist Abū Muḥammad al-Qāsim al-Ghassānī (d. 1019/1610), *balādhur* was natively grown in China, where it was used to dye hair black, in India and on Sicily's Mount Etna. Al-Ghassānī saw this nut, which resembled a chestnut in colour and was shaped like a bird's heart, for sale in the Sūq al-ᶜAṭṭārīn (Drug and Perfume Market) in Fez. It was so acrid that al-Ghassānī warned that it 'burned the user's tongue, as though it were wine made from mountain grapes'.[61]

The anacardium nut was also useful for calming the nerves. An anecdote, probably apocryphal, attributed to al-Jāḥiẓ illustrates the potential for developing a dependency on *balādhur* to regulate one's mood. The famous writer allegedly said: '*Balādhur* never overpowered me, and I only ever argued with someone when I stopped feeling its effects. It is good for the nerves. You know what they say: "It is important people who are really bad for the nerves"'![62] Such a claim suggests a tenuous line between benignly benefiting from its tranquillising effects and depending on it to such an extent that one becomes accustomed to the drug-induced state – in this case, calmness.[63] The concept of addiction certainly existed in 8th/14th- and 9th/15th-century Egypt. The Shāfiᶜī jurist al-Zarkashī (d. 794/1392) said of hashish: 'Among the greatest physical harm caused by it is the fact that habitual users of it are hardly ever able to repent of it because of the effect it has upon their temper'. The Cairene poet al-Badrī, to whose work Chapter 3 will be devoted, noted that 'one of the properties of hashish is that its user cannot give it up'.[64] Tellingly, the Andalusian scholar Ibn Daqqāq (d. 380/990 or 991) and the North African jurist Ibn Jummah (d. 470/1077 or 1078) used so much *balādhur* that they became irascible.[65] However, these observed behavioural changes may have had less to do with use or overuse of the drug and more to do with withdrawal symptoms experienced from not using it.

Ibn Khallikān (d. 681/1282) reported that Ibn Shaddād (d. 632/1234) saw four or five jurists gathered at Madrasat al-Niẓāmiyya in Baghdad to discuss appropriate dosages for anacardium.

> Because it strengthens one's memory and comprehension, they had gathered with one of the physicians. They asked him about the amount of it that humans can use and about how to use it. Then they bought the amount that the physician had told them and drank it somewhere outside the school. Insanity overtook them. They dispersed and they did not know what had come over them. After some days, one of them – a tall fellow – came to the madrasa. He was naked, and wore nothing to cover his genitals. On his head was a large turban (*biqyār kabīr*) with a long piece of it hanging down, which was not custom. He threw it [the piece] behind him, and it reached his ankles. He was silent, exuding peace and dignity, not talking, not joking. One of the jurists present approached him and asked him about his condition. He said to them: 'We gathered together and drank the *balādhur* nut. My friends became crazy and I was the only one to escape. My mind grew strong and clear.' The people mock him, and he is unaware of it. He firmly believes that he has escaped what afflicted his friends.[66]

The calming effect of *balādhur* is evidenced in this anecdote and in the one about al-Jāḥiẓ, though the above story also illustrates the known side-effect of insanity, which the narrator perceptively defined as simply shameless flouting of cultural norms. Reports of the serious harm suffered after taking *balādhur* circulated in anecdotes and biographies throughout the Mediterranean and in the Middle East. ᶜAbd al-Raḥmān b. Mahdī (d. 198/813) and Abū Dāwud al-Ṭayālisī (d. 203 or 204/819 or 820) were companions in Basra and colleagues in hadith-transmission who reportedly drank *balādhur* to improve their memories. Al-ᶜIjlī (d. 261/874) claimed that 'ᶜAbd al-Raḥmān [b. Mahdī] drank *balādhur* then developed tuberculoid leprosy (*baraṣ*), and Abū Dāwud [al-Ṭayālisī] drank it and developed lepromatous leprosy (*judhām*)'.[67] Al-Ṭayālisī apparently suffered even beyond the onset of this illness, as he reportedly died at the age of 70 'after drinking a medicine made of the semecarpus anacardium nut';[68] and the grandfather of the historian al-Balādhurī apparently 'died mentally deranged through inadvertent use of *balādhur* . . ., a drug believed beneficial for one's mind and memory'.[69] This last man's accidental overdose and the attendant dementia came to mark the entire family in name. Ibn al-Jawzī (d. 597/1201) suffered far less dramatically from his use of the drug, as his beard thinned in patches. Though not a dire health concern, the cultural association of thin-beardedness and emasculation would have made such a condition rather embarrassing.[70] The Granadan poet Abū Isḥāq al-Sāḥilī (d. 747/1346) lost mental stability for a short time after ingesting *balādhur* and started claiming that he was a prophet.[71] The 10th/16th-century Jewish physician Judah Aryeh of Modena, in northern Italy, warned against the overuse of anacardium because he had 'seen and known many people who because of a frequent use of [different] oils and because of the eating of all kinds of *balādhur* lost their mind and went crazy, or got sick and died before their time and were not remembered any more'.[72]

In the Middle Ages, dementia was so widely recognised as a side-effect of taking *balādhur* that some people manipulated public goodwill through deception. Al-Bayhaqī (d. early 4th/10th century) described a band of 3rd/9th-century beggars who, in a manipulative display, rubbed clay all over their bodies and feigned eating *balādhur*, so as to appear insane.[73] The Syrian author al-Jawbarī (d. after 619/1222) speculated that Jewish physicians provided duplicitous women with *balādhur* so that they would administer it to their husbands to render them passive, lethargic and confused.[74]

Al-Ḥijāzī's Overdose on **Balādhur**

Al-Ḥijāzī was narrowly spared death and lived another fifty years, but he was one of the unfortunate ones who lost his mind for an unspecified period of time in his early twenties, then regained mental stability, though he ultimately lost some cognitive power, preventing him from memorising as before.[75] No longer able to perform at the same level, he was forced to leave his religious studies behind and began to pursue literary studies full time. His loss of memory was not the only side-effect of his overindulgence in anacardium nut. According to a modern Indian pharmacological work, an overdose of the drug can lead to the eruption of red, inflamed sores that itch and burn.[76] Al-Ḥijāzī's outbreak of boils in Ramaḍān 815/1412 or 1413 was so excruciating that he found himself unable to sleep for ten days. On the tenth day of sleeplessness, he wrote to his friend Ṣalāḥ al-Dīn al-Asyūṭī (d. 859/1455) about the harrowing experience that became a test of patience. The letter is in rhymed prose (*saj*ᶜ) with some interspersed verses. Following an ornately rhetorical opening, al-Ḥijāzī wrote:

> Praise unto God. May He take me into account in whatever He wills. There is no strength except through God. 'Truly, the steadfast will be paid their reward without measure' [Qur'an 13: 39] . . .
>
> I have spent ten nights without being refreshed by sleep, and I have had nothing to eat. So here, in this holy month I am fasting both night and day. The fire of this boil has covered up my heart's good fortune as though it were a salamander/phoenix [*samandal*]. And why should it not be this way since it too is alive inside the fire?
>
> Night grew long, and through it a boil afflicted me.
> It kept me from falling asleep, and I could not bear it.
> It felt as though knowing the time were a temptation, so here I am
> Keeping an eye on the night stars, waiting for the dawn.[77]

In classical Arabic, *samandal* can mean either 'salamander' or 'phoenix'. The connection between the two meanings stems from the belief that the salamander cannot be killed by fire; in fact, the animal's cold body temperature was said to extinguish flames.[78] This belief even appears in contemporary Arabic, where one term for 'amphibian' (*amphi* = both, *bio* = life) is a direct translation from the Greek – *dhāt ᶜumrayn*, meaning 'having two lives'. By drawing a comparison between surviving his fiery boils and a salamander's surviving a fire, al-Ḥijāzī may have led his friend to conjure associations with *balādhur*, the source of his suffering, since *balādhur* was commonly prescribed as an antidote to the lethal effects of the salamander's cold humour.[79] The narrator al-Suyūṭī interjects after the above epigram that al-Ḥijāzī 'then lost his mind from a boil whose burning bore a hole in his skin like a live coal'.[80] While a known side-effect of *balādhur* was dementia or insanity, al-Suyūṭī may have felt obliged by friendship or professional loyalty to attribute his teacher's mental decline to a physical condition rather than to overuse of a dangerous drug. Al-Ḥijāzī himself never mentions *balādhur* in the letter, but the connection between his drug use, the boils and his loss of reason is made explicit in al-Sakhāwī's obituary notice.

The letter continues with details of his suffering and eventual despondency, with the writer likening the boils

> to an ordinary horseman who makes life hateful to me, attacking my soul again and again. I did not find a way out of practising patience . . . This difficult ordeal has made death easy for me . . . I gave up all hope of health . . . but I did not perish. Tears flowed from my eyes, as there was an obstacle between me and sleep . . . A night of worry about the boil followed without interruption . . . I bore it stoutly until the dawn overcame the night . . . My body wasted away in these ten days and nights from lack of food and sleep. Unfortunately, the truth is that crying did not make me fatter or spare me from hunger. But I swear by the dawn and the ten days and nights that my heart has already broken this fast. Though I was cut off from anything ruling over me and I was cast a long way off, my spirit has soared. I am greater than someone who has not known suffering or who does not know the difference between convalescence and illness.[81]

Being afflicted with boils taught al-Ḥijāzī piety, patience and perspective. Illness and suffering elevated him above the fray of ordinary believers, and he gained a renewed appreciation for life.

Khabar al-jism*: Sharing 'A Story about the Body'*

Al-Ḥijāzī once told his friend al-Biqāᶜī: 'Strange things have happened to me in my life', then proceeded to recount for him humorous stories about nearly suffocating from a headlong fall into a melon when he was just a boy, nearly drowning in an enormous water jug at the Baybarsiyya when he was a man, and having a new suit of clothes become progressively dirtier from blood splattered during a slaughter, the sticky juice of watermelon rinds and various other substances while walking through Cairo one day. After finishing these tales, al-Ḥijāzī confided in his friend: '"A lot of people think that I fabricate many of the things that happen to me", but he swore by God that all of it had happened to him and that he had not contrived any of it'.[82] The improbability of al-Ḥijāzī's experiences and stories gave his contemporaries reason to doubt their veracity; and certain elements of this letter suggest that it was not composed spontaneously during his period of deep suffering, but were deliberately composed later. Portions are written in rhymed prose (*sajᶜ*), and metred verses are interspersed throughout the prose. Though it is unlikely that this letter, which was reproduced by al-Suyūṭī, is an authentic, verbatim rendering of the original, the circumstances detailed within it have been substantiated by such reputable sources as al-Sakhāwī, al-Suyūṭī and al-Asyūṭī.

The recipient of this letter, al-Asyūṭī, replied to his friend with a sympathetic message. After an ornate rhetorical address, he reminded al-Ḥijāzī of the Prophet's affirmation that 'there is no type of illness or pain that afflicts a believer without it becoming a penance for his sins'.[83] These brief remarks are the only portion of the text addressed directly to al-Ḥijāzī. Following this section, al-Asyūṭī characterised the letter as 'an honoured composition that contained a complaint about the pain of boils [that] has reached me from our lord, a man who holds the reins of explication and is pointed at with the fingertips [a gesture suggesting a person's fame]'. The letter itself is described as more than simply a complaint letter, for al-Ḥijāzī has 'expressed a story about the body using dissimilarity and substitutions (*bi'l-taghayyur wa'l-abdāl*), giving insight on the particularities of illness (*ḥurūf al-iᶜtilāl*) after he had lost all remembrance of good health'.[84] Al-Asyūṭī recognised the spiritual significance of his friend's ordeal, but is quite clear in describing it as *khabar al-jism*, 'a story about the body'.

Since patient histories from Mamluk Cairo have not been recovered, and Arabic auto-narratives of illness are a rare genre, this letter represents a rare instance of individual self-expression of physical suffering. While al-Ḥijāzī's letter is not a formal narrative of symptoms and complaint, his prose and poetry offer a view of one man's construction of his ill body and his fury at the circumstances.

Here, a portrait of illness is so starkly rendered that al-Asyūṭī wonders who could possibly read al-Ḥijāzī's words unmoved, and marvels at his endurance during such an extraordinary physical trial. Al-Ḥijāzī connected with an unidentified mamluk who had experienced a similar bout of agony.

> His pain and sleeplessness persisted during the hottest part of the day. The carcasses of animals surrounded him, many of which had turned to stone. He sought refuge from the sun under rocks, though the stones had cracked open in the heat. The deaf man (*al-aṣamm*) is he who does not pity someone painfully afflicted, and the mute man (*al-abkam*) is he who does not open his mouth though his body has something to say. I remained silent about a symptom until it was manifested on my body, about a physical anomaly until I stood up and collapsed on the ground, about something found on the heart until it was found in the eye.[85]

In early 9th/15th-century Cairo, the Mamluk military corps consisted of mostly Turkic-speaking male slaves and their children (*awlād al-nās*), who were of Kurdish, Circassian and Turkish descent, and therefore linguistically and culturally isolated from the Arabic-speaking residents of the city. Since Mamluk sultans were drawn from either the pool of active mamluks or their sons, the mamluk soldiers had a more immediate identification with the power structure than with the masses. A culture of distrust characterised the relationship between the two groups. Arabic-speaking and mamluk social networks had few overlaps, so the communion of the mamluk and al-Ḥijāzī over their shared physical experiences and consequent social isolation is especially remarkable.[86] Al-Asyūṭī reports that the mamluk had suffered much ('his pain was long') and had been abandoned by his friends. His suffering was lightened when al-Ḥijāzī shared with him 'a symptom (*ᶜard*) of the body. Their souls suddenly came to know each other, and their spirits intermingled. Their bodies were associated with each other in good times, and their body parts were attracted to each other for their shared misfortunes.'[87] Their bodies formed the common grounds for companionship.

Al-Ḥijāzī's Literary Training and Production

> 'I am he whose literature the blind saw and whose words the deaf heard.'
>
> Al-Mutanabbī[88]

Al-Ḥijāzī's literary training included studies of Ibn Rashīq's treatise on literary composition titled *al-ᶜUmdah*, the Qur'an, *Nūr al-ᶜuyūn* (Light of the Eyes), *al-Tanbīh* (Allusions) and Ḥarīrī's *maqāmāt*, 'except for the insignificant ones among them'.[89] Among his own literary works are a seventy-volume work on the art of composition entitled *Tadhkira fī al-adīb* and an examination of poetic metre in the Qur'an (*Qalāʾid al-nuḥūr min jawāhir*), which his contemporary Shihāb al-Dīn b. ᶜArabshāh al-Dimashqī (791–854/1389–1450) recited to him. Al-Ḥijāzī apparently judged his recitation satisfactory and authorised Ibn ᶜArabshāh to teach it to others.[90] Our al-Ḥijāzī also wrote works of literary commentary (*Al-Qawāᶜid fī al-maqāmāt, Sharḥ al-muᶜallaqāt*) and anthologies of poetry (*Kitāb rawḍ al-ādāb, Al-Lumaᶜ al-shihābiyya min al-burūq al-ḥijāziyya*) that his students updated with his later verses. An autograph copy of his 275-folio *dīwān* at the Escorial Library in Spain includes samples of his poems in many genres.[91] On 17 Muḥarram 826/9 January 1422, al-Ḥijāzī completed *Kitāb Rawḍ al-ādāb* (Book of the Garden of Civilities), a compilation of Arabic 'verse, prose, love poems, praise poems, riddles, literary debates, oral strophic poems, *muwashshaḥāt*, anecdotes, among other genres' from the pre-Islamic era through his own lifetime, even including some of his own work.[92] He also anthologised a diverse collection of anecdotes into a volume titled *Nawādir al-akhbār wa-ẓarāʾif al-ashᶜār* (Anecdotal Reports and Charming Poetry).[93]

He was widely praised for his literary gifts. Al-Sakhāwī described him as the 'master littérateur of the age'; and, as befits someone with that title, his poetry enjoyed considerable popularity and a wide circulation.[94] One finds a sample of his verses in 'The Story of the Two Viziers: Nūr al-Dīn ᶜAlī al-Miṣrī and Badr al-Dīn Ḥasan al-Baṣrī' in a 17th- or 18th-century Egyptian manuscript of *The Thousand and One Nights*.

Say thou to skin 'Be soft,' to face 'Be fair,'
And gaze, nor shall they blame howso thou stare:
Fine nose in Beauty's list is high esteemed;
Nor less an eye full, bright and debonair:
Eke did they well to laud the lovely lips
(Which e'en the sleep of me will never spare);
A winning tongue, a stature tall and straight;
A seemly union of gifts rarest rare:
But Beauty's acme in the hair one views it;
So hear my strain and with some few excuse it![95]

The same story in the earliest known manuscript of the *Nights*, an 8th/14th-century Syrian text in the Bibliothèque Nationale de France, omits this poem and includes no discussion of the aesthetic merits of hair nor any mention of al-Ḥijāzī. These textual differences support the scholarly opinion that the *Nights* was largely amended in late Mamluk Cairo, and it is this form that has been transmitted to modern audiences.[96] Patrice Coussonnet, for instance, has analysed specific elements of this story across the various editions and manuscripts and has concluded that the final recension is actually from early 9th/15th-century Cairo, placing its completion just at the apex of al-Ḥijāzī's literary career.[97]

Along with representing the heights of Cairo's literary culture, al-Ḥijāzī was also a dedicated observer of current events. On occasion, historians cited verses that he had composed as social commentaries, as will be seen.[98] But he has also been recognised for the meticulous records he assembled of the Nile's water levels between the years 1/622 and 874/1470 and for his detailed descriptions of the Nile and the Nilometer, which had pre-Islamic origins.[99]

Al-Ḥijāzī's status as a writer was sufficiently strong that sometime between 815/1412 or 1413 and 852/1449 he was named one of the seven best poets living in Cairo. Because all seven poets were named Shihāb al-Dīn, an honorific meaning 'shooting star of the faith', they were known collectively as the 'Seven *Shihāb*s', meaning 'Seven Shooting Stars'.[100] Al-Ḥijāzī composed twin collections of romantic epigrams: *Al-Kunnas al-jawārī fī al-ḥisān min al-jawārī* (Retrograde Running Stars [Q 81: 16]: On Beautiful Young Women), a compendium of *muʾannathāt*, or love poetry addressed to women; and *Jannat al-wildān fī al-ḥisān min al-ghilmān* (The Paradise of Youths: On Beautiful Young Men), an anthology of *mudhakkarāt*, or love poetry addressed to men. The latter work represents one of many contemporary books on this same subject.[101] Al-Ṣafadī's *Al-Ḥusn al-ṣarīḥ* has already been mentioned, but ᶜUmar b. al-Wardī's *Al-Kalām ᶜalá miʾat ghulām* (Musings on One Hundred Young Men), Muḥammad al-Nawājī's *Marātiᶜ al-ghizlān fī al-ḥisān min al-ghilmān* (Pastures of Gazelles: On Beautiful Young Men) and Aḥmad b. al-Mullā's (d. 1003/1594 or 1595) *ᶜUqūd al-jumān fī waṣf nubdha min al-ghilmān* (Pearl Necklaces: A Description of a Few Young Men) are additional poetry collections on male beauties. Al-Nawājī's work served as a model for al-Ḥijāzī's complementary collections *Al-Kunnas al-jawārī* and *Jannat al-wildān.*[102] These two anthologies, like his *Kitāb rawḍ al-ādāb*, feature epigrams to bakers, hunters, flautists and other men and women of professions.[103] His *Kunnas al-jawārī* includes epigrams about women who are bald (*qurᶜāʾ*), mentally ill, blind or deaf, who cast harmful spells with their eyes and who have the speech impediment of switching the letters ك (a 'k' sound) and ء (a glottal stop). His *Jannat al-wildān* contains epigrams about men who are mentally ill, deaf, blind, one-eyed, ophthalmic (*armad*) or feverish (*maḥmūm*) or who have the power to kill others with a glance, and those who confuse the letters س (a soft 's' sound) with ث (a soft 'th' sound) and ر (an 'r' sound) with ع (a voiced pharyngeal fricative).[104]

The challenge of writing an effective epigram lies in condensing emotion and sometimes wit into only two lines of verse. In al-Ḥijāzī's verses, the symbols of beauty, seduction and sexual attractiveness are inverted. Rather than deploying the standard trope of love as a wounding force, he worked in the well-established Arab literary tradition of *taghayyur*, or praising the undesirable and demeaning the beautiful, evoking unexpected emotions on mundane topics. Al-Ḥijāzī masterfully evoked the playful seduction of a mentally ill (*majnūn*) woman. The Arabic term for mental illness, *junūn*, derives from the word for demon or invisible spirit (*jinn*), because the illness was sometimes equated with demonic possession. So, al-Ḥijāzī describes a man's love for a woman so enchantingly beautiful that even the *jinn* fell in love with her, possessing her body and driving her to illness. No human or spirit could resist her charms, no matter what her mental state.

> I was concerned about the woman who went mad,
> And I started to waste away over her.
> By reason she has captivated a man,
> As she continued to enchant the jinn.[105]

Similarly, in portraying love for a mentally ill man, it is the afflicted one who maintains control of the courtship. The speaker is 'shackled by his love', and when he 'recite[s] poetry for him sweetly, he plunged me into his mind'.[106] In a reversal of the archetype of the lover ill from the fervour of his love, here it is the beloved who suffers from a mental illness as a result of a *jinn's* obsession with her.

Another theme in these poems is that of the person with the blighted body being shielded from hearing, seeing or understanding the pain that people with unmarked bodies encounter. In these epigrams, al-Ḥijāzī employs the standard motif of two lovers weathering the mockery, gossip and/or reproach of their detractors. Of a deaf man, he writes:

> My reproachers have found fault with a beloved who has become
> Deaf. I said, 'Speak censure.
> It can cause no harm, because he
> Is deaf and cannot hear the slanderers' words.'[107]

And, regarding two deaf women, he muses about communicating through sign language and becoming figuratively deaf:

> I was infatuated with a young lady who could not hear
> The words of slanderers when obscene language increased.
> You make my heart skip when you are joined to me
> And you deafen my mind with your absence.[108]

I became very attached to a deaf woman
Whose face is to me like a halo around a full moon.
Because of her deafness, I say, 'Beware the detractors',
Though I conveyed my speech to her through gestures.[109]

Deafness affords a particular protection for the male lover, who can remain blissfully oblivious of the turmoil that their relationship is causing in the community.[110] In the case of the female beloved, her lover does not attempt to shield her from public reactions to their courtship, even using sign language to communicate this fact to her. In an oral society like Mamluk Cairo, deafness would have been considered a distinct and significant social disadvantage. As such, eroticising or privileging deafness may have had a stronger impact on a contemporary reader or lector of these verses than on a modern one. Still, the imagery is striking; and the motif of a disability or blight protecting someone from the undesirable aspects of the world sometimes reappears in modern literature.[111]

Other verses raise questions about the speaker's gaze. The following epigram about a bald woman seems fairly straightforward, as unrequited love was a common poetic theme.

There is a young lady who has no hair on her head,
But in her eyes is languor.
What pleasure her desire would give me.
I am dying of grief, and she knows nothing of it.[112]

Is the speaker referencing a figurative baldness, wherein the traditional veil covers the hair, creating the appearance of hairlessness? Or does the speaker, in fact, mean a woman with 'no hair on her head'? This latter possibility raises many questions of the male speaker's access to the woman in question. In a culture where respectable Muslim women are veiled in public spaces and when they are around men who are not close family members, an unknown man peering beneath the veil suggests a violation of privacy through subterfuge, class difference or surveillance. Other possibilities are that the bald woman is a slave, a non-Muslim or both. Perhaps he happened to feel her head and determined that there was no loose hair or knotted bun on her head.

Lastly, illness or blights can also serve to increase the desirability of the love object, inverting social and literary expectations of a physically whole and healthy beloved. On a man stricken with fever, he mused:

Like a rose, his fever has returned
Doubly strong to the cheek of my beloved.
God has augmented his beauty
With this illness. Now diminish the fever![113]

Rosy cheeks were a widely recognised mark of beauty for men and women in Mamluk Cairo, but an accentuation of this feature through illness probably marks a departure from archetypal representations of beauty.

In all these verses, the symbols of beauty, seduction and sexual attractiveness are inverted, representing an antinomian approach to body normatives. Al-Ḥijāzī has advanced an alternative vision of devotion, dignity and desirability here, departing from predominant writings of sexual culture that valorised ideal standards of beauty. There exists a well-established Arab literary tradition of praising the undesirable and demeaning the beautiful – an exercise known as *taghayyur*.[114] A mark of a writer's technical agility and skill was his ability to evoke unexpected emotions on mundane topics. Al-Thaᶜālibī compiled an anthology on this subject called *Taḥsīn al-qabīḥ wa-taqbīḥ al-ḥasan* (Beautifying the Ugly and Uglifying the Beautiful). Geert Jan van Gelder has found antecedents of this tradition in ancient Greek practices, and considers poems of the type that al-Ḥijāzī wrote representative of *taghayyur*. He attributes al-Jāḥiẓ's essay on blacks and whites to his interest in this technique;[115] and, while this may be part of al-Jāḥiẓ's motivation, it cannot account for all of it. Al-Jāḥiẓ's subjectivity, the zeitgeist of the medieval Middle East and evidence of black discontent at the time (for example, black slave revolts in lower Iraq) are elided in this evaluation, but bringing in a historical perspective illuminates how al-Jāḥiẓ's epistle is relevant to period concerns. Likewise, identifying aspects of al-Ḥijāzī's life makes his writings on blighted and disabled bodies more than just a literary exercise. As skilful as he is at *taghayyur*, he is even more skilful at de-stigmatising the gaze of unblighted people towards blighted ones and acknowledging the sexuality and desirability of marked people.

Friendships

The eldest of the seven Shihābs was the esteemed Shihāb al-Dīn b. Ḥajar al-ᶜAsqalānī, who is largely remembered today for his theological and legal writings and activities. Aside from being popularly known for his poetry, Ibn Ḥajar himself appears to have been rather proud of his work, even though he reportedly stopped composing poems by 816/1413 or 1414.[116] 'The importance that Ibn Ḥajar assigned to his own poetic production is shown by the fact that he himself composed three different recensions of his *Dīwān*,[117] a work that includes verses about the Prophet, panegyrics to caliphs, princes and other elites, and love poems. The following love poem is even dedicated to a one-eyed male youth, whose afflicted eye is as dark as an eclipsed sun:

My lover has been afflicted in the centre of this beauty
In the eye of perfection, just as when the sun passes through an eclipse.
Scorching fires have ruined his eye. Still, I ask detractors:
Is a piece of paper ever rejected for the fault of a single letter?
His face is public beauty, and his first beard growth resembles
Rows of handwriting. This eye (*ᶜayn*) is a letter that has lost its lustre.[118]

By rejecting the equation of sexual attractiveness with physical perfection, the poem's speaker is realigning beauty norms, allowing one to find beauty among the 'ruins' of an afflicted eye. The poem also shows how physical difference can be acknowledged for what it is without sensationalising or denigrating it. This sentiment was not for Ibn Ḥajar simply a poetic conceit. While teaching at al-Azhar mosque, he once had a cross-eyed student who attended his lectures. One day, another student wrote on the wall next to the cross-eyed boy's seat: 'There is no power or strength except with God' (*lā ḥawla wa-lā quwwata illā billāhi*). In Arabic, the second word could also be read *ḥawala*, meaning 'cross eyes'. The cross-eyed student read the graffiti as a taunt about his physical condition. Embarrassed and upset, the student sought a legal opinion on the matter from his teacher, expecting him to censure the graffiti-writer. Instead of condemning the perpetrator, Ibn Ḥajar wrote a legal opinion consisting of the same words as the graffito message: *lā ḥawla/ḥawala wa lā quwwata illā billāhi*. Ibn Ḥajar does not explain whether he intends the second word to read 'power' or 'cross eyes', because either interpretation would be acceptable. Either one, he wrote, can be considered 'one of the treasures of heaven'.[119]

The other five men who shared this name were Shihāb al-Dīn b. al-Shāb al-Tāᵓib (d. 832/1429), Shihāb al-Dīn b. Ṣāliḥ (d. 861/1456 or 1457), Shihāb al-Dīn b. Mubārak Shāh al-Dimashqī (d. 862/1458), Shihāb al-Dīn b. Abī al-Saᶜūd (d. 868/1464 or 870/1466) and Shihāb al-Dīn al-Manṣūrī (d. 887/1482).[120] The designation of this literary group as the Seven Shooting Stars was an identity that they all readily assumed, and their bonds of friendship appear to have been rather firm.[121] They composed verses to console each other about illnesses, eulogies to commemorate their lives, commentaries on current events that personally affected them and friendly letters on a host of subjects. Their shared name engendered a number of puns. Once, four of them – Ibn Ḥajar al-ᶜAsqalānī, al-Ḥijāzī, Ibn Ṣāliḥ and Ibn Abī al-Saᶜūd – wrote scathing reviews for an epigram that one Walī al-Dīn had composed about the strength of a man whose tooth had been pulled because of an illness. Ibn Ḥajar, for one, felt that the poet had 'shitted out this short poem', and Cairenes joked that Walī al-Dīn had been hit by four shooting stars.[122] The Shihābs banded together in a firm display of solidarity.

Al-Ḥijāzī had certainly meditated on the obligations and meaning of friendship in *Nawādir al-akhbār*. Dedicating an entire section to the subject, he cited a number of earlier Muslim thinkers who voiced contradictory opinions. Al-Ḥijāzī himself concluded that neither distance nor adversity should separate friends, as this bond was too precious to go unnurtured. One of his close friends, al-Ṣayrafī, described him as 'an excellent man who behaves humbly and affectionately to his friends and avidly desires visits from them'.[123] These two men spent many days and nights together at al-Ṣayrafī's home.

Another group of seven Shihābs exhibited similar dynamics of identifying intensely with the group. Al-Sakhāwī related an anecdote about this particular group of men:

> One time our shaykh [Ibn Ḥajar al-ᶜAsqalānī] was sitting with al-Shihāb b. Taqī, al-Shihāb al-Shayrajī [sic], al-Shihāb al-Rīshī, al-Shihāb al-Ḥijāzī, and another al-Shihāb. So along with the subject of this biography, there were seven people. Al-Ḥijāzī said, 'O Mawlānā, you (m. pl.) have named your comets "The Seven Planets", who are gathered here today'. Then our shaykh said suddenly, 'Whoever comes among the comets will be consumed in the fire'. How excellent is the speaker! Whoever claims knowledge of what he does not know lies about what he knows. What do you think of someone who is unbearable to everyone?[124]

Although two of the members of 'The Seven Shooting Stars' were also named as part of 'The Seven Planets', the groups were distinct from each other through their different collective foci. The former group shared literary interests, and the latter centred their religious lives around the Baybarsiyya. Al-Shihāb al-Rīshī was an astronomer (*muwaqqit*) at al-Muʾayyad mosque sometime after 812/1410. Al-Shihāb b. Yaᶜqūb was Ibn Ḥajar's *naqīb* (deputy) and was frequently in his teacher's company.[125] Al-Ḥijāzī told al-Sakhāwī that one day he was reciting the Qur'an to a large group while standing by a window at the Baybarsiyya, as was his duty. This position was a respected one at the Baybarsiyya, and reciters earned thirty dirhams monthly. The institution's endowment deed stipulated that the Qur'an be read before one of the five lower windows in the vestibule of the mausoleum, all of which faced al-Darb al-Aṣfar. One window had even been brought from one of the Abbasid palaces in Baghdad, a forceful reminder of the intersections of royal power and religious life in Mamluk Cairo.[126] Suddenly, Ibn Ḥajar and al-Shihāb b. Yaᶜqūb came by, just as the group was reciting Qur'an 4: 6: 'He will teach you the interpretation of sayings, and make His favour complete to you and the children of Yaᶜqūb'. Ibn Ḥajar took notice of this recitation and met with al-Ḥijāzī afterwards to ask whether the recitation had been deliberate or accidental. Al-Ḥijāzī swore to him that it was accidental, and Ibn Ḥajar was encouraged by this omen.[127] Whether al-Shihāb b. Yaᶜqūb had been appointed *naqīb* before or after this event is unclear, but evidently these three men all had some ties to the Baybarsiyya. Of course, this was not necessarily an exclusive affiliation. Later in his life, al-Ḥijāzī spent most days at *majālis* at the Qarāsunquriyya madrasa, an institution next door to the Baybarsiyya that even shared with it a nearly contiguous façade, and in the evenings he would retire to the home of his friend Qāḍī Muwaffaq al-Dīn (d. 877/1472 or 1473) at Birkat al-Raṭl.[128] The length of time that al-Ḥijāzī spent at al-Qarāsunquriyya is unknown, as the available sources are sparsely distributed, but al-Ḥijāzī's affiliation with this particular madrasa extended over decades. Al-Biqāᶜī had a conversation with al-Ḥijāzī on 14 Dhū al-Qaᶜda 837/22 June 1434, at the Qarāsunquriyya, and he also once remarked that al-Ḥijāzī was a resident there in Jumādā I 864/February 1460.[129]

As for the six eminent poets whom he called friends, his affection for them is most obviously evidenced in his poetry and letters. He composed two verses after a fire raged in Būlāq in 862/1457 destroying more than 300 housing units:

> My grief is for Old Cairo (*miṣr*) and her residents
> And a tear for her has been freed from my eye
> For her who witnessed the crowds of the dead and its horrors, and
> Who suffered sorrowfully through the agony of the fire.[130]

The fire broke out just before the death of his fellow poet Shihāb al-Dīn b. Mubārak Shāh al-Dimashqī; so, if he composed these verses after his friend's death, the sorrow expressed in the poem could have had double resonances.

As for these friends showing support and love for one another, we have the example of al-Manṣūrī dedicating two verses to al-Ḥijāzī upon hearing of what would be his final illness:

> People say that al-Shihāb is ailing, and I say, 'What a pity!
> What does Aḥmad think about not being free of illness (*ᶜilal*)?'
> The measure of the spiritual link between man and God comes from the sacrifice that releases the bond,
> And its distinguishing mark is in the arts of learning and of labour.[131]

In a thematic echo of al-Ḥijāzī's letter to al-Asyūṭī, al-Manṣūrī has constructed sickness as a form of pious suffering, making al-Ḥijāzī an object of sacrifice who demonstrates his love of God through pursuits of learning and the poetic craft. The illness that claimed al-Ḥijāzī's life was a long and intense gastrointestinal disease, and his companions stayed with him through it.[132] Taqī al-Dīn Abū Bakr al-Badrī, a friend and pupil of al-Ḥijāzī, who will also be the subject of Chapter 3, said that he 'watched closely over him in the illness that carried him to his grave'.[133] Al-Ḥijāzī certainly considered his legacy after his death, and wrote:

> They say: 'When a dead man has not left behind any memories,
> He is forgotten'. So I say to them: 'In some of my poems,
> My friends will remember me after death
> Through what I leave of my thoughts'.[134]

After this long illness, al-Ḥijāzī died on Wednesday, 7 Ramaḍān 875/28 February 1471, in his home, which was located near Sultan Barqūq's (d. 801/1399) tomb in the Qarāfa cemetery.[135] The poet al-Shihāb al-Manṣūrī eulogised al-Ḥijāzī in thirteen lines of poetry that begin: 'The loss I feel for al-Ḥijāzī has grown and plunged me into sadness'.[136]

After the sixth Shihāb of their group died, the last remaining member, al-Manṣūrī, composed fifteen lines eulogising all six of them. In his estimation, Cairo's literary scene had just suffered a devastating blow, marking a decline in the poetry of the era. 'The heavens of style have been deprived of the radiance of the shooting stars (*shuhub*) / And now, the horizons of poetry and literature have darkened'.[137] Al-Manṣūrī's experiences with this close-knit group of friends imbue these brief lines with a depth that aptly commemorates the love and respect he felt for them and gives dimension to intimate aspects of everyday life.

Notes

1. Ibn Ḥibbān (d. 354/965) related a weak hadith on the authority of ᶜĀʾisha that the Prophet declared blue eyes a sign of good luck.
2. ᶜAbd al-Raḥmān al-Thaᶜālibī, *Al-Jawāhir al-ḥisān fī tafsīr al-Qurʾān* (Exquisite Jewels: On Quran'ic Exegesis), ed. ᶜAmmār al-Ṭālbanī (Algiers: Al-Muʾassasat al-waṭaniyya li'l-kitāb, 1985), 3:61.
3. Burhān al-Dīn Ibrāhīm b. ᶜUmar al-Biqāᶜī, *Naẓm al-durar fī tanāsub al-āyāt wa-suwar* (Pearl Necklace: On the Link between Qurʾanic Verses and Chapters) (Hyderabad: Maṭbaᶜa majlis dāʾirat al-maᶜārif al-ᶜuthmāniyya, 2006) 5:45.
4. Andreas Tietze, *Muṣṭafā ᶜĀlī's Description of Cairo of 1599: Text, Transliteration, Translation, Notes* (Vienna: Verlag der Österreichischen Akademie der Wissenschaften, 1975), p. 42.
5. Al-Suyūṭī was the only biographer to have recorded al-Ḥijāzī's great-

grandfather's name as Ḥusayn, rather than Ḥasan. See Jalāl al-Dīn al-Suyūṭī, *Naẓm al-ᶜiqyān fī aᶜyān al-aᶜyān*, ed. Philip K. Hitti (New York: Syrian-American Press, 1927), p. 63.

6. Aḥmad b. ᶜAlī Ibn Ḥajar al-ᶜAsqalānī, *Inbāᵓ al-ghumr bi-anbāᵓ al-ᶜumr*, ed. Ḥasan al-Ḥabashī (Cairo: s.n., 1969), 1:350.
7. Of al-Ḥijāzī's dozens of biographers, Ibn Khalīl (d. 920/1514) is the only one to give his birth year as 795/1392. See his *Nayl al-amal fī dhayl al-duwal*, ed. ᶜUmar ᶜAbd al-Salām Tadmurī (Ṣaydā/Beirut: Al-Maktabat al-ᶜaṣriyya, 2002), 6:438.
8. Taqī al-Dīn Aḥmad al-Maqrīzī, *Kitāb al-sulūk li-maᶜrifat duwal al-mulūk* (The Guide to the Knowledge of Royal Dynasties), ed. Muḥammad Muṣṭafá Ziyāda and Saᶜīd ᶜAbd al-Fattāḥ al-ᶜAshūr (Cairo: Lajnat al-taᵓlīf wa'l-tarjama wa'l-nashr, 1934), 3:577.
9. Al-Badrī, *Ghurrat*, fo. 158b. Because of the popularity of intercrural sex between men in this period, men's thighs often served as a focus of erotic interest in male homoerotic literature.
10. It is worth noting that 'the 11th-century geographer al-Bakri . . . reported that the people in northern Morocco did not allow the physically defective to dwell in their country because it corrupted their progeny'. Cited in Shoshan, 'The State', p. 336.
11. Rukn al-Dīn Baybars al-Manṣūrī al-Dawādar, *Zubdat al-fikra fī taᵓrīkh al-hijra*, ed. Donald S. Richards (Beirut: Al-Sharikat al-muttaḥida li'l-tawzīᶜ, 1998), p. 106; Badr al-Dīn Maḥmūd al-ᶜAynī, *ᶜIqd al-jumān fī taᵓrīkh ahl al-zamān*, ed. Muḥammad Muḥammad Amīn (Cairo: Hayᵓat al-miṣriyya al-ᶜāmma li'l-kitāb, 1987), 1:428. The accounts by these authors are identical, suggesting an earlier common source or al-ᶜAynī's direct borrowing of Baybars al-Manṣūrī's words.

    Susan M. Schweik has investigated a similar phenomenon in United States history in her *The Ugly Laws: Disability in Public* (New York: New York University Press, 2009). In the 19th and 20th centuries, laws were passed in urban centres such as Chicago, Philadelphia and New York that forced disabled mendicants off the streets because of their supposed unsightliness.
12. Al-Maqrīzī, *Kitāb al-sulūk* [repr. 1956], 2:322–3.
13. Ibid., 3:772; Muḥammad b. ᶜAbd al-Raḥīm Ibn al-Furāt, *Tāᵓrīkh Ibn al-Furāt*, ed. Constantine Zurayq (Beirut: Al-Maṭbaᶜa al-amīrkāniyya, 1936–), 9:310–11; Muḥammad b. Aḥmad al-Ḥanafī Ibn Iyās, *Badāᵓiᶜ al-zuhūr fī waqāᵓīᶜ al-duhūr*, ed. Muḥammad Muṣṭafá (Cairo: s.n., 1960), 1.2:454; Ibn Ḥajar al-ᶜAsqalānī, *Inbāᵓ* [1969], 3:121. In reading these same passages, Adam Sabra has understood *jadhmāᵓ*, which can mean 'amputees', to indicate 'thieves whose hands had been amputated in punishment'. See his *Poverty and Charity in Medieval Islam: Mamluk Egypt, 1250–1517* (Cambridge: Cambridge University Press, 2000), p. 60. On the meaning of *jadhmāᵓ* as 'lepers', see *EI*^{2}, s.v. 'Djudhām'.

14. ʿAlī b. Dāwūd al-Ṣayrafī, *Nuzhat al-nufūs wa'l-abdān fī tawārīkh al-zamān* (The Recreation of Bodies and Souls: On Histories of the Period), ed. Ḥasan Ḥabashī (Cairo: Wizārat al-thaqāfa, markaz taḥqīq al-turāth, 1970–94), 3:408–9. The figure of the able-bodied beggar who played on public sympathies by feigning mental and physical illnesses occupied a prominent place in Arabic literatures. In his shadow play *ʿAjīb wa-gharīb*, Ibn Dāniyāl (d. 710/1310) humorously described one swindling beggar's application of sticky ointments to his eyes to appear blind.
15. Ibn Taghrībirdī, *Al-Nujūm al-ẓāhira fī mulūk miṣr wa'l-qāhira* (The Shining Stars: On the Kings of Egypt and Cairo) (Cairo: s.n., 1929), 14:359.
16. Shoshan, 'The State', pp. 337–8.
17. Al-Sakhāwī, *Kitāb al-tibr al-masbūk fī tawārīkh al-mulūk* (Cairo: Maktabat al-kulliyāt al-azhariyya, 1972), p. 302. Ibn Taghrībirdī gave his name as Saʿdān and described him as a black slave. For an analysis of the various tellings of the Saʿdallāh affair in Mamluk chronicles, see Shaun Marmon, 'Black Slaves in Mamlūk Narratives: Representations of Transgression', *Al-Qanṭara* 28.2 (2007), pp. 452–6.
18. Al-Sakhāwī, *Kitāb al-tibr*, p. 302.
19. Ibid., p. 302 (*wa-fīhim al-kathīr min al-zamanī wa-dhawī al-ʿāhāt wa'l-amrāḍ*); Ibn Taghrībirdī (d. 874/1470), *Ḥawādith al-duhūr fī madá al-ayyām wa'l-shuhūr* (Cairo: Lajnat iḥyāʾ al-turāth al-islāmī, 1990), 1:200–1, 203; Ibn Taghrībirdī, Al-Nujūm, 15:406–7.
20. Ibn Iyās, *Badāʾiʿ*, 2.5:2, 253.
21. Owen Jarus, 'Long Pilgrimages Revealed in Ancient Sudan Art', *Live Science*, 3 November 2011. <http://www.livescience.com/16854-sudan-yields-medieval-art-signs-long-pilgrimages.html>. This article is a synopsis of Bogdan Zurawski's lecture 'Kings and Pilgrims: Excavating the Holy Sites of Banganarti and Selib' on 25 September 2011 at the Royal Ontario Museum in Canada.
22. Al-Sakhāwī, *Al-Ḍawʾ al-lāmiʿ li-ahl al-qarn al-tāsiʿ* (Beirut: Dār maktabat al-hayāt, 1966), 2:147. Muslim infants customarily have their heads shorn when they are one week old, and the weight of the hair in silver is donated to charity. Though not explicitly mentioned, it is likely that Shihāb al-Dīn underwent this ritual on this day.
23. Susan Jane Staffa, *Conquest and Fusion: The Social Evolution of Cairo, A.D. 642–1850* (Leiden: E. J. Brill, 1977), pp. 111–12; Nasser O. Rabbat, *The Citadel of Cairo: A New Interpretation of Royal Mamluk Architecture* (Leiden: E. J. Brill, 1995), p. 238.
24. Al-Maqrīzī, *Kitāb al-khiṭaṭ al-maqrīziyya* (Cairo: s.n., 1959), 2:427–8.
25. For more images and architectural details about the Baybarsiyya, see K. A. C. Creswell, *The Muslim Architecture of Egypt* (New York: Hacker Art Books, 1979), 2:249–53 + plates 95–8, 112–13, 121; Henri Stierlin and Anne Stierlin, *Splendours of an Islamic World: Mamluk Art in Cairo, 1250–1517* (New York: Tauris Parke Books, 1997), pp. 26–9.

26. Al-Sakhāwī, *Al-Ḍawʾ*, 8:179.
27. ^{c}Alī b. Dāwūd al-Ṣayrafī, *Inbāʾ al-haṣr bi-anbāʾ al-^{c}aṣr*, ed. Ḥasan Ḥabashī (Cairo: Dār al-fikr al-^{c}arabī, 1970), p. 258.
28. Al-Sakhāwī, *Al-Ḍawʾ*, 2:147–8.
29. Michael Chamberlain, *Knowledge and Social Practice in Medieval Damascus* (New York: Cambridge University Press, 1994), pp. 7, 114.
30. Taqī al-Dīn Ibn Fahd al-Hāshimī, *Laḥẓ al-alḥāẓ bi-dhayl ṭabaqāt al-ḥuffāẓ* (Beirut: Dār iḥyāʾ al-turāth al-^{c}arabī, s.d.), pp. 339–45; Ibrāhīm b. Ḥasan al-Biqā^{c}ī, *^{c}Inwān al-zamān bi-tarājim al-shuyūkh wa'l-aqrān*, ed. Ḥasan Ḥabashī (Cairo: Dār al-kutub wa'l-wathāʾiq al-qawmiyya, 2001), 1:131–2; Al-Sakhāwī, *Al-Jawāhir*, 1:317, 428–31.
31. Al-Sakhāwī, *Kitāb al-tibr*, p. 233.
32. Al-Sakhāwī, *Al-Jawāhir*, 1:317.
33. Aftab Aḥmad Raḥmānī, *The Life and Works of Ibn Hajar al-Asqalani* (Bangladesh: Islamic Foundation Bangladesh, 2000), p. 109.
34. Al-Sakhāwī, *Al-Jawāhir*, 1:428. It is also cited in al-Badrī, *Al-Durr*, 1:188. It is likely that the reference to the eye (*^{c}ayn*) in the final hemistich is a subtle attack on one of al-^{c}Asqalānī's chief rivals, the scholar Badr al-Dīn Muḥammad al-^{c}Aynī (d. 855/1451), so named because he was a native of ^{c}Ayntāb, a city in eastern Anatolia. The convention of placing a double entendre at the end of a poetic line is known as *tawriyya.* Cf. a sample of al-^{c}Asqalānī's poetry in Raḥmānī, *Life*, p. 209. For more on these two scholars, see Anne Broadbridge's rich portrait of scholarly social networks, 'Academic Rivalry and the Patronage System in Fifteenth-Century Egypt: Al-^{c}Ayni, Al-Maqrizi, and Ibn Hajar al-^{c}Asqalani', *MSR* 3 (1999), pp. 85–107; and Al-Badrī, *Al-Durr*, 1:187.
35. Al-Sakhāwī, *Al-Jawāhir*, 3:1,053.
36. My translation of Leonor Fernandes, 'The Foundation of Baybars al-Jashankir: Its Waqf, History, and Architecture', *Muqarnas* 4 (1987), p. 39, column 2, lines 31–2. Additionally, appointees to military and bureaucratic posts may have been subject to similar restrictions. David Ayalon has cited numerous instances in which Mamluk *amir*s were dismissed for illness or advanced age in his 'Discharges from Service, Banishments and Imprisonments in Mamlūk Society', *Israel Oriental Studies* 2 (1972), p. 26, fn. 9. The author of an 11th/17th-century Andalusian text on cannon noted that only men of sound health were permitted to operate the cannon. They could not be 'deaf nor weak nor paralyzed nor one-eyed nor drunk'. See Nabil Matar, 'Confronting Decline in Early Modern Arabic Thought', *Journal of Early Modern History* 9.1–2 (2005), p. 68.
37. Ayalon, 'Discharges', p. 27.
38. Boaz Shoshan, *Popular Culture in Medieval Cairo* (Cambridge: Cambridge University Press, 1993), pp. 52–3.
39. Fernandes, 'Foundation', p. 27.
40. Rispler-Chaim, *Disability*, p. 25.

41. Al-Sakhāwī, *Al-Jawāhir*, 3:1,045.
42. Ibid., 3:1,212. Aftab Aḥmad Raḥmānī understands this passage to mean that Uns Khātūn cared for disabled people. See Raḥmānī, *Life*, p. 95.
43. Fernandes, 'Foundation', p. 25.
44. Raḥmānī, *Life*, p. 43.
45. Cited in K. A. C. Creswell, *Muslim Architecture*, 2:253.
46. Ibrāhīm b. Ḥasan al-Biqāʿī, *ʿUnwān al-ʿunwān bi-tajrīd asmāʾ al-shuyūkh wa-baʿḍ al-talāmidha wa'l-aqrān* (Beirut: Dār al-kitāb al-ʿarabī, 2002), p. 36; Al-Sakhāwī, *Al-Ḍawʾ*, 2:147.
47. Al-Sakhāwī, *Al-Ḍawʾ*, 8:179.
48. Al-Ṣayrafī, *Inbāʾ*, p. 259.
49. Al-Sakhāwī, *Al-Ḍawʾ*, 2:148; ʿUmar Ibn Fahd al-Hāshimī, *Muʿjam al-shuyūkh*, ed. Muḥammad al-Zāhī (Riyadh: Manshūrāt Dār al-Yamāma li'l-baḥth wa'l-tarjama wa'l-nashr, 1982), p. 345.
50. Ibn al-Ukhuwwa (d. 729/1329), *The Maʿālim al-Qurba fī Aḥkām al-Ḥisba of Ḍiyaʾ al-Dīn Muḥammad ibn Muḥammad al-Qurashī al-Shāfiʿī, known as Ibn al-Ukhuwwa*, ed. and trans. Reuben Levy (London: Luzac & Co., 1938), p. 60.
51. Al-Sakhāwī, *Al-Ḍawʾ*, 2:147–9.
52. Ibid., 2:148. Ibn Hishām al-Lakhmī (d. 577/1182) noted in his book on provincial Arabic expressions that Andalusians pronounced this word *balādhūr*. See his *Madkhal ilá taqwīm al-lisān wa-taʿlīm al-bayān*, ed. Maʾmūn b. Muḥyī al-Dīn al-Jannān (Beirut: Dār al-kutub al-ʿilmiyya, 1995), p. 201.
53. Ignaz Goldziher, 'Muhammedanischer Aberglaube über Gedächtniskraft und Vergesslichkeit, mit Parallelen aus der jüdischen Litteratur', in *Festschrift zum siebzigsten Geburtstage A. Berliners* (Frankfurt am Main: J. Kauffmann, 1903), pp. 131–55; Gerrit Bos, 'Jewish Traditions on Strengthening Memory and Leone Modena's Evaluation', *Jewish Studies Quarterly* (1995), pp. 39–58.
54. Gerrit Bos, '*Balādhur* (Marking-Nut): A Popular Medieval Drug for Strengthening Memory', *BSOAS* 59.2 (1996), pp. 229–36.
55. Abū Muḥammad al-Qāsim al-Ghassānī, *Ḥadīqat al-azhār fī māhiyyat al-ʿushb wa'l-ʿaqqār* (Flower Gardens: The Essence of Herbs and Drugs), ed. Muḥammad al-ʿArabī al-Khaṭṭābī (Beirut: Dār al-gharb al-islāmī, 1985), p. 65.
56. A 31-year-old man was treated in Burnley, England, for 'redness, itching and blistering [on his forearm] followed by skin necrosis' after having applied marking-nut extract to the area in order to remove a tattoo. A friend had procured the extract from Pakistan. After treating the eczema, the dermatologists found the man's arm had healed 'without scarring, any visible remnants of the tattoo, or the need for debridement'. See A. Hafejee et al., 'Traditional Tattoo Treatment Trauma', *British Journal of Dermatology* 153, suppl. 1 (2006), p. 62.

57. H. W. Bailey, *Zoroastrian Problems in the Ninth-Century Books* (Oxford: Clarendon Press, 1943), p. 81.
58. ^{c}Alī b. Sahl Rabbān al-Ṭabarī, *Firdaws al-ḥikma fī al-ṭibb* (Paradise of Wisdom on Medicine), ed. Muḥammad Zubayr al-Ṣiddīqī (Berlin: Maṭba^{c} Āftāb, 1928), p. 456.
59. Abū Naṣr al-^{c}Aṭṭār al-Isrāʾīlī (d. 658/1260), *Kitāb minhāj al-dukkān wa-dustūr al-a^{c}yān fī a^{c}māl wa-tarkīb al-adawiyya al-nāfi^{c}a li'l-abdān*, ed. Ḥasan Zaghla (Frankfurt: Ma^{c}had Taʾrīkh al-Ulūm al-^{c}Arabiyya wa'l-Islāmīyah fī iṭār Jāmi^{c}at Frānkfūrt, 1997), pp. 36, 154.
60. See Ibn al-Bayṭār, *Kitāb al-jāmi^{c} li-mufradāt al-adwiyya wa'l-aghdhiyya* (Beirut: Dār al-Madīna, s.d.), 1.1:113.
61. al-Ghassānī, *Ḥadīqat*, p. 65; Staph, 'Dell'anacardio', trans. Giuseppe Belluomini, *Annali di medicina omiopatica per la Sicilia* 4 (1838), pp. 318–60.
62. Abū al-Qāsim Muḥammad b. ^{c}Umar al-Zamakhsharī (d. 538/1144), *Rabī^{c} al-abrār fī nuṣūṣ al-akhbār* (Vernal Gardens for the Virtuous and Texts of Anecdotes), ed. ^{c}Abd al-Amīr Mihnā (Beirut: Muʾassassat al-a^{c}lamī li'l-maṭbū^{c}āt, 1992), 5:55. This anecdote is found in chapter 77, which is titled 'On illnesses, diseases, physical blights (*^{c}āhāt*), medicine, drugs, caring for the sick and the like'.
63. As recently as the 1980s and 1990s, schoolboys in northern Yemen were using *balādhur* as a study aid, and the broader Yemeni community regarded it as an addictive substance. Moshe Piamenta, *A Dictionary of Post-classical Yemeni Arabic* (Leiden: E. J. Brill, 1990), 1:38.
64. Franz Rosenthal, *The Herb: Hashish versus Medieval Muslim Society* (Leiden: E. J. Brill, 1971), p. 97.
65. Ibn Bashkuwāl (d. 578/1183), *Kitāb al-ṣilah fī taʾrīkh aʾimmat al-andalus wa-^{c}ulamāʾihim wa-muḥaddithīhim wa-fuqahāʾihim wa-udabāʾihim*, ed. Francisco Codera y Zaidin (Madrid: Rojas, 1882), 1:287. Halima Ferhat, in her rush to depict these scholars as dangerous and dishonourable, asserts that *balādhur* made these men violent, without considering the possibility of withdrawal symptoms creating their harsh tempers. Furthermore, the editor offers an alternative reading of the Ibn Bashkuwāl passage, which would make it read 'It is said that he drank *balādhur* for his memory, and it benefitted him. It sharpened his memory.' In the other version, the last sentence reads: 'It caused a violent disposition'. See her *Le Maghreb aux XIIIème siècles: les siècles de la foi* (Casablanca: s.n., 1993), pp. 32–3.
66. Ibn Khallikān, *Wafayāt al-a^{c}yān wa-anbāʾ abnāʾ al-zamān*, ed. Iḥsān ^{c}Abbās (Beirut: Dār ṣādir, 1968–77), 7:94.
67. Al-Dhahabī, *Kitāb tadhkirat al-ḥuffāẓ* (Hyderabad: Maṭbā^{c}a dāʾirat al-ma^{c}ārif al-niẓāmiyya, 1914–15), 1:331.
68. EI^2, s.v. 'Al-Ṭayālisī'.
69. EI^2, s.v. 'Al-Balādhurī'.
70. Al-Dhahabī, *Kitāb tadhkirat*, 4:140; ^{c}Abd al-Raḥmān b. Aḥmad Ibn Rajab

(d. 795/1392 or 1393), *Al-Dhayl ᶜalá ṭabaqāt al-ḥanābila* (Continuation of *Ṭabaqāt al-ḥanābila*), ed. Muḥammad Ḥamīd al-Faqī (Cairo: Maṭbaᶜat al-sunna al-muḥammadiyya, 1952–3), 1:413. I am grateful to Mr Maxim Romanov of the University of Michigan for this second reference.

71. Ismāᶜīl b. Yūsuf Ibn al-Aḥmar al-Naṣrī (d. 807/1404 or 810/1407), *Nathīr farāʾid al-jumān fī Naẓm fuḥūl al-zamān* (Beirut: Dār al-thaqāfa li'l-ṭibāᶜa wa'l-nashr wa'l-tawzīᶜ, 1967), pp. 308–9. Cited in John O. Hunwick, 'An Andalusian in Mali: A Contribution to the Biography of Abū Isḥāq al-Sāḥilī, c. 1290–1346', *Paideuma* 36 (1990), pp. 59–60.
72. Quoted in Bos, '*Balādhur*', p. 234.
73. C. E. Bosworth, *The Mediaeval Islamic Underworld: The Banū Sāsān in Arabic Society and Literature* (Leiden: E. J. Brill, 1976), 1:46–7.
74. ᶜAbd al-Raḥmān al-Jawbarī, *Mukhtār kashf al-asrār wa-hatk al-astār* (Select Work on the Uncovering of Secrets and the Tearing Away of Veils) (Beirut: Dār taḍmūn, 1992), pp. 56, 122.
75. Al-Ṣayrafī, one of al-Ḥijāzī's close friends, wrote an obituary in which he claimed that al-Ḥijāzī possessed 'clarity of mind, lightness of spirit and sweetness of memory', ascribing a sunnier legacy to his friend. See al-Ṣayrafī, *Inbāʾ*, p. 258.
76. Bos, '*Balādhur*', p. 234.
77. Al-Suyūṭī, *Naẓm*, pp. 65–6.
78. For the magical properties of the salamander, see Ibn Waḥshiyya (d. 3rd/9th c.), *Medieval Arabic Toxicology: The Book of Poisons of Ibn Waḥshiyya and Its Relation to Early Indian and Greek Texts*, trans. Martin Levey (Philadelphia: American Philosophical Society, 1966), pp. 56–8. For the salamander as Ottoman poetic motif, see Walter Andrews and Mehmet Kalpaklı, *The Age of Beloveds: Love and the Beloved in Early-Modern Ottoman and European Culture and Society* (Durham: Duke University Press, 2005), p. 96, fn. b, and p. 972.
79. Ibn Waḥshiyya, *Book of Poisons*, p. 58.
80. Al-Suyūṭī, *Naẓm*, p. 66.
81. Ibid., pp. 66–7.
82. Al-Biqāᶜī, *ᶜInwān*, 1:220–2.
83. Al-Suyūṭī, *Naẓm*, p. 68. Variations of this hadith are found in *Ṣaḥīḥ al-Bukhārī*, vol. 7, nos 545, 551 and 571.
84. Al-Suyūṭī, *Naẓm*, p. 68.
85. Ibid., *Naẓm*, p. 69.
86. David Ayalon, 'The Muslim City and the Mamluk Military Aristocracy', *Proceedings of the Israel Academy of Sciences and Humanities* 2 (1968), p. 323.
87. Al-Suyūṭī, *Naẓm*, p. 69.
88. For more about this verse, and the blind poet Abū al-ᶜAlāʾ al-Maᶜarrī's (d. 419/1057) application of it to himself, see Franz Rosenthal, '"Blurbs" (*taqrîẓ*) from Fourteenth-Century Egypt', *Oriens* 27 (1981), p. 195, fn. 35.

89. Al-Sakhāwī, *Al-Ḍawʾ*, 2:147.
90. Ibid., 2:148. Ibn ʿArabshāh was taken prisoner by the Mongols during their siege of Damascus in 803/1401. The experience of captivity remained with him for a long time, and he eventually wrote a scathing biography of Timur-e Lang (Tamerlane).
91. J. R. Smart, 'The Muwaššaḥāt of al-Šihāb al-Ḥijāzī', in Federico Corriente and Angel Sáenz-Badillos (eds), *Poesía estrófica; actas del Primer Congreso Internacional sobre Paralelos Romances (Madrid, diciembre de 1989)* (Madrid: Instituto de Cooperación con el Mundo Arabe, 1991), pp. 347–56.
92. The colophon of Leiden Cod. Or. 423 has this completion date. Al-Biqāʿī, *ʿInwān*, 1:220.
93. Abdul Qayyum, 'Al-Ḥijāzī, the Author of *Nawādir al-akhbār*', *Islamic Culture* 18 (July 1944), pp. 257, 260–1.
94. Al-Sakhāwī, *Al-Jawāhir*, 3:1,082; al-Sakhāwī, *Al-Ḍawʾ*, 11:197; al-Sakhāwī, *Al-Dhayl al-tām ʿalá Duwal al-islām li'l-Dhahabī*, ed. Ḥasan Ismāʾīl Marwa (Beirut: Dār Ibn al-ʿImād, 1992–), 2:246; al-Sakhāwī, *Wajīz al-kalām fī al-Dhayl ʿalá Duwal al-islām*, ed. Bashār Maʿrūf (Beirut: Muʾassassat al-risāla, 1995), 2:824.
95. Richard F. Burton (trans.), *The Book of the Thousand Nights and a Night: A Plain and Literal Translation of the Arabian Nights Entertainment* (London: The Burton Club, 1900). See also Muhsin Mahdi, *The Thousand and One Nights* (Leiden: E. J. Brill, 1995), p. 124.
96. Robert Irwin, *The Arabian Nights: A Companion* (New York: Routledge, 1994).
97. Patrice Coussonet, 'Pour une lecture historique des "Mille et Une Nuits": Essai d'analyse du conte des deux vizirs égyptiens', *Institut des Belles Lettres Arabes* (1985), pp. 85–115.
98. Al-Sakhāwī, *Kitāb al-tibr,* pp. 267–8.
99. See his *Nayl al-rā'id fī al-nīl al-zā'id*, Bankipore Public Library, Bankipore, India, MS. 1069. For examples of modern scientific and historical citations, see Mamdouh M. A. Shahin, *Hydrology and Water Resources of Africa* (New York: Springer, 2002), p. 294, and Paul P. Howell and John A. Allan, *The Nile: Sharing a Scarce Resource: A Historical and Technical Review of Water Management and of Economical and Legal Issues* (New York: Cambridge University Press, 1994), p. 37.
100. Ibn Iyās, *Badāʿīʾ* 3:58; Al-Suyūṭī, *Naẓm*, p. 36. Shihāb al-Dīn al-Manṣūrī is identified as one of the seven *Shihābs* (*aḥad al-shuhub al-sabiʿa*) in Ibn al-Mullā al-Ḥaṣkafī (d. 1003/1595), *Mutʿat al-adhhān min al-Tammatuʿ bi'l-iqrān bayna tarājim al-shuyūkh wa'l-aqrān* [= extracts from Ibn Ṭūlūn's *Al-Tammatuʿ bi'l-iqrān bayna tarājim al-shuyūkh wa'l-aqrān*], ed. Ṣalāḥ al-Dīn Khalīl al-Shaybānī al-Mawṣilī (Beirut: Dār ṣādir, 1999), 2:873.
101. The editor worked from Muḥammad Amīn al-Kutubī's 1908 edition, which

was rife with diacritical and orthographic errors, of three of al-Ḥijāzī's short treatises. In addition to the two that ᶜAkkāwī edited, there was another entitled *Qalāʾid al-nuḥūr min jawāhir al-buḥūr*. See Rajāb ᶜAkkāwī, 'ᶜAmalnā fī risālatayn', in Shihāb al-Dīn al-Ḥijāzī, *Al-Kunnas al-jawārī fī al-ḥisān min al-jawārī, wa-bi-dhaylihi, Jannat al-wuldān fī al-ḥisān min al-ghilmān*, ed. Rajāb ᶜAkkāwī (Beirut: Dār al-ḥarf al-ᶜarabī, 1998), p. 18.

102. Thomas Bauer, 'Mamluk Literature: Misunderstandings and New Approaches', *MSR* 9.2 (2005), p. 123.
103. For more on the types of workers featured in *Kitāb rawḍ al-ādāb*, see Joseph Sadan, 'Kings and Craftsmen, a Pattern of Contrasts: On the History of a Medieval Arabic Humoristic Form (Part I)', *SI* 56 (1982), p. 33. Cf. also the *shahrangiz* poetic genre in Persian, Turkish and Urdu literatures, which praises male beauties of various crafts and professions.
104. Ibn Sūdūn al-Bashbughāwī (810–68/1407–64)'s play 'Narrative of the Baghdadi Hunchback' spoofs a similar phenomenon, the tendency in Baghdadi Arabic to replace ر with غ. See Arnoud Vrolijk, *Bringing a Laugh to a Scowling Face: a study and critical edition of the "Nuzhat al-nufūs wa-muḍḥik al-ᶜabūs" by ᶜAlī Ibn Sūdūn al-Bashbughāwī (Cairo 810/1407 – Damascus 868/1464)* (Leiden: Research School CNWS, School of Asian, African, and Amerindian Studies, 1998), p. 141 of the English commentary and pp. ١٥٨–١٥٥ of the Arabic edition.
105. Al-Ḥijāzī, *Kunnas*, p. 29.
106. Ibid., p. 125.
107. Ibid., p. 125.
108. Ibid., p. 30.
109. Ibid., pp. 30–1.
110. The scholar Maḥmūd b. al-Baylūnī (d. 1599) remarked to his biographer al-Ghazzī that his being hard-of-hearing was a gift from God, as it permitted him to ignore idle gossip and to listen only to recitations of the Qur'an. See Sara Scalenghe, 'Being Different: Intersexuality, Blindness, Deafness, and Madness in Ottoman Syria', PhD dissertation, Georgetown University, 2006, pp. 168–9.
111. A similar sentiment is found in this Egyptian short-story excerpt: 'Ali can talk himself into believing that it is a hundred times better to be blind than sighted. It is better to be blind because a blind man can love through his ears. His hearing is sharpened and he packs his memory with smells and delicate sounds . . . A blind man – in Ali's analysis – has only the injuries he might incur bumping into an iron railing, tripping over a stone or brick, or a careless movement from the razor to worry about. The injuries of a sighted man, on the other hand, consist in the consciousness of his own feebleness every time he looks at the stone or hole that tripped him despite being in perfect physical health.' From Ashraf Abdelshafy, 'Imagination of the Blind', *Banipal* 25 (Spring 2006), pp. 105–6.
112. Al-Ḥijāzī, *Kunnas*, p. 31.

113. Ibid., p. 130.
114. Renaissance English writers of prose, poetry and drama praised the 'deformed mistress' in works that 'appear to reappraise aesthetic norms and the constraints they place upon women, arguing for the appeal and value of features generally considered ugly. [Rather,] this form of writing ironically works to confirm the ugliness of the female body further, once again locating beauty in male art rather than in female nature.' See Naomi Baker, *Plain Ugly: The Unattractive Body in Early Modern Culture* (Manchester and New York: Manchester University Press, 2010), p. 139.
115. Geert Jan van Gelder, 'Beautifying the Ugly and Uglifying the Beautiful: The Paradox in Classical Arabic Literature', *Journal of Semitic Studies* 48.2 (2003), p. 339.
116. Sabri Khalid Kawash, 'Ibn Ḥajar al-Asqalānī (1372–1449 A.D.): A Study of the Background, Education, and Career of a ᶜĀlim in Egypt', PhD dissertation, Princeton University, 1969, p. 214.
117. Thomas Bauer, 'Ibn Ḥajar and the Arabic Ghazal of the Mamluk Age', in Thomas Bauer and Angelika Neuwirth (eds), *Ghazal as World Literature* (Beirut: Ergon Verlag, 2005), 1:35.
118. Ibn Ḥajar al-ᶜAsqalānī, *Dīwān Shaykh al-Islām Ibn Ḥajar al-ᶜAsqalānī*, ed. Firdaws Nūr ᶜAlī Ḥusayn (Cairo: Dār al-faḍīla, 2000), p. 262. The Arabic word for eye (*ᶜayn*) and the 18th letter of the Arabic alphabet (*ᶜayn*) are homonyms.
119. Al-Sakhāwī, *Al-Jawāhir*, 3:1,039.
120. Ibn Iyās, *Badāᶜīᵓ*, 3:58. For Ibn al-Shāb al-Tāᵓib, who was also a Sufi and a *khāṭib*, see Carl Brockelmann, *Geschichte der arabischen Litteratur* (Leiden: E. J. Brill, 1943–), 2:147ff.; Ibn al-ᶜImād, *Shadharāt al-dhahab fī akhbār man dhahab* (Damascus/Beirut: Dār Ibn Kathīr, 1986–), 7:198. For a description of Ibn Abī al-Saᶜūd as *muwaswis* (mumbling to himself and obsessed by demonic delusions), see al-Biqāᶜī, *Iẓhār al-ᶜaṣr li-asrār ahl al-ᶜaṣr: tāᵓrīkh al-Biqāᶜī*, ed. Muḥammad Sālim b. Shadīd al-ᶜAwfī (Giza: Hajar li'l-ṭibāᶜa wa'l-nashr wa'l-tawzī, 1992–), 1:208; and also al-Suyūṭī, *Naẓm*, p. 36, where he is referred to as Shihāb al-Dīn Aḥmad b. Ismāᶜīl al-Saᶜūdī and is explicitly named as one of the seven Shihābs. For al-Manṣūrī, who moved to Cairo from Manṣūra in 825/1422 and remained there until his death, see al-Sakhāwī, *Al-Ḍawᵓ*, 2:150–1; al-Suyūṭī, *Naẓm*, p. 77; Brockelmann, *GAL Supplement* (Leiden: E. J. Brill, 1943–), 2:12; and Fuᵓād Afrām al-Bustānī (ed.), *Dāᵓirat al-maᶜārif: qāmūs ᶜāmm li-kull fann wa-maṭlab*, (Beirut: s.n., 1956), 4:116.
121. Modes of social configuration in Mamluk and early Ottoman academic circles are interesting sites of friendship analysis, especially as they relate to categories of physical difference. Bonds were formed according to professional guilds, fraternal orders, clans and tribes, among other group identifiers, but social clusters were occasionally based on physical characteristics or nicknames. Ibrāhīm al-Kharīzātī al-Ṣāliḥī al-Uṭrūsh (d. 15 Rabīᶜ II

933/18 January 1527) is identified by one biographer as 'one of the partially deaf anecdotalists (*aḥad al-mudṭaᶜīn al-uṭrūsh*)'. He eventually lost his mind and fell into ruin, taking his meals at the Salīmiyya hospice. See Ibn al-Mullā al-Ḥaṣkafī, *Mutᶜat*, 1:248. Samer M. Ali mentioned that the only deaf littérateur he had encountered in the sources was Muḥammad b. Saᶜīd al-Aṣamm. Though Ali wonders how he could possibly have heard, recited or narrated anecdotes, it is possible to imagine a writer using gestures, sign language or lip-reading to communicate. See his *Arabic Literary Salons in the Islamic Middle Ages: Poetry, Public Performance, and the Presentation of the Past* (Notre Dame: University of Notre Dame Press, 2010), pp. 45 and 223, fn. 44.

For 10th/16th-century Syrian uses of the word *uṭrūsh*, see Muḥammad b. Ibrāhīm Ibn al-Ḥanbalī (d. 971/1563), *Baḥr al-ᶜawwām fīmā aṣāba fīhi al-ᶜawāmm* (Cairo: Dār al-thaqāfat al-ᶜarabiyya, 1990), p. 255.

122. Al-Sakhāwī, *Al-Jawāhir*, 2:883.
123. Al-Ḥijāzī, *Nawādir al-akhbār wa-ẓarāʾif al-ashᶜār*, Panjab University Library, India, fos 7a–10a; Al-Ṣayrafī, *Inbā'*, p. 258.
124. Al-Sakhāwī, *Al-Jawāhir*, 2:883. For al-Shihāb b. Taqī's (d. 844/1440) biography, see Al-Sakhāwī, *Al-Ḍawʾ*, 1:229–30, 2:78–80. The name 'al-Shihāb al-Shayrajī' should read 'al-Shihāb al-Sayrajī'. This man was a friend of Ibn Ḥajar al-ᶜAsqalānī. He was born in 778/1376 and died in Muḥarram 862/November 1457. For his biography, see al-Suyūṭī, *al-Naẓm*, pp. 90–2; Al-Sakhāwī, *Al-Ḍawʾ*, 2:249. Al-Shihāb al-Rīshī was born in the Egyptian village of Kūm Rīshī in 775/1373 or 1374. He died in Cairo on 11 Muḥarram 852/17 March 1448, four years before his son Muḥammad was led to prison in chains (Al-Biqāᶜī, *Iẓhār*, 1:245). For al-Shihāb al-Rīshī's biography, see Al-Sakhāwī, *Al-Ḍawʾ*, 2:2; Al-Biqāᶜī, *ᶜUnwān*, pp. 20–1; and Al-Biqāᶜī, *ᶜInwān*, 1:58, fn. 105.
125. Al-Biqāᶜī wrote biographical notices for both al-Shihāb b. Yaᶜqūb and his wife Zaynab bint ᶜAbd al-Raḥīm b. al-Ḥusayn b. ᶜAbd al-Raḥīm, the daughter of al-Zayn al-ᶜIrāqī, for which see his *ᶜUnwān*, pp. 42–3, 82.
126. Leonor Fernandes, *The Evolution of a Sufi Institution in Mamluk Egypt: The Khanqah* (Berlin: K. Schwartz, 1988), p. 27.
127. Al-Sakhāwī, *Al-Jawāhir*, 2:651, 3:1,041.
128. Al-Ṣayrafī, *Inbāʾ*, 259; Al-Sakhāwī, *Al-Ḍawʾ*, 5:4.
129. Al-Biqāᶜī, *ᶜInwān*, 1:221; Al-Biqāᶜī, *Iẓhār*, 3:221.
130. Al-Suyūṭī, *Naẓm*, p. 77. Ibn Taghrībirdī wrote of this fire in his *Al-Manhal al-ṣāfī wa'l-mustawfā baᶜda al-wāfī*.
131. Ibn Iyās, *Badāᶜīʾ*, 3:57. In the 1894 edition (2:126), the poem's third line reads: 'the sacrifice that *permits* the bond'. Al-Manṣūrī also wrote a poem about his own long bout with hemiplegia (*fālij*), which immobilised him and confined him to his home, where he was entirely dependent on a male servant (*Badāᶜīʾ*, 2:213–14).
132. Al-Ṣayrafī, *Inbāʾ*, pp. 258–9; Shihāb al-Dīn Aḥmad Ibn al-Ḥimṣī

(d. 934/1527), *Ḥawādith al-zamān wa-wafayyāt al-shuyūkh wa'l-aqrān*, ed. ᶜUmar ᶜAbd al-Salām Tadmurī (Ṣaydā/Beirut: Al-Maktabat al-ᶜaṣriyya, 1999), 1:195.

133. Al-Badrī, *Al-Durr*, 2:281. This is an edited version of a lithograph of a 23 Rajab 1276/24 January 1860 manuscript printed in Cairo under the title *Kitāb siḥr al-ᶜuyūn*. The author's and copyist's names are not found in this manuscript, and the colophon indicates that it was copied for the Egyptian writer ᶜAbd al-Hādī Najā al-Ibyārī (d. 1305/1888).
134. Ibid.; Al-Sakhāwī, *Al-Ḍawᵓ*, 2:148.
135. Al-Biqāᶜī, *ᶜUnwān*, p. 36.
136. Ibn Iyās, *Badāᶜīᵓ*, 3:57–8. In the 1894 edition (2:126), only the first eight lines are included.
137. Ibid., 3:58–9. In the 1894 edition (2:126), only the first five lines are included.

3

Recollecting and Reconfiguring Afflicted Literary Bodies

The *adab* anthology (*majmūʿa*), such as proliferated in the Mamluk era, challenges modern literary historians' conceptions of authorship, authorial style and originality. Abdelfattah Kilito has argued that, in classical Arabic literature, 'individual style hardly exists. Instead, each genre possesses its own "composition", a set of recurrent features common to a number of works. Given these features, the reader can easily determine the genre to which a given text belongs and move from that text to the consideration of related texts.'[1] In the Mamluk period, anthologies incorporated various organisational, structural and schematic features. Thomas Bauer, in a thorough investigation of available sources, has identified four typologies of the Mamluk anthology:

1. the anthology organised around a single theme, as in al-Ṣafadī's anthology of epigrams about skin moles, titled *Kashf al-ḥāl fī waṣf al-khāl*;
2. the anthology structured as a commentary on another work, as in al-Ṣafadī's *Ghayth al-musajjam fī sharḥ Lāmiyyat al-ʿajam*, which is a commentary on Muʾayyad al-Dīn al-Ṭughrāʾī's (d. 515/1121) poem *Lāmiyyat al-ʿajam*;
3. the anthology of an author's works, as in a *dīwān* of poetry;
4. and the anthology that blends two or more of these characteristics, resulting in works that are not easily classifiable or are notable exceptions to the above three categories.[2]

In all of these types of anthologies, the conceptual work of the anthologist lies mostly in his mode of composition – collecting and reorganising literary fragments – as this process created new spatial and temporal contexts in which to appreciate literature. This trend of reorganising and reconfiguring known information and texts came to characterise other literary forms of the period. In fact, after reviewing Arabic-language Mamluk and Ottoman literary works, one modern scholar concluded that they mostly consisted of '"literature of recollection": dictionaries, commentaries upon literature, manuals of administrative practice, above all historiography and geography'.[3] Genres of writing that centred on collecting information and organising it according to a scheme (thematic or alphabetical, say), in order to preserve them for posterity, became hallmarks of the age. In this way, remembrance and the reordering of knowledge for public consumption formed a significant basis of scholarly production. When one speaks of 'literatures of recollection', one is referring to works based on memory, introspection and reminiscence. However, the term 'recollection' means more than just 'remembrance', as it can also be defined as 'reassemblage' or 're-membering', which captures the sense of reordering information to inform audience reactions to it. In this chapter, the friendly and professional ties binding Shihāb al-Dīn al-Ḥijāzī to his pupil Taqī al-Dīn al-Badrī al-Dimashqī (d. 894/1489) will be reconstructed, and their roles in generating a particular discourse on marked bodies explored.[4] First, the formative influence of al-Ḥijāzī is rather apparent in portions of al-Badrī's two anthologies *Ghurrat al-ṣabāḥ fī waṣf al-wujūh al-ṣibāḥ* (The Shining Dawn: On the Description of Fair Faces) and *Al-Durr al-maṣūn, al-musammá bi-Siḥr al-ᶜuyūn* (The Guarded Pearl, also known as The Magic of the Eyes); and al-Badrī masterfully integrates past and contemporary voices into a canon of literature about blighted bodies.[5] In al-Badrī's *Ghurrat al-ṣabāḥ*, an anthology of romantic and erotic verses addressed to men, afflicted male bodies are framed as beautiful, seductive and sympathetic, offering a novel, aestheticised portrait of physical difference. *Al-Durr al-maṣūn* exemplifies the process of fashioning literary canons on particular themes – in this case, body parts.

Historical Context

Although al-Badrī enjoyed a strong reputation as an author of literary and historical works, his biography was not as widely recorded as al-Ḥijāzī's, so, in a departure from Chapter 2, this chapter will be constructed less as a close entanglement of biography and a particular historical moment and more as an investigation of the shared intellectual life of this particular teacher and student through a close reading of al-Badrī's anthologies.

Situating the anthology *Ghurrat al-ṣabāḥ* in the context of al-Badrī's professional and personal biographies illuminates several influences for its composition. Al-Badrī was born in Rabīᶜ I 847/1443 in Damascus and grew up there. Al-Badrī visited Cairo many times with his father, but did not stay there long enough to set up a home. He moved between the two cities, working intermittently in Egypt and Syria as a copyist and a professional witness. The instability and lack of prestige in his professional life suggest humble origins. To reinforce this impression, his biographers do not mention any shaykhs with whom he studied as a youth, or masters who authorised him as a young man to teach, which was an uncommon gap in a scholar's intellectual biography. What has been recorded of his formal education took place when he was in his forties. Al-Badrī forged his own professional path as an adolescent, operating just outside the traditional elite process of inheriting social connections from one's family. His adolescence was distinguished by a lack of access to the best teachers and no affiliation with elite religious institutions. What is known is that he married young and became a widower while still a teenager. Although his wife left him an ample inheritance, he found himself impoverished for a time after her death. He then put his affairs in order, travelled to Mecca and later moved to Syria, where he wrote *Kitāb rāḥat al-arwāḥ fī al-ḥashīsh wa'l-rāḥ* (The Book of Comfort of Souls: On Hashish and Wine), the most extensive Arabic-language treatise on the history and uses of hashish and wine in the Middle East.[6] This book was probably his earliest one, which he claimed to have written in 867/1462–3 at the age of 20; and, with its publication, he established himself as a formidable literary presence in Cairo. He cited al-Ḥijāzī's poetry and direct reports of his anecdotes in various sections of this work, which suggests that the two writers met during al-Badrī's late adolescence.[7] His *Kitāb rāḥat al-arwāḥ* defined his career and legacy; and, a decade later in his topographical treatise *Nuzhat al-anām fī maḥāsin al-shām* (The Recreation of Mankind: On the Beauties of Damascus), he still referred to it as a relevant text.[8] He also wrote *Ghurrat al-ṣabāḥ fī waṣf al-wujūh al-ṣibāḥ* (The Shining Dawn: On the Description of Fair Faces) in Damascus, telling al-Sakhāwī that it was completed around 865/1460 or 1461; but Franz Rosenthal has challenged the accuracy of al-Sakhāwī's report. Based on clues within the text, he argues that it was composed between 868/1464 and 871/1467, when al-Badrī would have been between the ages of 24 and 27.[9] However, Rosenthal's dating cannot be completely accurate, as al-Bāᶜūnī, who penned a blurb for this book, died in 870/1465.

In addition to these works, Ibn Ṭūlūn (d. 953/1546) described him as the author of 'a well-known poetry collection and a history entitled *Tabṣirat ūlī al-abṣār fī inqirāḍ al-ᶜumariyyin bi'l-layl wa'l-nahār*', as well as of at least eleven other books on such subjects as Damascene topography and agriculture, moon phases, local history, contemporary literary tastes, caliphs, table companions and close friends.[10]

The emergence of his writing career from unconventional beginnings set the tone for the rest of his career. Al-Badrī wrote books in a number of genres, including history, geography, poetry and prose, but the intertextuality within his corpus of works created generic overlaps. In addition to referencing his past writings, he tended to quote the same authors in all of his works, like Ibn Qalāqis (d. 567/1172), Ibn Nubātah (d. 768/1366), Ibn Makānis (d. 822/1419) and Ibn Ḥajar al-ᶜAsqalānī (d. 852/1449). Drawing from a fixed corpus of writers did not limit his literary production or his choice of subjects. What contacts al-Badrī did make in this period must have been hard won. The Cairene poet Shihāb al-Dīn al-Ḥijāzī was probably his first real connection to elite scholarship, and this association gave him access to a wide set of influential intellectuals. Among his more famous teachers were Shihāb al-Dīn al-Manṣūrī, the last living member of Cairo's seven *Shihāb*s, al-Samhūdī (d. 912/1506) and al-Sakhāwī. Rather than having followed the typical scholar's path of studying under them in his youth, he only met the latter two in the final two or three years of his life.

Mamluk Cairo and Damascus

The Mamluk capital cities of Cairo and Damascus were administratively, economically, militarily and culturally significant in the sultanate, even more so than the Hijaz, which, although the site of Islam's two holiest cities, was semi-autonomous. As such, Cairo and Damascus served as twin academic pillars that were closely identified with the Mamluk sultanate. Cairo functioned as al-Badrī's intellectual centre, although Damascus was his birthplace, and the dual importance of these locales in his life moved him to take both cities' names into his own *nisba*. Even in his topographical work on Syria, he made references to and comparisons with Cairo.[11] His hybrid identity was not an unusual one, as itinerancy and interregional movement characterised many scholars' lives. The early Mamluk poet Ibn Nubātah himself took advantage of his ties to Cairene and Damascene intellectual circles to meld two of their literary forms into a new hybrid school of literary practice. Known as the School of Licit Magic (*madrasat al-siḥr al-ḥalāl*), its hallmark was blending the Egyptian and Syrian forms of *tawriyya* (double entendre). Among his students and adherents were Zayn al-Dīn b. al-Wardī (d. 749/1349), al-Ṣafadī (d. 764/1363), who himself wrote a treatise on *tawriyya*, and Burhān al-Dīn al-Qīrāṭī (d. 781/1379).[12] Of this school, 'the "seven *Shihāb*s" were its most prominent students'.[13] The influence of this school of thought and of Shihāb al-Dīn al-Ḥijāzī, one of the seven *Shihāb*s, on al-Badrī's *Ghurrat al-ṣabāḥ* is evident, as al-Badrī frequently cites therein the works of these older poets. Al-Badrī even gives prominence to al-Ḥijāzī's verse. More indicative of al-Ḥijāzī's influence than these citations is his generously worded blurb for *Ghurrat al-ṣabāḥ*, which will be examined in the following section.

Al-Badrī was in Cairo in Ramadan 875/February 1471 at the time of al-Ḥijāzī's death, caring for him in his final days.[14] There is some evidence that he remained in the region of Egypt and Syria until at least 25 Dhū al-Ḥijja 876/3 June 1472, when Shah Suwwār b. Dhī al-Qādir, a rebellious vassal to the Egyptian Mamluk sultanate, was captured by Mamluk forces at his fortress in Zamantu, a city on Anatolia's south-eastern border with Syria. On 18 Rabiᶜ I 877/23 August 1472, Shah Suwwār and his sixteen-person entourage were led into Cairo. All but one of them were strung up on hooks on Bāb Zuwayla, the southern gate of the old Fatimid city. Their bodies were left suspended there for a day and a half. Al-Badrī composed a couplet about the event, which he wrote from the perspective of the deceased Shah Suwwar, suggesting that al-Badrī witnessed the gruesome punishment. He wrote: 'the angels who thrust the damned into Hell are at Bāb Zuwayla, and they have seized my life with hooks'.[15] The public spectacle of capital punishment was a frequent and well-attended occurrence in Mamluk Cairo, and Bāb Zuwayla was the official site where the bodies of captives and political prisoners were paraded and was also the location where sultans entered and exited the city. Displaying flayed and mutilated bodies reminded the sultan's subjects of the ruler's power and the corporeal consequences of disobedience. That al-Badrī could assume in his poetry the voice of a disgraced, deceased political dissident indicates an ability to imagine and/or appropriate other men's pain and life experiences. This window into al-Badrī's historical writing shows his willingness to insert his own voice into the historical record and even manipulate the voices of deceased actors by imagining their words. Whether motivated by the literary challenge, by social conscience, by empathy or by something else entirely, his responses to suffering bodies are echoed in a chapter in *Ghurrat al-ṣabāḥ* about afflicted body parts.

In Rabīᶜ II 877/September 1472, just one month after the incident at Bāb Zuwayla, Shams al-Dīn al-ᶜAynṭābī al-Amshāṭī (d. 902/1496) was appointed chief Ḥanafī judge of Cairo, replacing the venerable Muḥibb al-Dīn b. al-Shiḥna, whom Sultan Qāytbāy had summarily dismissed after disagreeing with one of his rulings. Al-Badrī composed verses to mark the occasion – and, given his allegiance to the Shiḥna clan, they were probably openly critical of Ibn al-Shiḥna's removal and implicitly critical of the new appointee. These verses did not come to al-Amshāṭī's attention until al-Badrī spoke ill of ᶜAbd al-Razzāq b. Yūsuf al-Qibṭī (d. 896/1491), al-Amshāṭī's housemate (*nazīl*) at al-Barqūqiyya Sufi lodge, by accusing him of 'a hideous thing'.[16] Al-Sakhāwī refrained from specifying the allegation in al-Badrī's biographical entry, averring that 'God knows best' about this affair, but he did write in al-Qibṭī's own entry that

> al-Amshāṭī . . . was highly revered until he had him [al-Qibṭī] live with him in one of the two rooms for shaykhs in al-Barqūqiyya. Things happened to him that may have been false or true. These allegations caused him to turn away from carrying out his office. His outward asceticism, piety and modesty were accused of being shams and exaggerations.[17]

Al-Amshāṭī was so outraged by this affront that he moved quickly to have al-Badrī brought to him; but he was nowhere to be found. He then declared al-Badrī unable to serve as a witness, but this prohibition only lasted a short time. Soon thereafter, one of al-Badrī's wives died, leaving him a large inheritance. In due time, he lost all his money. He travelled to Mecca, then lived in Syria, then moved to Medina in 892/1486–7. In Medina, he copied the works of al-Samhūdī, a blind religious scholar who had moved to the city the same time as he. Al-Badrī remained in Medina for less than one year, and by 893/1487 or 1488 had moved to Mecca to hear hadith from al-Sakhāwī. He wrote the following in praise of his teacher:[18]

> *judda lī sarī*^{can} *bi'l-ḥadīthi ijāza*^{tan}
> *yā kāmil*^{an} *dum wāfiru al-i*^{c}*ṭā*$^{\circ}$*i*
> He toiled long and fast so I could have an *ijāza* for hadith.
> O, my cup runneth over from this award!

This praise poem is cleverly constructed in metre, if not in message. Three poetic metres are named in the poem: *sarī*^{c}, *kāmil* and *wāfir*. A fourth metre, *rajaz*, is not named, though an allusion is made to it with the word *ijāza* – a near rhyme. The phrase *judda lī sarī*^{can} roughly scans as *sarī*^{c}; *bi'l-ḥadīthi ijāza*^{tan} scans as *rajaz*. But *bi'l-ḥadīthi ijāza*^{tan} / *yā kāmil*^{an} scans as *kāmil*. Finally, *dum wāfiru al-i*^{c}*ṭā*$^{\circ}$*i* scans as *wāfir*.

He worked as a merchant in Mecca; and in Dhū al-Ḥijja 893/November 1488, the final month of the hijri calendar and also the month of Muslim pilgrimage, he may have been working in a *ḥānūṭ*, a room beneath a religious building that merchants rented as shops, warehouses or stand-alone stores. The rented rooms funded building upkeep in Mecca during the pilgrimage festivities. Al-Badrī fell ill in Mecca that month and travelled from the city in this weakened state. He was aboard a vessel sailing on the Red Sea at the beginning of Muḥarram 894/December 1489. He had disembarked at Al-Ṭūr port on the Sinai peninsula and had reached the city of Gaza when death overcame him in Jumādā I or II, at the age of 47. Two or more children and maybe his father survived him.[19] The news only reached al-Sakhāwī four or five months later, in the month of Shawwāl.

Ghurrat al-ṣabāḥ fī waṣf al-wujūh al-ṣibāḥ

The British Library holds the sole surviving manuscript of *Ghurrat al-ṣabāḥ*, a copy dated 5 Dhū al-Ḥijja 875/25 May 1471 – mere months after the death of al-Ḥijāzī.[20] It is a compilation of mostly Ayyubid and Mamluk *mudhakkarāt* (romantic or erotic verses addressed to men), though several earlier poets, like Imām al-Shāfiᶜī (d. 204/820), ᶜAlī b. al-Jahm (d. 249/863) and al-Waʾwāʾ (d. c. 385/995), are also notably included. The anthology itself is prefaced by endorsements (*taqāriẓ*, sing. *taqrīẓ*) from five of al-Badrī's contemporaries, some of whose poems appear in this anthology:

1. Shihāb al-Dīn al-Ḥijāzī, whose blurb is dated 16 Jumādā II 871/23 January 1467;
2. Shihāb al-Dīn al-Manṣūrī (d. 887/1482);
3. ᶜAbd al-Barr b. al-Shiḥna (d. 921/1515 or 1516);
4. Abū Bakr Muḥammad b. ᶜUmar b. al-Naṣībī (d. 916/1510); and
5. Aḥmad b. Muḥammad al-Awtārī (d. after 878/1473).

Al-Sakhāwī mentioned five other eminent writers who had also written blurbs for al-Badrī's collection, including Burhān al-Dīn al-Bāᶜūnī (d. 870/1465), al-Bāᶜūnī's two unidentified brothers, Shams al-Dīn Muḥammad b. Abī Bakr al-Qādirī (b. 824/1421, death date unknown) and the historian-poet Badr al-Dīn Muḥammad b. Qurqmās al-Sayfī al-ᶜAlāʾī (d. 942/1535). Al-Sakhāwī himself was also asked to compose a *taqrīẓ* (alt. *taqrīḍ*) for the collection; and he claimed to have produced a lovely one, but this text has not been recovered.[21] Although none of these latter five endorsements appears in the London manuscript, they may have been appended to other versions of the work or published together as a separate pamphlet. Certainly, all of the blurbs offered uniform praise using stock imagery for al-Badrī and his anthology, so they are not useful for assessing the literary value of the work or the ability of the author. Rather, as Rosenthal has remarked, the blurb

> tells us something about literary habits and modes of thought, and it has the potential to add to our knowledge of the organisation of past intellectual life and the relationships among intellectuals and their role in society. The medieval Arabic 'blurb' sheds some light on the social motivations behind literary activity and the development of ways to propagate literary products.[22]

The blurbs for *Ghurrat al-ṣabāḥ* offer insight into hierarchies within al-Badrī's professional networks. As for the preserved *taqāriẓ*, Al-Ḥijāzī's was written earliest and would have carried a lot of weight in Mamluk literary circles. Because he had already written *Jannat al-wildān*, a well-received collection of love poems addressed to male youths, his endorsement of a similarly themed work carried considerable authority. The two men's shared interests in homoeroticism has led Franz Rosenthal to raise the question of who influenced whom, ultimately concluding that 'the possibility that al-Ḥijāzī could have conceived the idea for his work upon hearing about al-Badrī's project can safely be excluded; more likely, it was he who suggested the project to al-Badrī'.[23] Another source of possible inspiration was al-Nawājī's anthology of homoerotic poems. Al-Badrī himself acknowledged no forebears or contemporaries who influenced or inspired his work, though he did remark in the foreword that 'one of the elites . . . asked me to compile a unique anthology for him about young boys'. However, he was so taken aback by the moral implications of writing about the subject that he needed time to reflect. 'I responded to his question after it had occurred to me that I had a duty to obey his example. So I gathered together for him these jewels and stars, luminous and splendid.'[24]

In the spirit of a mentor eminently proud of his pupil's achievements, al-Ḥijāzī used ornate rhetoric and hyperbole to describe the scope of al-Badrī's composition, situating it as a strong contribution to literature that would have deeply impressed past writers:

> If Ibn Qalāqis [d. 567/1172] had heard al-Badrī's composition, then he would have lowered his head shamefully and been humbled. If Ibn al-Khaṭīb [d. 776/1374] had seen the grandeur of his minaret (*manār*), then he would have said that this man is an unparalleled compiler. If Ibn Mammātī [d. 606/1209] had beheld his collection, he would have been revived. Would that he had had food (*al-mammāt*)![25]

Comparing the current author to past luminaries was a generic convention among writers of such endorsements in 8th/14th- and 9th/15th-century Cairo, and in 795/1393 Ibn Ḥajar al-ᶜAsqalānī even employed a similar 'allusion to a shared literary heritage' in a blurb for Ibn Damāmīnī's (d. 827/1424) *Nuzūl al-ghayth* (The Rainfall).[26] Al-Ḥijāzī's endorsement carried such force because it depicted *Ghurrat al-ṣabāḥ* as a composition that had the power to humble, embarrass, impress and even spare past literary giants from fatal illnesses. By invoking the memory of these literary predecessors, al-Ḥijāzī amplified the worth of this individual work. The reading and listening publics were not the only intended audiences for al-Ḥijāzī's writings. The compiler himself, al-Badrī, paid close attention to his teacher's comments about Ibn Qalāqis, later echoing his teacher's language in the conclusion of his circa 893/1487 anthology *Al-Durr al-maṣūn*, but inverted the imagery about Ibn Qalāqis.[27] Writing nearly twenty-one years after al-Ḥijāzī had completed his endorsement, al-Badrī concluded the lengthy work thus: 'Let us content ourselves, in this book of ours, with Ibn Qalāqis's words that made heads bow to him. According to what the pen has recorded [that is, historical records], people pointed to him with their fingertips [indicating that he was a famous, remarkable man].'[28] Al-Ḥijāzī deeply admired Ibn Qalāqis's poetry and included numerous samples of his verse in his anthology *Rawḍ al-ādāb*.[29] Al-Badrī, too, felt an attachment to Ibn Qalāqis and paid homage to him and, by extension, to al-Ḥijāzī's mentorship.

Following the endorsements and al-Badrī's foreword comes the anthology itself, *Ghurrat al-ṣabāḥ*, which is arranged in seventeen thematic chapters:[30]

1. Men's names
2. Adjectives deriving from the names of locations, religions etc.
3. Clothes and jewellery
4. Political elites
5. Soldiers
6. Archers and hunters
7. Public officials
8. Merchants and jewellers
9. Labourers and porters
10. Petty merchants and those who eke out a living
11. Sellers of fruits and flowers
12. Artisans and merchants
13. Laudable physical attributes
14. Afflicted limbs and body parts
15. Miscellanea
16. Beauty moles
17. Beard down.

Chapter 14, titled 'Those with Afflicted Limbs and Body Parts', comprises twenty-five folios and approximately 160 poems, ranging in length from one to four lines. The title words focus attention to the body part bearing the blight, thereby constructing bodily organs and limbs as aesthetic subjects; and each epigram stunningly reconfigures each afflicted part as beautiful. How does writing the body in parts alter the boundaries of the discursive body, and what critical work is done in aestheticising body parts?

Among the earliest poets featured are Imām al-Shāfiʿī (d. 204/820) and ʿAlī b. al-Jahm (d. 249/863), who appear alongside some of al-Badrī's contemporaries, like al-Ḥijāzī. Additionally, the authors come from all over the Arabic-speaking world. In fact, the three authors just mentioned hail from Baghdad, Basra and Cairo respectively. Some of them had afflicted and missing body parts themselves. In 812/1409, the Mamluk sultan al-Nāṣir Faraj accused the Damascene poet Aḥmad b. Yūsuf al-Zuᶜayfarīnī (d. 830/1426) of treason and ordered the removal of a portion of his tongue and all of the fingers of his right hand. Al-Maᶜarrī, who only has one poem featured in this chapter, was blinded at the age of four after suffering complications from smallpox.[31]

The Mamluk era ushered in a flood of literature related to blighted bodies, distinguished from Abbasid lists, anecdotes and occasional poetry by its inclusion in new genres. Al-Ṣafadī's *Nakt al-himyān ᶜalá nukat al-ᶜumyān* consists of 313 biographical entries about prominent blind men, and his much later *Al-Shuᶜūr bi'l-ᶜūr* consists of entries about one-eyed men and women. According to al-Sakhāwī, al-Ṣafadī wrote as yet unrecovered histories about weak-sighted and hunchbacked people.[32] One of al-Ṣafadī's poems that al-Badrī included in his collection is emblematic of the most pervasive literary impulse in *Ghurrat al-ṣabāḥ* – a reconfiguration of normative body aesthetics and an inversion of the standard trope in love poetry of a healthy beloved and the lover whose intense affections make him ill. Al-Ṣafadī wrote:

As for the lame man, I could not free myself from his love.
How much the reproachers censured me for it and aggravated the situation.
So I answered their reproaches, 'What is the shame in the matter?
Rather, this angel's very beauty is that he is lame.'[33]

Al-Badrī's method of compilation innovatively gives these poems new significances. Writing about early modern and modern English anthologies, Anne Ferry has noted that 'the unique role and presence of the anthologist can give a different direction to the experience of reading a poem than if it were read elsewhere'.[34] Selecting and splicing together material from different genres, periods and places are liberties uniquely accorded to the anthologist; and al-Badrī in this capacity was able to create a new context and moment in which to appreciate the verses. *Ghurrat al-ṣabāḥ* effectively obliterates the historical, social and literary contexts in which these verses were originally written. At times, the effect is carried into individual poems, where it is difficult to place the bodies described in any social context. The experience of reading a single poem on blights in a poet's *dīwān* differs significantly from reading the same poem alongside similarly themed works by other authors. With anthologies, the process of extracting and reassembling is essential to the genre. So, what can one learn from the material he chose to include?

In an epigram or short poem, an author can only present a succinct and sometimes partially developed scene or idea. These literary snippets allow his audiences to absorb the material quickly. In one example, al-Badrī included the following verse: 'I asked him about his hand, asked him what had caused it pain. / He said, "My hand is broken", and I responded, "So is my heart".'[35] Terribly moved by the suffering of the unnamed man, the speaker reveals empathy, solidarity and compassion in a single line of verse. With such brief poems as this one, more text fits onto a single folio, giving a visual sense of copious, easy-to-digest poetic samples. In this way, anthologies influence audience responses to the material at hand. Al-Badrī's work had the potential to create new associations with standard texts by reconfiguring their spatial arrangements. These new sites of analysis make possible an innovative presentation of blighted bodies, as al-Badrī has rendered past utterances about blights legible to his 9th/15th-century audience. Poetic traditions are re-archived, informing the ways in which their particular subjects are remembered. While anthologising does not necessitate the creation of original material, the opportunity to fashion new canons, thereby establishing new sites of collective memory, stands as a rather broad project with major social, political and literary significance. Indeed, al-Badrī's reassembly of this set of poems presents a sense of continuity, as he has constructed a quasi-narrative about the cycle of life, illness and death. From beginning to end, chapter 14 follows a teleological arch of illness, opening with poems praising medical workers who treat afflicted patients, moving then to men with various afflictions, sufferers of declining health, death, burial and men visiting their beloveds' tombs. The author's conceptualisation of illness follows the model for progression of disease in Prophetic medicine (*al-ṭibb al-nabawī*). Al-Badrī wrote in *al-Durr al-maṣūn*, an anthology he later composed about the eye: 'Every illness shifts, and it has four stages: onset, increase, end and decline'.[36] The associations from poem to poem are not always thematic. Most often, each successive verse was chosen either for its thematic relevance to the previous one or for its having been written by the same author as the previous one. Rosenthal found this organisational principle somewhat disruptive, remarking that 'the decision as to where to put some of the epigrams seems at time to have caused a small problem for him'.[37] The chapter's final poems praise young boys who have been orphaned by illness and who, in their isolation, seek solace with the poems' male speakers. The attention of the adult speakers on the now extremely vulnerable boys represents a striking and haunting end to the chapter. In one such poem, the speaker remarks on the 'blessed water' coursing down the orphan's face around his cheek moles, compares his front teeth to 'stringed pearls', claims to be wasting away from his affection for him and is ultimately moved to 'cry in solitude over an orphan'. The death of ill bodies creates new focus on young, isolated, vital bodies.

Throughout this anthology, the reassembly of poems about bodies and their body parts comes together to create a hybrid corpus of work and a composite human body that is the sum of its individual diseased parts. The technique is reminiscent of that of ancient Greek sculptors who chose

> the best parts of various models in order to produce an image so beautiful that it could not exist in nature: They would take the form from one, the small of the back from another, the face from a third, and so on. In this way a sculpted or painted body was a kind of compendium, a collection of parts which, taken together, created an ideal impression.[38]

Al-Badrī gamely adapted this visual conceit to his literary project; he has not only reassembled a set of poems, but also re-membered a *segmented human body* into an idealised composite whole. This act of 'textual fragmentation of the body', to borrow Terry Wilfong's phrase, is gendered male in this anthology, but al-Ḥijāzī and other authors wrote about women's blighted body parts too.[39] In Wilfong's study of Coptic communities in Egypt from 400 to 1000 CE, he read isolated body parts to understand how they were differently valorised in magical, medical, religious, poetic, visual and historical sources and in the confined spaces of convents, monasteries and homes. The variance of constructions of segmented male and female bodies and the impossibility of deriving a single unitary theory of the body arise from Wilfong's study. In much the same way, al-Badrī has not advanced a unified vision of disability aesthetics or male-male homoerotics in this period, but has produced a worthy contribution to the genre of literature about body parts, like al-Nawājī's (d. 859/1455) study of birthmarks, and literary traditions about blights.

Ghurrat al-ṣabāḥ resituated knowledge about blighted bodies. By focusing on the literary body, al-Badrī heightened the abilities, identities, cultural and aesthetic ascriptions and fetishes of individual body parts; and the technique works to tremendously strong effect in the literary construction of a wholly diseased male body and also for the entire anthology. In *Ghurrat al-ṣabāḥ*, illnesses and afflictions play out over every inch of the human body; and, in the end, every part of this wholly afflicted body dies. The multi-layered, seductive and symbolic forces of body parts find expression in this miscellany dedicated to male homoerotics of blighted bodies.

Here is an outline of chapter 14 of al-Badrī's *Ghurrat al-ṣabāḥ*, 'Those with Afflicted Limbs and Body Parts':

Folio	Subject of poem	Poet
152b	Doctor	Zayn al-Dīn b. al-Wardī (d. 749/1349)
	Doctor	Daftarkhwān (d. 7th/13th century)
153a	Doctor	Jamāl al-Dīn b. Maṭrūḥ (d. 649/1251)
	Medical student	Jamāl al-Dīn b. Maṭrūḥ (d. 649/1251)
	Eye doctor	Ṣalāḥ al-Dīn al-Ṣafadī (d. 764/1363)
	Eye doctor	Ṣalāḥ al-Dīn al-Ṣafadī (d. 764/1363)
	Eye doctor	Daftarkhwān (d. 7th/13th century)
	One who performs cupping	ᶜIzz al-Dīn al-Mawṣilī
	Barber	Ibn al-Faḍl b. Abī Wafāᵓ
53b	Student of bloodletting	Ibn al-Faḍl b. Abī Wafāᵓ
	Sub-chapter entitled 'The Afflicted'	
	Hunchback	Unattributed
	Hunchback	Maḥāsin al-Shawā (d. 635/1237)
	Hunchback	Ibn al-Mazīz
	Flat-nosed	Unattributed
	Blind	Zayn al-Dīn b. Labbaykum
	Blind	ᶜAlā al-Dīn al-Wadaᶜī
154a	Blind	Ibn Nubātah (d.768/1366)
	Blind	Unattributed
	One-eyed	Zayn al-Dīn b. al-Wardī (d. 749/1349)
	One-eyed	Zayn al-Dīn b. al-Wardī (d. 749/1349)
	One-eyed	Shihāb al-Dīn al-Ḥijāzī (d. 875/1471); see also *Kunnas*, p. 129
	One-eyed	Ibn Abī Ḥajala (d. 766/1375)
	One-eyed	Ibn al-ᶜAfīf al-Tilimsānī (d. 688/1289)
154b	Eye	Burhān al-Dīn al-Qīrāṭī (d. 781/1379)
	Jaundice	Ibn Sanāᵓ al-Mulk (d. 609/1211)
	Cross-eyed	Unattributed
	Cross-eyed	Ṣadr al-Dīn b. al-Wakīl (d. 716/1316)
	Close-set eyes[40]	Abū al-Ḥasan al-Muqrī (d. 402/1011)
	Having a contorted eye	Abū al-Ḥasan al-Muqrī (d. 402/1011)
	Deaf (*atrash*)	Abū al-Ḥasan al-Muqrī (d. 402/1011)
155a	Deaf (*dhā ṣamam*)	Shihāb al-Dīn al-Ḥijāzī (d. 875/1471); see also *Kunnas*, p. 125
	Deaf (*aṣamm*)	Ibn Ḥajar al-ᶜAsqalānī (d. 852/1449)
	Deaf (*aṣamm*)	Zayn al-Dīn b. Labbaykum
	Who fell off a roof and hit the ground	Unattributed
	Stutterer	Unattributed
	With a chipped front tooth	Shihāb al-Dīn al-Thaqafī

	Stutterer	Unattributed
155b	Stutterer	Sarī al-Dīn ʿAbd al-Barr b. al-Shiḥna al-Ḥanafī (d. 921/1515)
	Lisp (*althaʿ*)	Sarī al-Dīn ʿAbd al-Barr b. al-Shiḥna al-Ḥanafī (d. 921/1515)
	Lisp	Shihāb al-Dīn al-Ḥijāzī, direct transmission (d. 875/1471); see also *Kunnas*, p. 126
	Lisp	Ibrāhīm al-Miʿmār (d. 749/1348)
	Lisp	Zayn al-Dīn b. al-Wardī (d. 749/1349)
	Lisp	Daftarkhwān (d. 7th/13th century)
	Lisp	Al-Qayyim al-Fākhūrī
156a	Lisp	Zayn al-Dīn b. al-Wardī (d. 749/1349)
	Lameness	Unattributed
	Lameness	Abū al-Barakāt al-Andalusī
	Lameness	Ṣalāḥ al-Dīn al-Ṣafadī (d. 764/1363)
	Lameness	Ibn Dāniyāl (d. 710/1310)
	Ophthalmia	Unattributed
156b	Ophthalmia	Ibn al-Muʿtazz (d. 296/908)
	Ophthalmia	Ibn Dāniyāl (d. 710/1310)
	Ophthalmia	Ibn al-ʿAṭṭār (d. 777/1375)
	Ophthalmia	Jamāl al-Dīn al-Nabulusī
	Eye reddened from ophthalmia	Shihāb al-Dīn al-Ḥijāzī, direct transmission (d. 875/1471); see also *Kunnas*, p. 130
	Eye reddened from ophthalmia	Al-Armawī
	Who complains about his eye	Unattributed
157a	Veiny eyes from ophthalmia	Unattributed
	Swollen eye	Majd al-Dīn b. Makānis (d. 822/1419)
	Broken tooth	Muḥibb al-Dīn al-Zuraʿī
	Freckle-faced	Ibn ʿArabī (d. 656/1258)
	Freckle-faced	Al-Nāṣir b. al-Naqīb (d. c. 687/1288)
	Freckle-faced	Zayn al-Dīn b. Labbaykum
	Halitosis	Ibn ʿArabī (d. 656/1258)
157b	Measles	Al-Sirāj ʿUmar al-Warrāq (d. 695/1296)
	Measles	Majd al-Dīn b. Makānis (d. 822/1419)
	Leprosy (*bahaq*)	Shihāb al-Dīn b. Yusuf al-Zuʿayfarīnī (d. 830/1426)
	Mange	Unattributed
	Itching skin eruption	Ibn al-ʿAṭṭār (d. 777/1375)

	Smallpox	Zayn al-Dīn b. al-Wardī (d. 749/1349)
	Smallpox	Majd al-Dīn b. Makānis (d. 822/1419)
158a	Adolescent acne	Ibn Luʾluʾ al-Dhahabī (d. 680/1281)
	Adolescent acne	Ṣalāḥ al-Dīn al-Ṣafadī (d. 764/1363)
	Bump on cheek	Majd al-Dīn b. Makānis (d. 822/1419)
	Bump on cheek	Ibn al-ᶜAfīf al-Tilimsānī (d. 688/1289)
	Bump on lip	Al-Badr Ḥasan al-Ghazzī al-Zuᶜarī (b. 1306, death date unknown)
	(*bi-khaddihi al-ᶜatash*)	Unattributed
	Smallpox	Ṣalāḥ al-Dīn al-Ṣafadī (d. 764/1363)
	Wounded mouth	Unattributed
158b	Plague boils on the leg	Al-Ṣalāḥ al-Ṣafadī (d. 764/1363)
	Plague boils on the leg	Al-Ṣalāḥ al-Ṣafadī (d. 764/1363)
	Stung by scorpion	Jamāl al-Dīn b. Maṭrūḥ (d. 649/1251)
	Bee-stung lips	Al-ᶜAlāʾ al-*m*di
	Enchanted (*masḥūr*)	Maḥāsin al-Shawā (d. 635/1237)
	Demon possession/mental illness	Maḥāsin al-Shawā (d. 635/1237)
	Demon possession/mental illness	Muḥammad al-Azharī
	Satan	Majd al-Dīn b. Makānis (d. 822/1419)
159a	Crucified	Muḥammad b. ᶜAbdallāh al-Aḥṭar
	Crucified	ᶜAmarah al-Yamanī, cited from *al-Murqiṣ wa'l-muṭrib*[41]
	Broken hand	Unattributed
	Broken hand	Zayn al-Dīn b. al-Wardī (d. 749/1349)
	Mute	Shihāb al-Dīn b. Yūsuf al-Zuᶜayfarīnī (d. 830/1426)
	Whose leg was cupped	Unattributed
	Who underwent cupping	Unattributed
	Who underwent cupping	Zayn al-Dīn b. Labbaykum
159b	Bloodletting	Al-Qayyim al-Fākhūrī
	Whose forearm was cupped	Unattributed
	Whose arm was cupped	Unattributed
	Attempted cupping	Unattributed
	Felt pain in his limbs	Unattributed
	Whose broken bones were set	Majd al-Dīn b. Makānis (d. 822/1419)
160a	Slashes on cheek	Unattributed
	Fractured forehead	Muḥyī al-Dīn b. ᶜAbd al-Ẓāhir (d. 692/1292)
	Bite on cheek	Unattributed

	Wounded cheek	Ṣalāḥ al-Dīn al-Ṣafadī (d. 764/1363)
	Wounded cheek	Ṣalāḥ al-Dīn al-Ṣafadī (d. 764/1363)
	Wounded cheek	Ibn Aybak al-Dimashqī (d. 801/1398)
160b	Wounded by brother	Ibn al-Muraḥḥal (d. 699/1300)
	Cut open his palm	Ibn al-ᶜAfīf al-Tilimsānī (d. 688/1289)
	Burned his hand in a fire	Nāṣir al-Dīn b. al-Naqīb (d. c. 687/1288)
	Wounded forehead	Ibn Ḥabīb al-Ḥalabī (d. 779/1377)
	Cauterised temple	Al-Badrī (d. 894/1489)
	Skin incision[42]	Ṣalāḥ al-Dīn al-Ṣafadī (d. 764/1363)
161a	Skin incision	Ibn Nubātah (d. 768/1366)
	Skin incision	Ibn al-ᶜAṭṭār (d. 777/1375)
	Skin incision	Maḥāsin al-Shawā (d. 635/1237)
	Molar pain	Unattributed
	Broken tooth	Al-Badrī (d. 894/1489)
	Pulled out tooth	Safī al-Dīn al-Ḥillī (d. 750/1349)
	Pulled out tooth	Daftarkhwān (d. 7th/13th century)
	Leprous or slain? (*muqaᶜṭal*)[43]	Muḥammad b. Aḥmad al-Ghassānī al-Waʾwāʾ al-Dimashqī (d. c. 385/995)
161b	Violent shaking and diarrhoea	Al-Sirāj al-Maḥḥār (d. 711/1311)
	Fever	Unattributed
	Fever	Ibn Ḥabīb al-Ḥalabī (d. 779/1377)
	Fever	Al-Qāḍī ᶜAbd al-Raḥīm al-Fāḍil (d. 596/1200)
	Fever	Ibn Sanāʾ al-Mulk (d. 609/1211)
162a	Fever	Shihāb al-Dīn al-Ḥājibī
	Fever	Same as preceding poem with a different speaker
	Fever	Najm al-Dīn b. Isrāʾil (d. 667/1268)
	Fever	Al-Sirāj ᶜUmar al-Warrāq (d. 695/1296)
	Fever	Daftarkhwān (d. 7th/13th century)
	Whom a doctor visited and treated	Unattributed
162b	Who fell ill from something he ate	Unattributed
	Fever	Ibn al-Muᶜtazz (d. 296/908)
	Healer (?)	Unattributed
	Sick (or healing?)	Imām al-Shāfiᶜī (d. 204/820)
	Who regained health	Unattributed

	Speaker honours lover through breaking fast, not through fasting	Burhān al-Dīn b. Shajā^{c}
	Who drank medicine	Unattributed
163a	Who drank medicine	Abū al-Ḥasan Muḥammad b. Muẓaffar
	Who drank medicine	Ibn Nubātah (d. 768/1366)
	Who drank medicine	Ibn al-^{c}Aṭṭār (d. 777/1375)
	Cauterised hand	Najm al-Dīn b. Isrā$^{\supset}$il (d. 667/ 1268)
	Cauterised hand	Tāj al-Dīn al-Naqīb
	Cauterised hand	Jamāl al-Dīn Mūsá b. Yaghmūr (d. 664/1265)
	Whose health improved, then declined	Unattributed
163b	Whose health improved, then declined	^{c}Alī b. al-Jahm (d. 249/863)
	Ill (*^{c}alīl*)	Unattributed
	Sick (*marīḍ*)	Ibn Sanā$^{\supset}$ al-Mulk (d. 609/1211)
	Ailing (*saqīm*)	Abū al-Faḍl b. al-Amīn, direct transmission
	Visiting a sick lover	Shams al-Dīn al-Qādirī (b. 824/1421, death date unknown)
	In the throes of death	Shihāb al-Dīn al-Ḥijāzī, direct transmission (d. 894/1471)
	Who was near death	Ibn al-^{c}Aṭṭār (d. 777/1375)
164a	Who embraced his dying lover	Ṣalāḥ al-Dīn al-Ṣafadī (d. 764/1363)
	A man turned towards the *qiblah*	Ṣalāḥ al-Dīn al-Ṣafadī (d. 764/1363)
	Eulogising a dead man	Shihāb al-Dīn al-Ḥijāzī, direct transmission (d. 875/1471)
	Eulogising a dead man	Shihāb al-Dīn al-Ḥijāzī, direct transmission (d. 875/1471)
	Eulogising a dead man	Shihāb al-Dīn al-Ḥijāzī, direct transmission (d. 875/1471)
	Eulogising a dead man	Ibrāhīm al-Mi^{c}mār (d. 749/1348)
	Crying for his love and devotion	Unattributed
	Beautiful black man crying behind a bier	Maḥāsin al-Shawā (d. 635/1237)

164b	Whom the earth took	Shihāb al-Dīn al-Ḥijāzī, direct transmission (d. 875/1471)
	Whom the earth took	Shihāb al-Dīn al-Ḥijāzī, direct transmission (d. 875/1471)
	Whom the earth took	Shihāb al-Dīn al-Ḥijāzī, direct transmission (d. 875/1471)
	Someone addressing his beloved's grave	Ṣalāḥ al-Dīn al-Ṣafadī (d. 764/1363)
	Qur'an-reciter (*muqrī*)[44]	Ibn al-ᶜAfīf al-Tilimsānī (d. 688/1289)
	On two lovers who visit their beloveds' tombs	Unattributed
165a	Whose grave sprouts a flower	Ṣalāḥ al-Dīn al-Ṣafadī (d. 764/1363)
	Whose grave sprouts a flower	Ṣalāḥ al-Dīn al-Ṣafadī (d. 764/1363)
	Orphan	Ṣalāḥ al-Dīn al-Ṣafadī (d. 764/1363)
	Orphan	Fakhr al-Dīn b. Makānis (d. 794/1392)[45]

Al-Durr al-maṣūn

Al-Badrī's choice of the eye as the subject of the anthology *al-Durr al-maṣūn* may reflect the pre-eminence of the field of ophthalmology in the medieval Islamicate world; the medical advancements achieved in this time surpassed the knowledge of neighbouring civilisations in both scope and depth. Arabs were renowned for their pre-eminence and expertise in the sciences of the eye, so al-Badrī had a wealth of information at his disposal and recourse to earlier works in the field when he began composing his own work. His massive anthology about the eye has been characterised as 'a synthesis of ophthalmological observations and poetry emulating al-Ṣafadī's *Ṣarf al-ᶜayn*'.[46] Al-Ṣafadī's large anthology comprises materials on Islamic jurisprudence, Arabic language, literature and alphabetically arranged selections of poetry, and al-Badrī's collection comprises much more than just eye-related medical information and verse. Historical anecdotes, prophetic hadith, Qur'anic scripture, fables, legal debates, letter magic, aphorisms and literary references to eyes round out *Al-Durr al-maṣūn*. Compiled between 893/1487 and 894/1488, towards the end of his life, the sum of the influence of al-Badrī's mentors is prominent in this text. A veiled reference to al-Ṣafadī appears in the opening pages of the book: 'I named this work *Siḥr al-ᶜuyūn* because the essence of a thing is its name, and by my life, it is known to literary critics and arbiters of refined literary taste who understand what there is of utility, double entendre, eloquence and harmony in this name'.[47] The reference to utility and double entendre mirrors the language of the title of al-Ṣafadī's treatise on double entendre and its uses as a poetic device – another subtle reference to the value that al-Badrī assigned to al-Ṣafadī and the School of Licit Magic.

If chapter 14 of *Ghurrat al-ṣabāḥ* represents a uniquely ordered selection of homoerotic poetry praising blighted bodies, then *al-Durr al-maṣūn* is its counterpart rooted in historically normative practices of writing about eyes, blighted or otherwise. Blights among the *ashrāf* are explored in traditional fashion as lists of names or partially narrativised lists. Here, al-Badrī explores etymologies, definitions and grammatical variations of blight-related terms. All in all, it is an expansive exploration of eyes from many perspectives – that of medical workers, jurists, religious scholars, men and women of letters, practitioners and believers of magic, and historians. Due to the range of viewpoints incorporated into this work, popular and elite registers of voices find representation in his compendium.

The first chapter of *al-Durr* centres on 'the power of vision', or the agency of the eye. Magical tables, incantations and diagrams of the magical properties of the eye concretise popular beliefs about the eye's ability to influence the physical world. The chapter closes with a story of violence against Zarqā᾽ al-Yamāma, a blue-eyed woman from the central Arabian region of al-Yamāma, who could see three days into the future and used her ability to protect her clan from surprise attacks. Interestingly, her rare ability is constructed not as supernatural foresight but rather as the result of vision so acute that 'she could spot a white hair in milk'.[48] One day, she claimed to see trees approaching their settlement to attack, and the people of al-Yamāma roundly denounced her as feeble-minded and insane. She was also accused of lying, then was seized and had her eyes gouged out. It turned out that the enemy horsemen had covered themselves and their riding animals with leaves to disguise their advance and, as a result, successfully ambushed the settlement and handily defeated the settlers.

This story raises a number of questions about the nature of the Blue-Eyed Woman's ability. The pairing of sharply piercing sight with clairvoyance may be a hyperbolic statement or an indication of how sight was configured. Relatedly, common Arab lore credited blind individuals with greater 'vision of the heart' or the ability to discern feelings and to access piety with greater ease. Figurative conceptions of sight (through time *and* space, and with organs other than the eyes) bespeak a view of the body that rejects neat compartmentalisations and boundaries of physical abilities. The heart can see, and the eye can discern the future. Zarqā᾽ al-Yamāma's eyes had agency and possessed abilities that belonged solely to the eyes. The blue colour of her eyes only heightened the 'otherness' of her abilities. A reinforced sense of her difference contributed to the violent reactions of her peers to her suspected lies. The punishment of removing offending body parts is rooted in Islamic jurisprudence, and the amputation of limbs was essentially an order of death for the body part that had transgressed moral order. No judge, however, ordered this woman's punishment; and her fellow tribespeople exacted this gruesome sentence as a form of impromptu justice against a woman who threatened their peace and their sense of honour and who transgressed physical and sexual norms. In later sections about the magical properties of the eye, women figure as the main possessors of these abilities. Even when they are shown to use 'licit magic', they are accused of being, or are found to be, treacherous.

The second chapter turns to the legal implications of evil eyes and includes various discussions on determining the blood price (*diya*) for injuries caused by evil eyes. In chapter 3 al-Badrī discusses eye-related illnesses and mentions descendants of the Prophet who were one-eyed and blind, as well as anecdotes about the Followers who were blind. Chapter 4 is about ophthalmology and cures of eye diseases.

In the fifth chapter, al-Badrī describes different parts of the eye, emphasising that even units of a whole can be particularised and divided into even smaller units. The eye is not a unitary organ, and many of its smaller components find recognition in this chapter. Indeed, al-Badrī writes about the inner corner of the eye, as well as the follicles on the eyelids from which eyelashes grow. Ibn Nubātah praised these follicles as the best part of a woman's eye.[49] The enchanting capabilities of women's eyes, which reference the book title, are detailed in random places throughout these volumes. In another instance, a man encounters a slave woman with eyes so beautiful that they compel him to pay 40,000 dirhams for her.[50] The sixth chapter features jokes and anecdotes about eyes, and the concluding chapters feature mostly love poetry about eyes.

The restoration of historical performances by anthologising multiple performances changes their original meanings and significations. Al-Badrī's anthologies resituated knowledge about blighted bodies. By focusing on the literary body, al-Badrī heightens the abilities, identities, cultural and aesthetic ascriptions and fetishes of individual body parts. When treated singly as subjects, limbs and organs transform into literary or historical subjects with agency and identity, calling into question the notion of a person's control over his or her own body. Control is an illusion when the constitutive parts of a body possess identities and wills. Ascribing agency to one part of the human body creates a particular relationship of the part to the whole, and the technique works to different effect in each anthology. In *Ghurrat al-ṣabāḥ*, illnesses play out over every inch of the human body; and, in the end, every part of this wholly afflicted body dies. In *al-Durr al-maṣūn*, the seductive, coercive, symbolic and magical forces of the eye find expression in this miscellany dedicated to this singular organ – the eye.

Notes

1. Abdelfattah Kilito, *The Author and His Doubles: Essays on Classical Arabic Culture*, trans. Michael Cooperson (Syracuse: Syracuse University Press, 2001), p. 2.
2. Thomas Bauer, 'Literarische Anthologien der Mamlūkenzeit', in Stephan Conermann and Anja Pistor-Hatam (eds), *Die Mamluken. Studien zu ihrer Geschichte und Kultur. Zum Gedenken an Ulrich Haarmann (1942–1999)* (Schenefeld: EB-Verlag, 2003), pp. 73–9. For more on Mamluk anthologies, see chapter 4 ('An Anthology as a Mirror of Literary Tastes') of Vrolijk's *Bringing a Laugh to a Scowling Face.*
3. Albert Hourani, *A History of the Arab Peoples* (Cambridge, MA: Harvard University Press, 1991), p. 200.
4. Brockelmann incorrectly listed his death date as 909/1503 in *GAL* 2:132 and *GAL Supplement* 2:163. Al-Sakhāwī, one of al-Badrī's teachers, rendered his full name Abū Bakr b. ᶜAbdallāh b. Muḥammad b. Aḥmad b. ᶜAbdallāh Taqī al-Dīn b. al-Jamāl al-Dimashqī al-Qāhirī al-Shāfiᶜī al-Shāᶜir al-Wafāʾī, noting additionally that he was known as Ibn al-Badrī and that his *kunya* was Abū al-Tuqā (Al-Sakhāwī, *Al-Ḍawᶜ*, 11:41). For additional notes on various versions of this author's name, see Charles Rieu and W. Cureton (eds), *Catalogus codicum manuscriptorum orientalium qui in Museo Britannico asservantur Pars secunda, codices arabicos amplectens* (London: British Museum, 1846–71), pp. 478–9.
5. Although I am unaware of contemporary Arabic anthologies of disability poetry, the genre is gaining prominence in the contemporary USA. See, for instance, Jennifer Bartlett et al. (eds), *Beauty is a Verb: The New Poetry of Disability* (El Paso, TX: Cinco Puntos, 2011), and the recently founded *Wordgathering: A Journal of Disability Poetry*.
6. For more on *Kitāb rāḥat al-arwāḥ*, see Rosenthal, *Herb*, pp. 13–15; Indalecio Lozano Cámara, 'Un Fragmento del *Kitāb rāḥat al-arwāḥ fī al-hašiš wa al-rāḥ*', *Miscelanea de Estudios Arabes y Hebraicos* 38 (1989–90), pp. 163–83; and idem, 'Un Nuevo Fragmento del *Kitāb rāḥat al-arwāḥ fī l-hašiš wa-l-rāḥ* de Taqī al-Dīn al-Badrī', *BEO* 49 (1997), pp. 235–48; Fabio Zanello, *Hashish e Islam: tradizione e consumo, visioni e prescrizioni nella poesia, nella letteratura e nelle leggi* (Rome: Cooper and Castelvecchi, 2003). Zanello's study derives mostly from Rosenthal's work, rather than from primary sources. Even though much of the material is borrowed, the study includes many inaccuracies. Zanello states, for instance, that al-Badrī is 'presumably Egyptian', (p. 42, fn. 17).

7. Lozano Cámara, 'Fragmento', p. 174.
8. Taqī al-Dīn al-Badrī, *Nuzhat al-anām fī maḥāsin al-shām* (Cairo: Al-Maṭba[c]at al-salafiyya, 1922–3), p. 62. In al-Badrī's autograph manuscript, which is catalogued as History MS no. 1642 in Cairo's Dār al-Kutub, the completion date is given as 877/1472.
9. Al-Sakhāwī, *Al-Ḍaw'*, 11:41; Franz Rosenthal, 'Male and Female: Described and Compared', in J. W. Wright and Everett K. Rowson (eds), *Homoeroticism in Classical Arabic Literature* (New York: Columbia University Press, 1997), pp. 50–1, fn. 45.
10. Ibn al-Mullā al-Ḥaṣkafī, *Mut[c]at*, 1:229. For a list of al-Badrī's works, see al-Badrī, *Al-Durr*, 1:9; Brockelmann, *GAL* 2:132 and *GAL Supplement* 2:163.
11. Al-Badrī, *Nuzhat*, p. 74. Al-Ḥijāzī probably would not have approved of the comparison, as he himself wrote a poem in which he proudly declared: 'I would not exchange my city for Damascus, / Because its flowers and almonds are not my land'. Poem cited in Aḥmad b. Muḥammad al-Maqqarī (d. 1041/1631 or 1632), *Al-Nafḥ al-ṭīb min ghuṣn al-andalus al-raṭīb* (The Sweet Fragrance from the Green Bough of Andalusia), ed. Iḥsan [c]Abbās (Beirut: Dār ṣādir, 1968), 2:405.
12. See al-Ṣafadī, *Faḍḍ al-khitām [c]an al-tawriyya wa'l-istikhdām* (Breaking the Seal on Double Entendre and Metalepsis), ed. al-Muḥammadī [c]Abd al-[c]Azīz al-Ḥinnāwī (Cairo: s.n., 1979); and Seeger A. Bonebakker, *Some Early Definitions of the Tawriya and Ṣafadī's Fadd al-Xitam [c]an at-Tawriya wa-l-Istixdam* (The Hague: Moulton & Co., 1966).
13. Aḥmad Ṣādiq al-Jammāl, *Al-Adab al-[c]āmmī fī miṣr fī al-[c]aṣr al-mamlūkī* (Cairo: Al-Dār al-qawmiyya, 1966), p. 59.
14. Al-Badrī, *Al-Durr*, 2:281.
15. Ibn al-Mullā al-Ḥaṣkafī, *Mut[c]at*, 1:229, citing al-Badrī's *Tabṣirat ūlī al-abṣār fī inqirāḍ al-[c]umariyyin bi'l-layl wa'l-nahār*, an unrecovered chronicle.
16. Al-Sakhāwī, *Al-Ḍaw'*, 11:41.
17. Ibid., *Al-Ḍaw'*, 4:196.
18. Ibn al-Mullā al-Ḥaṣkafī, *Mut[c]at*, 1:230–1.
19. Al-Sakhāwī , *Al-Ḍaw'*, 11:42.
20. A detailed description of this manuscript (British Library MS 1423, add. 23,445) is to be found in Rieu and Cureton (eds), *Catalogus*, 2:654–5, and Rosenthal, 'Male', p. 50, fn. 45.
21. Al-Sakhāwī, *Al-Ḍaw'*, 11:41. For *taqrīẓ* and its alternative spellings in the late medieval Arabic world, see Ibn al-Ḥanbalī, *Baḥr*, p. 221, and Rudolf Vesely, 'Das Taqrīẓ in der arabischen Literatur', in Conermann and Pistor-Hatam (eds), *Die Mamluken*, pp. 379–85. Also, Franz Rosenthal has noted in '"Blurbs"', p. 178: 'Arabic lexicographers tried to restrict *qarraẓa* to "praise of the living". There was no real basis for this restriction, and it was not generally accepted. Nor was there any consensus as to whether the roots *qarraẓa*

and *qarraḍa* were to be kept apart. To the Semitist, no original distinction seems to exist between [the roots] *qrṣ*, *qrḍ*, and *qrẓ*.'

22. Rosenthal, '"Blurbs"', p. 189.
23. Rosenthal, 'Male', p. 33.
24. Al-Badrī, *Ghurrat*, fo. 7b.
25. Al-Badrī, *Ghurrat*, fo. 4b. Ibn Mammātī died impoverished and starving in Aleppo. His patronymic was purportedly inherited from his grandfather, who was known for his charitable donations of food to the poor.
26. Rosenthal, '"Blurbs"', pp. 189, 195.
27. Dating the text is possible because, within the text, al-Badrī reported the death of al-Salāmī b. Muḥammad b. Muḥammad b. ᶜAbdallāh in 893/1487 or 1488, and al-Badrī himself died the following year in 894/1489. See al-Badrī, *Al-Durr*, 2:197.
28. Al-Badrī, *Al-Durr*, 2:281.
29. Muḥammad Zakariyya ᶜInānī, *Al-Nuṣūṣ al-ṣiqilliyya min shiᶜr Ibn Qalāqis al-Iskandarī (567 AH) wa-āthārihi al-nathriyya* (Sicilian Texts in the Poetry of Ibn Qalāqis al-Iskandarī [d. AH 567] and His Prose Works) (Cairo: Dār al-maᶜārif, 1982), p. 11.
30. The bulk of these chapters' verses addresses men of professions, a common motif in Middle Eastern literatures, as evidenced in the *shahrangiz* poetic genre in Persian, Turkish and Urdu literatures, which praises male beauties of various crafts and professions.
31. Taha Thalji Tarawneh, *The Province of Damascus during the Second Mamluk Period (784/1382–922/1516)* (Jordan: Publications of the Deanship of Research and Graduate Studies, Muᵓtah University, 1994), p. 176.
32. Rosenthal, *History*, p. 432.
33. Al-Badrī, *Ghurrat*, fo. 156a. Cf. Qur'an 70: 4, 'the angels ascend' (*taᶜruju al-malāᵓikatu*). Al-Ṣafadī's *Al-Ḥusn al-sarīḥ fī miᵓat malīḥ* includes even more love verses addressed to physically different men.
34. Anne Ferry, *Tradition and the Individual Poem: An Inquiry into Anthologies* (Stanford: Stanford University Press, 2001), p. 7.
35. Al-Badrī, *Ghurrat*, fo. 159a.
36. Al-Badrī, *Al-Durr*, 1:91. The third term, which literally translates as 'end', may have referred to what we today would call a 'peak in illness'.
37. Rosenthal, 'Male', p. 34.
38. Françoise Barbe-Gall, *How to Read a Painting* (London: Francis Lincoln Ltd, 2010), p. 142.
39. Terry Wilfong, 'Reading the Disjointed Body in Coptic: From Physical Modification to Textual Fragmentation', in Dominic Montserrat (ed.), *Changing Bodies, Changing Meanings: Studies on the Human Body in Antiquity* (London and New York: Routledge, 1998), p. 118.
40. In al-Muqrī's lifetime, close-set eyes would have still been perceived as physically undesirable, in contrast to the large eyes that were commonly praised in Arab poetry. A Mamluk-era poem on close-set eyes, such as

those written by Ibn Nubātah or Muḥyī al-Dīn ^{c}Abd al-Ẓāhir, would not have suggested physical aberration, as beauty norms were shifting in this period. According to Aḥmad Ṣādiq al-Jammāl, 'We know that Arabic literature is filled with descriptions of young boys, women and large eyes, but customs changed here [in early Mamluk Egypt] as poets started composing love poems about close-set eyes . . . We see that the ethnic heritage of the Mamluks left its traces in Egyptian poetry' through the celebration of hallmarks of Turkish beauty (close-set eyes) and through the use of Turkish words. See al-Jammāl, *Al-Adab*, pp. 46–7.

41. The copyist rendered the title *Al-Murqiṣ wa'l-muṭrib*, but this title by Ibn Sa^{c}īd (d. after 683/1284) has also been transmitted as *^{c}Unwān al-murqiṣāt wa'l-muṭribāt* and *Al-murqiṣāt wa'l-muṭribāt.*
42. In this series of poems about skin incisions, the beloved is doing the cutting.
43. *Muqa^{c}ṭāl* was the collective noun form of two types of leprosy, *baraṣ* and *judhām*. See Michael Dols, 'Leprosy in Medieval Arabic Medicine', *Journal of the History of Medicine and Allied Sciences* 34.3 (July 1979), p. 321. The German scholar G. J. Wetzstein postulates that this euphemism for leprosy derived from an assumption that lepers were punished (*qatala*) by God: see 'Aus einem briefe des Herrn Consul Wetzstein an Prof. Fleischer', *ZDMG* 23 (1869), pp. 310–11.
44. 'Muqri's often exhibited a physical handicap associated with their profession: blindness. Not all muqri's were without sight, but individuals who had suffered the misfortune and who had retentive powers were often encouraged to find their vocation in the recitation of scripture.' See Carl F. Petry, *The Civilian Elite of Cairo in the Later Middle Ages* (Princeton: Princeton University Press, 1981), p. 263.
45. On this author, see Brockelmann, *GAL* vol. 2, 15 no. 3a; *Supplement* vol. 2, 7 no. 3a.
46. Andras Hamori and Thomas Bauer, 'Anthologies', in EI^{3}, ed. Gudrun Krämer et al. (Leiden: E. J. Brill, 2008). Brill Online, University of Michigan-Ann Arbor. <http://www.encislam.brill.nl.proxy.lib.umich.edu/subscriber/entry?entry=ei3_COM-0031>. Last accessed on 13 March 2008. Bauer also briefly describes *Al-Durr al-maṣūn* in his 'Literarische Anthologien der Mamlukenzeit', p. 119.
47. Al-Badrī, *Al-Durr*, 1:15.
48. Ibid., 1:59. On Zarqāʾ al-Yamāma, see Sahar Amer, 'Medieval Arab Lesbians and Lesbian-Like Women', *Journal of the History of Sexuality* 18.2 (2009), pp. 218–19.
49. Al-Badrī, *Al-Durr*, 1:159.
50. Ibid., 2:9.

4

Transgressive Bodies, Transgressive Hadith

Anthony Grafton argues that 'to the inexpert, footnotes look like deep root systems, solid and fixed; to the connoisseur, however, they reveal themselves as anthills, swarming with constructive and combative activity'.[1] The classical Arabic equivalent of the footnote was the *isnād*, or chain of transmitters that preceded texts of Arabic literary anecdotes, historical reports and excerpted speech in medieval texts. The *isnād* functioned essentially to authenticate narratives and speech through oral testimonies of learned figures, rather than through reference to written records. Although manuscript production was robust in the Islamicate Middle Ages, 'a book could not adequately substitute for the authority of learned gifted personalities', who embodied knowledge and transmitted it through personal contact.[2] The *isnād*, like the footnote, often carried subtle significations, so that, before such knowledgeable audiences as hadith specialists or historians, the *isnād* could entertain, subtly polemicise, discredit, taint or authenticate a report.

The Shāfiᶜī historian ᶜAbd al-Karīm al-Rāfiᶜī (d. 623/1226) certainly understood the potential for entertainment in a well-crafted *isnād*. Among the various hadith he compiled, one report is gamely introduced as follows:

> Abū Dharr [d. 32/652] heard from Abū al-Ḥasan Muḥammad b. ᶜUbayd Allāh b. Sulūqā, who said: '[A hadith] was related to me by the stooped man, who narrated from the cold-sufferer, who narrated from the ill man, who narrated from the hemiplegic man, who narrated from the gap-toothed man, who narrated from the hunchbacked man, who narrated from the deaf man, who narrated from the blind man [*al-ḍarīr*], who narrated from the bleary-eyed man, who narrated from the one-eyed man, who narrated from the lame man, who narrated from the blind man [*al-ᶜamá*], who said: "The Prophet performed ablution by washing only once"'.

The combination of the twelve ambiguously identified transmitters, the emphasis on the physical defects of these men and the staid, uncontroversial hadith that appears in several canonical hadith collections makes a confused impression.

In the very next sentence, al-Rafiᶜī identified each man thus: 'The stooped man is Abū ᶜAlī b. Abī al-Ḥusayn al-Iṣbahānī; the cold-sufferer, Abū ᶜAlī al-Ṣūlī; the sick man, Aḥmad b. Muḥammad b. Sulaymān; the hemiplegic, Muḥammad b. Muḥammad b. Sulaymān al-Ṭūsī; the gap-toothed, al-Ḥasan b. Mihrān; the hunchback, ᶜAbdallāh b. al-Ḥusayn Qāḍī al-Maṣīṣa; the deaf, ᶜAbdallāh b. Naṣr al-Anṭākī; the blind, Abū Muᶜāwiya (d. 195/810); the bleary-eyed, Sulaymān b. Mihrān (d. 148/765); the one-eyed, Ibrāhīm al-Nakhaᶜī (d. c. 69/717); the lame, al-Ḥakam b. Mihrān; and the blind, ᶜAbdallāh b. ᶜAbbās (d. 68/688)'.[3] All twelve men were regarded as trustworthy narrators of hadith, as evidenced by their biographies and their inclusion in works praising sound hadith specialists. This hadith on ablution is also considered sound, appearing as it does in al-Bukhārī's collection of hadith, which Sunnis regard as reliable. The reliability of the named men and the wide acceptance of this hadith serve as foils to the foregrounding of the transmitters' afflicted bodies, forcing readers to realign their professional expectations of disabled hadith-transmitters and to acknowledge the inclusion of disabled men among the ranks of prestigious scholars.

The Life of Ibn ᶜAbd al-Hādī

Ibn al-Mubarrad (sometimes rendered Ibn al-Mibrad) was the patronymic for Jamāl al-Dīn Yūsuf b. ᶜAbd al-Hādī al-Ḥanbalī (d. 909/1503), a historian and legal scholar who was born in Damascus in 840 or 841/1437. When Ibn Ṭūlūn asked him about the origins of this patronymic, which means 'the son of the man with a handsome face', Ibn ᶜAbd al-Hādī claimed that his grandfather Aḥmad's paternal uncle gave him this name as a show of respect.[4] Our Ibn ᶜAbd al-Hādī grew up in al-Ṣāliḥiyya, a village just outside the city walls of Damascus and situated on the slope of Mount Qāsiyūn. (Today, the city's boundaries have expanded to include al-Ṣāliḥiyya as a quarter within Damascus proper.) The community was established by the Banū Qudāma, a clan that fled Palestine during the Crusades, and the Banū ᶜAbd al-Hādī were among the more prominent families of the Ṣāliḥiyya quarter. When the Banū Qudāma first arrived, they lived temporarily in the Abū Ṣāliḥ mosque. To honour the significance of this shelter, the neighbourhood was named after the mosque. Ibn Ṭūlūn presented an alternative possibility for the origins of the quarter's name: its founder was a man named Ṣilāḥ.[5] Whatever the origins of the name, the area soon gained a reputation as a scholarly community with Ḥanbalī leanings. Of the six men profiled in this study, the only non-Shāfiᶜīs are the two from al-Ṣāliḥiyya – Ibn ᶜAbd al-Hādī and Ibn Ṭūlūn, who were both Ḥanbalīs. The neighbourhood also acquired strong pious and Sufi associations. Notably, the important Sufi figure Muḥyī al-Dīn b. ᶜArabī (d. 638/1240) is buried at the Jāmiᶜ Salīmiyya/Sulaymiyya there. According to our al-Badrī, al-Ṣāliḥiyya was 'filled with Sufi lodges (*zawāyā*), tombs and Qur'anic schools'.[6] This neighbourhood also boasted numerous gardens, markets and mosques. For both men, Damascus and its environs were their intellectual centres, and Ibn ᶜAbd al-Hādī's identification with the quarter was such that he composed poetry about the splendours of al-Ṣāliḥiyya and wrote a local history of the quarter entitled *Taʾrīkh al-Ṣāliḥiyya* (The History of al-Ṣāliḥiyya).[7] His influence on the historical writings of Ibn Ṭūlūn was tremendous[8] and is seen, in part, in Ibn Ṭūlūn's continuation of Ibn ᶜAbd al-Hādī's local history, which he titled *Qalāʾid al-jawhariyya fī taʾrīkh al-Ṣāliḥiyya* (Jewelled Necklaces: On the History of al-Ṣāliḥiyya).[9] What has survived of Ibn ᶜAbd al-Hādī's text is found in this work by Ibn Ṭūlūn and in Ibn Kinnān's (d. 1153/1740) *Al-Murūj al-sundusiyya al-fasīḥa fī talkhīs Taʾrīkh al-Ṣāliḥiyya* (Vast Silken Fields: A Summary of the History of al-Ṣāliḥiyya). Both books focus on the neighbourhood's origins, mosques, markets, Qur'an schools, Sufi lodges, prominent clans and notable residents. In addition to representing his native quarter textually, Ibn ᶜAbd al-Hādī was even elected neighbourhood spokesperson by his fellow residents, making him the political embodiment of the people of al-Ṣāliḥiyya.

There is considerable evidence that Ṣāliḥīs considered themselves a rarified corner of the Mamluk Empire. For one, in 903/1497, armed rebels representing the governor of the province of Damascus and amir Āqbirdī al-Dawādār requested that the residents of al-Ṣāliḥiyya abandon support for the Mamluk sultan al-Nāṣir Muḥammad. That their allegiance was sought indicates the politically strategic importance of the quarter in the province of Damascus. Ultimately, the populace refused to form an allegiance with the rebels.[10]

Male and female inhabitants of al-Ṣāliḥiyya often adopted strong ties to the neighbourhood, taking the *nisba*s of al-Ṣāliḥī and al-Ṣāliḥiyya respectively, in addition to or instead of al-Dimashqī or al-Dimashqiyya. This practice of naming probably 'reflects the awakening consciousness of the inhabitants to their quarter' and its relationship to the metropolis.[11] A separate identity was being asserted here that situated them in a very distinct and distinguished physical, social and intellectual space. Mikhail Bakhtin famously observed that 'the most intense and productive life of culture takes place on the boundaries'.[12] Here, in a liminal geographic and social space along an urban border, a new awareness of the constitution of the body politic led to novel appreciations for bodies on the margins.

Ibn ᶜAbd al-Hādī grew up in al-Ṣāliḥiyya under the guidance and support of his father Badr al-Dīn and his paternal grandfather Shihāb al-Dīn. He transmitted hadith to Aḥmad b. Muḥammad al-Shuwaykī (d. 939/1532), ᶜAbd al-Raḥmān al-Kutubī (d. 932/1525), Muḥammad b. ᶜAbd al-Raḥmān al-Mardāwī (d. 909/1503), Najm al-Dīn al-Mātānī (d. 960/1552) and the famous historian Ibn Ṭūlūn. He also taught his own children, grandchildren, wives, concubines, clients and relatives and his children's wives and concubines.[13] In a book about the forty masters who helped to direct his intellectual career, Ibn Ṭūlūn noted that our Shihāb al-Dīn al-Ḥijāzī had certified Ibn ᶜAbd al-Hādī to teach hadith.[14] Although most of al-Ḥijāzī's students were of Cairene origin, he did attract students from all over the central Islamic lands, including Mesopotamia, Syria, the Hijaz and rural Egypt.[15] Mamluk and early Ottoman scholars recognised al-Ḥijāzī's contributions to hadith studies and other fields of Islamic studies, as he was frequently cited as instructing many luminaries in this field.[16] When most of Yūsuf b. ᶜAbd al-Hādī's biographers have mentioned al-Ḥijāzī, they have offered no biographical identifiers, leading to multiple identifications of this figure by modern scholars.[17] One researcher has conjectured that the teacher might have been Aḥmad al-Shihāb al-Ḥijāzī (d. 893/1488), a scholar who lived in Old Cairo.[18]

Ibn ᶜAbd al-Hādī's personal library included approximately 600 of his own works and another 2,400 by other authors. Most of his works are currently held at al-Asad Library in Damascus. He composed a number of works about ailments and the ailing body. He wrote treatises about medical treatments for two types of leprosy (*Adwiyat al-bahaq wa'l-baraṣ*),[19] coughs (*Adwiyat al-wāfida ᶜalá al-hummā al-bārida*) and eye diseases (*Al-Funūn fī adwiyat al-ᶜuyūn*). He also wrote about death resulting from the plague and other epidemics (*Funūn al-manūn fī al-wabāʾ wa'l-ṭāᶜūn*). His interest in this last subject was shared by many other Mamluk and Ayyubid writers, as Michael Dols has shown – perhaps because, like many of these other men, plague had personally affected members of his immediate family.[20] Of his thirteen wives and concubines, Ibn ᶜAbd al-Hādī's favourite was his second wife, Bulbul bint ᶜAbd Allāh, who was mentioned earlier in this chapter as the subject of one of his books. She bore him two children – ᶜĀʾisha and ᶜAbd al-Hādī – before dying of the plague in 883/1478 or 1479. After her death, he took into his household another concubine, who was also named Bulbul. She bore six children by him, among them Badr al-Dīn Ḥasan, an adolescent son who died of the plague in 897/1492. Remarkably, nine more of Ibn ᶜAbd al-Hādī's children died from plague infections in this same year.[21]

The vulnerability of life, particularly of children's lives, led many bereaved fathers in the late Mamluk period to write about their grief and the saving grace of religious devotion.[22] Al-Sakhāwī, for instance, wrote one after his son's death in 863 or 864/1458 or 1459 from the plague.[23] Ibn ᶜAbd al-Hādī completed his treatise *Al-Irshād ilá ḥukm mawt al-awlād* (Guidance on Children's Deaths) in late 897/1492, the devastating year in which he lost ten children. The approximately 500-page work is divided into fifty-eight chapters and treats an assortment of topics. The Prophet Muḥammad lost an infant son named Ibrāhīm, so relevant hadiths are discussed here, along with poetry, historical anecdotes on grief and loss, popular responses to children's deaths, advice on exhibiting patience and steadfastness in the face of tragedy, and actions from which parents must refrain in their grief. Disciplining the body encouraged stoicism and acceptance of the reality of a child's death. Ibn ᶜAbd al-Hādī advised parents not to scar themselves, shed tears, slap or scratch their cheeks, shave their beards, rend their clothes or blacken their faces. These ritualistic acts expressed mourning and anger and also served to venerate the dead in early modern Islamdom.[24] Ibn ᶜAbd al-Hādī's recommendations demand even greater personal restraint of the mourner than do the commands for the bereaved issued by the Prophet Muḥammad, who reproached a woman for weeping openly when her granddaughter died. She asked him if he ever cried, and he responded: 'I do not weep (loudly) but silently when I feel moved'.[25] Bodily practice informed piety and served as an index of religious formation. The rest of this lengthy book was dedicated to Ibn ᶜAbd al-Hādī's own children; and, upon his death, the book was inherited by his surviving offspring and later Ibn Ṭūlūn.

Kitāb al-ḍabṭ

Ibn ᶜAbd al-Hādī also described bodies as indices of religious formation in an earlier work of his, an eleven-folio work titled *Kitāb al-ḍabṭ wa'l-tabyīn li-dhawī al-ᶜilal wa'l-ᶜāhāt min al-muḥaddithīn* (The Book of Correctness and Clarity of Hadith-Transmitters Who Had Defects [in Their Hadith] and Physical Blights). An autograph copy dated 889 or 890/1484 or 1485 is today housed in al-Asad Library in Damascus.[26] The title contains a clever double entendre, as the term *ᶜilal* signifies both illnesses and defects in hadith resulting from faulty transmissions or outright fabrications. (The title contains a hint of tension, as the term *al-ḍabṭ* refers specifically to the correctness of hadith-transmitters.) Ibn ᶜAbd al-Hādī's work aligns defects of hadith with defects of the body. Unsound, transgressive bodies transmit unsound, transgressive hadith through ineptitude or conscious deception. By combining 'defects/illnesses and physical blights' in the manuscript title, Ibn ᶜAbd al-Hādī evoked the long Arabic tradition – spanning the 2nd/8th to his own – of commentaries on *ᶜilal al-ḥadith*, or defects in hadith; but the work is an exercise in *ᶜilm al-rijāl*, or the evaluation of hadith-narrators. Literature in this genre originated in the 2nd/8th century and grew tremendously throughout the Islamic Middle Ages.[27] The earliest known work on the subject was written by Hishām b. Ḥassān (d. c. 147/764), but Ibn ᶜAbd al-Hādī appended a chain of transmitters to the colophon of this manuscript that identified al-Bukhārī as the source of this work. Consultations of al-Bukhārī's *Ṣaḥīḥ* and *Al-Ḍuᶜafāᵓ al-ṣaghīr* did not offer up any likely sources for Ibn ᶜAbd al-Hādī's work, so al-Bukhārī's as yet unrecovered *Kitāb al-ᶜilal* or *Al-Ḍuᶜafāᵓ al-kabīr* probably contains the root of this 9th/15th-century work.

Ibn ᶜAbd al-Hādī offered only a succinct introduction to his work in which he explained: 'I will mention herein hadith – transmitters who were among the people of ailments and physical blights (*aṣḥāb al-awjāᶜ wa'l-ᶜāhāt*) . . . and will arrange them alphabetically'. Following this opening, Ibn ᶜAbd al-Hādī listed forty-five men – none of whom, incidentally, appeared in al-Rafiᶜī's *isnād* – who lived in the first 255 years of Islamic history and numbered among 'the blind[,. . .] the hemiplegic, the wall-eyed, the flat-nosed and the large-mouthed',[28] as well as the bleary-eyed, the hunchbacked, the lame, the leprous and the one-eyed. The life dates of the named men support Ibn ᶜAbd al-Hādī's claim that al-Bukhārī, who died in 256/870, originally transmitted this information.

The intended audience for this work were probably fellow legal scholars, though it seems not to have circulated widely. Ibn ᶜAbd al-Hādī's contemporaries and successors do not cite it; and, as will be seen in Chapter 5, his student Ibn Ṭūlūn appears not to have mentioned it to a friend who had written his own book about eminent Muslims with *ᶜāhāt*. Researching the works of the men and the single woman named in the *isnād* turns up no writings about disabled hadith-transmitters, though some, such as Abū Bakr b. al-Muḥibb al-Maqdisī al-Ḥanbalī (d. 789/1387), wrote books about weak hadith and weak hadith-transmitters.

In spite of Ibn ᶜAbd al-Hādī's expressed intentions in the introduction, it is only loosely organised alphabetically. The list of names is divided into sections bearing letter names as headings. The letters *ẓāᵓ*, *hāᵓ*, *wāw* and *yāᵓ* are not at all represented in the text; many headings are empty, with space left to fill in names, as was common in medieval Arabic manuscripts; and, from folio 161b to 164a, the author briefly confused the alphabetical order of the headings, so that one reads the following sequence: *dāl*, *dhāl*, *sīn*, *dhāl*, *rāᵓ*, *shīn*. Although the *dhāl* heading appears twice, no names are listed under either heading. This structural confusion is heightened by the difficulty of Ibn ᶜAbd al-Hādī's handwriting. He used diacritical marks sparingly and wrote sloppily, prompting even native readers of Arabic to comment on the palaeographical challenges they have faced when deciphering his writing.[29] The letter ل in its terminal and independent forms is written like ك , and the tail of the م in its terminal and independent forms curves like the Latin letter 'c'. And lastly, the author never writes the *hamza*.

There are also signs that *Kitāb al-ḍabṭ* was carelessly and hastily composed or was perhaps only intended as a draft. For one, the name 'Ḥārith' appears twice in the manuscript and is both times misspelled.[30] Secondly, the author made several marginal and interlinear corrections to rectify mis-alphabetisation. Thirdly, there are several cross-outs. Under the *khāʾ* heading, the author mistakenly wrote 'Razīq the Blind on the authority of Abū Hurayra', then crossed out the name, later placing it under the correct heading.[31] The cacography, frequent errors and conspicuously unfinished portions of this short manuscript create a harried impression that strangely complements the subject of this work, since, unlike al-Rafiᶜī's *isnād*, all of the men in *Kitāb al-ḍabṭ* were widely viewed unfavourably as hadith-transmitters.

In sharp contrast to the earlier portions of the manuscript, the concluding folio consists entirely of four *isnād*s tracing the transmission of this list of traditionists back to al-Bukhārī, a widely respected 3rd/9th-century traditionist who reportedly had his own defect: a stutter (*ᶜī fī lisānihi*).[32] Apparently, a physical defect did not automatically disqualify one's hadith-transmissions; having a physical defect and defective hadith were understood as coincidental phenomena. The chains of narration read as follows:

1. Abū ᶜAbdallāh Muḥammad b. [ᶜAlī] al-Buqsumāṭī al-Baᶜlī al-Ḥanbalī (d. after 870/1465)[33] → Abū al-Faraj b. al-Zaᶜbūb al-Baᶜlī al-Ḥanbalī (d. 778/1377)
2. al-Qāḍī al-Quḍāt [Taqī al-Dīn] Abū Bakr b. al-Ṣadr al-Ṭarābulusī al-Ḥanbalī (d. 871/1467) → Abū ᶜAbdallāh Muḥammad b. al-Yūnāniyya al-Baᶜlī al-Ḥanbalī (707–83/1307–81 or 1382)[34]
3. Abū al-ᶜAbbās Aḥmad b. Zayd al-Mawṣilī al-Ḥanbalī (d. 870/1465) → ᶜĀʾisha bint ᶜAbd al-Hādī al-Maqdisiyya al-Ḥanbaliyya (d. 816/1413) → al-Ḥajjār (d. 730/1329) → al-Qāḍī Abū Jaᶜfar al-Ḥanbalī *and* Abū ᶜAbdallāh al-Ṣāliḥī al-Ḥanbalī → Abū Bakr b. al-Muḥibb al-Maqdisī al-Ḥanbalī (d. 789/1387) → Qāḍī al-Quḍāt al-Maqdisī al-ᶜUmarī al-ᶜAdawī al-Ḥanbalī (probably al-Qāḍī Sulaymān, d. 718/1315)→ Abū ᶜAbdallāh al-Ḥusayn b. al-Mubārak al-Zabīdī al-Ḥanbalī (d. 649/1251)
4. al-Qāḍī Sulaymān (628–718/1230–1315) → Abū al-Faraj ᶜAbd al-Raḥmān b. Muḥammad al-Maqdisī al-Ḥanbalī (d. 682/1283) *and* Abū ᶜAbdallāh

Muḥammad b. ᶜAbd al-Wāḥid al-Maqdisī al-Ḥanbalī (d. 643/1245) → Abū al-Faraj ᶜAbd al-Raḥmān b. ᶜAlī al-Ḥanbalī (d. 597/1201), who said that he and Ibn al-Zabīdī heard it from → Abū al-Waqt ᶜAbd al-Awwal b. ᶜIsá al-Sijzī (d. 553/1158) → [alternative link interpolated: Abū al-Ḥasan al-Dāwudī (d. 467–9/1074–6)] → Abū al-Faraj *and* Muḥammad b. ᶜAbd al-Hādī al-Ḥanbalī *and* Abū al-Ḥusayn Muḥammad b. Muḥammad al-Ḥanbalī → Abū Yaᶜlá Muḥammad b. al-Farrāᵓ al-Ḥanbalī (d. 458/1066)

a. → al-Dāwudī (d. 467/1074) → Abū Muḥammad al-Sarahsī (d. 381/991) → Abū ᶜAbdallāh Muḥammad b. Yūsuf b. Maṭar al-Firabrī (d. 320/932)

b. → Abū al-Fatḥ b. Abī al-Fawāris (d. 412/1022) → al-Sarahsī (d. 381/991) → al-Firabrī (d. 320/932) → Abū ᶜAbdallāh b. Ismāᵓil al-Bukhārī (d. 256/870).

Lists such as this one reflected debates in the sphere of legal scholarship, where the reliability of transmitters who had impaired hearing and sight was endlessly questioned. Al-Ṣafadī, for one, argued that blind people, like sighted women of the early Islamic period, were disadvantaged in hearing and relating hadith, but could certainly rise to the occasion and transmit hadith well. Sighted women could not see their teachers or audience, as they heard and related from behind curtains, and blindness was the curtain for unsighted men.[35] In the sphere of hadith-transmission, the blighted body served as a contested site of moral reckoning and cultural valuation, where societal values were writ small. However, in medieval pictorial and textual depictions of the Prophet Muḥammad's life, disabled people figure comfortably among his Companions. In this miniature painting from a late 10th/16th-century Ottoman manuscript, the Prophet is seated in a pulpit, preaching at a mosque. His son-in-law ᶜAlī and his grandsons Ḥasan and Ḥusayn are seated on the floor to the right of the Prophet. The Prophet's face is veiled, and all members of his family have flame halos around their heads. To the left of the Prophet, at the base of the pulpit, is seated an older male adult dwarf. His age is conveyed by his white moustache and beard. The Ottoman inscriptions above and below the scene and on the reverse of the page make no reference to the dwarf. In the bottom left corner of the painting sits a bare-legged man with a beggar's bowl next to him. Men of various social classes, ages and backgrounds are depicted as gathering to hear the Prophet speak, and it would have been auditors such as these who would have reported the sayings and actions of the Prophet and recited learned Qur'anic verses. Textual sources attest to the presence of disabled people in the life of the Prophet, and this Ottoman miniature simply illustrates this fact.

Figure 4.1 'Prophet Muḥammad Preaching'. (Source: Metropolitan Museum of Art, 55.121.40, Baghdad, late 10th/16th century. Image copyright © The Metropolitan Museum of Art/Art Resource, New York.)

ᶜĀhāt in Late Mamluk/Early Ottoman Damascus

As in Egypt, plague raged intermittently in 9th/15th and 10th/16th-century Syria, devastating families and communities, stalling crop production and raising the prices of commodities. Physical disabilities were visible elements of the Syrian landscape. Ibn Ṭūlūn reports that in Ramaḍān or

Shawwāl 908/March 1503 'it became known in Damascus that in the village of Qaṭanā there is a source of water that cures *al-ᶜāhāt*. Droves of people – men and women – flock there to perform ablutions, naked or otherwise, in its cold waters. This occurred with many groups [of people] who had severe impairments.'[36] Against the backdrop of public-health crises and economic instability, communities of scholars and friends unified around shared devotions to learning and social companionship, and their works began to reflect the experiences of people confronting disease, pain and death all too often in their daily lives.

Mamluk Syria consisted of the provinces of Hama, Safed, al-Karak, Damascus, Aleppo and Tripoli. Under both the Mamluks and Ottomans, Damascus was the largest, most populous and most strategically important province of the region, and its history was correspondingly the most extensively recorded of all of the Syrian provinces. After the Ottoman takeover of Syria in 922/1516, the new conquerors saw fit to consolidate the administrative geographies of the Mamluk sultanate, leaving only three large provinces: Damascus, Aleppo and Tripoli. This act of redistricting was precipitated by detailed censuses taken of the newly acquired areas. On 2 Ramaḍān 922/28 November 1516, the day after Sultan Selīm triumphantly entered Damascus, a census was taken of the city.[37] Later 10th/16th-century Ottoman cadastral registers for Damascus are extant. They recorded the numbers of Muslim, Christian and Jewish male heads of households, and each confessional group was subdivided into various categories. These detailed records specified whether a head of household was a *mujarrad* (bachelor or foreigner), religious functionary, descendant of the Prophet Muḥammad or disabled. Four categories of disability were recognised by the census authorities: blindness, lameness, mental illness/demon possession and severe lameness to the point of losing mobility (*mukassaḥ*), and they were exempt from certain taxes.[38] This imperial documentation reveals the significance of people of blights in legal contexts and offers insights into how individual human bodies related to the Damascene body politic. Under Ḥanafī law, a person must possess full reason or sanity to carry out a required duty, thus preventing a mentally ill or possessed person from being required to pay *zakat*, or the charitable tax, which typically amounted to a yearly donation of 2.5 per cent of one's assets. The dictates of Shiᶜi, Mālikī, Ḥanbalī and Shāfiᶜī law all differ from Ḥanafī law on this point, as they oblige the mentally ill or demon-possessed individual to pay *zakat*.[39] The other sensory- and mobility-related disabilities are not exempt from paying these charitable donations.

Conclusion

All in all, the visibility of *ahl al-ᶜāhāt* in public, domestic and political spaces forced medieval Muslim subjects to reckon with notions of physical difference and illness, ultimately using them as 'a kind of metaphor for a significant group of concepts, values, and ideals in medieval Islamic civilization'.[40] In the case of Ibn ᶜAbd al-Hādī's *Kitāb al-ḍabṭ*, a work that participates in and merges the Arabic traditions of listing the names of people with *ᶜāhāt* and of evaluating the reliability of hadith-transmitters, the transgressive, blighted body is aligned with transgressive, faulty transmissions of Islamic traditions. The ideal maintainer and propagator of religious truth has a whole male body. In their circumstances and their bodies, women, like some disabled men, were inherently disadvantaged in hearing and relating hadith. Some were able to do so well, but disabled and female traditionists were regarded with much suspicion.

Notes

1. Anthony Grafton, *The Footnote: A Curious History* (Cambridge, MA: Harvard University Press, 1999), p. 9.
2. Ali, *Arabic*, p. 39.
3. ᶜAbd al-Karīm al-Rāfiᶜī, *Al-Tadwīn fī akhbār qazwīn* (Record of Events in Qazwin), ed. ᶜAzizallāh al-ᶜAṭāradī (Beirut: Dar al-kutub al-ᶜilmiyya, 1987), 2:63–4.
4. Ibn al-Mullā al-Ḥaṣkafī, *Mutᶜat*, 2:839.
5. Ibn Ṭūlūn, *Al-Qalā'id al-jawhariyya fī ta'rīkh al-Ṣāliḥiyya* (Jewelled Necklaces: The History of al-Ṣāliḥiyya), ed. Muḥammad Aḥmad Dahmān (Damascus: s.n., 1949–56), 1:24–5; Muḥammad b. ᶜĪsá Ibn Kinnān, *Al-Murūj al-sundusiyya al-fasīḥa fī talkhīs Ta'rīkh al-Ṣāliḥiyya* (Wide Silken Meadows: A Summary of the History of al-Ṣāliḥiyya), ed. Muḥammad Aḥmad Dahmān (Damascus: Maṭbaᶜa al-taraqī, 1947), p. 15; ᶜAbd al-Qādir b. Muḥammad al-Nuᶜaymī, *Al-Dāris fī ta'rīkh al-madāris* (The Student: On the History of Madrasas) (Damascus: Maṭbaᶜat al-tarqī, 1948), 1:477.
6. Al-Badrī, *Nuzhat*, p. 320. Portions of this text (pp. 24ff.) have been translated into French as *Description de Damas*, ed. and trans. H. Sauvaire (Paris: Imprimerie Nationale, 1896), 2:407–41. The authorship of *Nuzhat al-anām* has been disputed, but, on p. 62 of *Nuzhat al-anām*, al-Badrī mentioned his *Rāḥat al-arwāḥ fī ḥashīsh wa'l-rāḥ*, a book on hashish and wine that he had written as a young man.
7. Ibn Ṭūlūn, *Al-Qalā'id*, 2:381–2.
8. EI^2, s.v. 'Ibn Ṭūlūn', 3:958.
9. The bulk of Ibn Ṭūlūn's autograph was edited and published in 1949 by

Muḥammad Aḥmad Dahmān, who had purchased the manuscript in 1927 from a dealer in Egypt. Only in the course of editing did Dahmān realise that several chapters were missing. Unbeknown to him, those chapters were rebound in another manuscript currently housed at Princeton University. I am preparing an article about these recovered pages and their significance for early modern Damascene history.

10. Toru Miura, 'The Ṣāliḥiyya Quarter in the Suburbs of Damascus: Its Formation, Structure, and Transformation in the Ayyūbid and Mamlūk Periods', *BEO* 47 (1995), p. 164.
11. Ibid., p. 131. For more on al-Ṣāliḥiyya, see Shākir Muṣṭafá, *Madīna li'l-ᶜilm: Āl Qudāma wa'l-Ṣāliḥiyya* (A Learned City: The Qudāma Clan and al-Ṣāliḥiyya) (Damascus: Dār Ṭalās, 1997); and Stefan Leder, 'Charismatic Scripturalism: The Hanbali Maqdisis of Damascus', *Der Islam* 74 (1997), pp. 279–304.
12. Mikhail Bakhtin, *Speech Genres*, ed. Carol Emerson and Michael Holquist (Austin: University of Texas Press, 1986), p. 2.
13. Muḥammad ᶜUthmān Shubayr, *Al-Imām Yūsuf b. ᶜAbd al-Hādī al-Ḥanbalī wa-atharuhu fī al-fiqh al-Islāmī* (Imām Yūsuf b. ᶜAbd al-Hādī al-Ḥanbalī and His Influence on Islamic Jurisprudence) (Amman: Dār al-furqān, 2001), p. 55. Yehoshu'a Frenkel has translated a certificate in which Ibn ᶜAbd al-Hādī's family members, including a five-day-old son, are named as audience participants in his 'Women in Late Mamluk Damascus in the Light of Audience Certificates (*Samāᶜāt*)', in Urbain Vermeulen and Jo van Steenbergen (eds), *Egypt and Syria in the Fatimid, Ayyubid and Mamluk Eras* (Leuven: Peeters, 2006), pp. 421–3. Fedwa Malti-Douglas, 'Yûsuf ibn ᶜAbd al-Hâdî and His Autograph of the *Wuqû' al-Balâ bil-Bukhl wal-Bukhalâ*', *BEO* 31 (1979), p. 29.
14. Ibn Ṭūlūn, *Kitāb al-arbaᶜīn ᶜan arbaᶜīn shaykh*[an], Al-Asad Library, Damascus, Syria, MS 958, fo. 46a; Ibn al-Mullā al-Ḥaṣkafī, *Mutᶜat*, 1:105, 107, 167, 256, 394; 2:529, 553, 590, 684, 780–1; Najm al-Dīn al-Ghazzī, *Kawākib al-sāʾira bi-aᶜyān al-miʾah al-ᶜashira*, ed. Jibrāʾil Sulaymān Jabbūr (Beirut: Al-Maṭbaᶜat al-amīrikāniyya, 1945), 1:252.
15. Muḥammad b. Abī Bakr al-Shillī (d. 1093/1681 or 1682), *Kitāb al-sanāʾ al-bāhir bi-takmīl al-Nūr al-sāfir fī akhbār al-qarn al-ᶜāshir*, ed. Ibrāhīm b. Aḥmad al-Maqḥafī (Sanaa: Maktabat al-irshād, 2004), pp. 231, 263, 272; Ibn al-Ḥimṣī, *Ḥawādith*, 1:196; ᶜAbd Allāh Murdād Abū al-Khayr, *Al-Mukhtaṣar min kitāb nashr al-nūr wa'l-zahr fī tarājim afāḍil Makka* (Abridgement of the Book of the Diffusion of Light and Flowers: On the Biographies of Virtuous Meccans), ed. Muḥammad Saᶜīd al-ᶜĀmūdī and Aḥmad ᶜAlī (Jiddah: ᶜĀlam al-maᶜrifa, 1986), p. 142.
16. Ibn al-Mullā al-Ḥaṣkafī, *Mut'at*, 1:105, 167, 256, 394; 2:529, 780–1.
17. Muḥammad Jamīl al-Shaṭṭī, *Mukhtaṣar ṭabaqāt al-ḥanābila* (Damascus: Maṭbaᶜat al-taraqī, 1920), p. 75; Muḥammad Asᶜad Ṭalas, 'Muqaddima', in Yūsuf b. ᶜAbd al-Hādī, *Thimār al-maqāṣid fī dhikr al-masājid* (Fruits of

Meaning: On Mosques), ed. Muḥammad Asʿad Ṭalas (Beirut: s.n., 1943), p. 13; Ṣalāḥ Muḥammad al-Khiyamī, 'Jamāl al-Dīn Yūsuf b. ʿAbd al-Hādī al-Maqdisī al-Dimashqī, al-mutawaffa sanat 909 H: ḥayāt wa-āthāruhu l-makhṭūṭa wa'l-maṭbūʿa', *Majallat Maʿhad al-Makhṭūṭāt al-ʿArabiyya* 26.2 (1982), p. 777.

18. Malti-Douglas, 'Yûsuf', p. 22.
19. The terms *bahaq* and *baraṣ* are difficult to define with any precision. In some contemporary Arabic dialects, *baraṣ* designates a white face covered with freckles. For a discussion of possible meanings of these terms, see C. Elgood, 'On the Significance of al-Baras and al-Bahaq', *Journal of the Proceedings of the Asiatic Society of Bengal* 27 (1931), pp. 177–81.
20. Michael Dols, *The Black Death in the Middle East* (Princeton: Princeton University Press, 1977).
21. Shubayr, *Al-Imām*, pp. 53–4. Badr al-Dīn Ḥasan must have died after 13 Jumādā I 897/25 March 1492, as his father related hadith to him on this day. See Frenkel, 'Women', p. 422.
22. Avner Giladi, 'Islamic Consolation Treatises for Bereaved Parents: Some Bibliographical Notes', *SI* 81 (1995), p. 197.
23. Avner Giladi, '"The Child Was Small . . . Not So the Grief for Him": Sources, Structure, and Content of al-Sakhāwī's Consolation Treatise for Bereaved Parents', *Poetics Today* 14.2 (1993), p. 371.
24. Ignaz Goldziher, *Muslim Studies*, ed. S. M. Stern, trans. S. M. Stern and C. R. Baker (Chicago: Aldine Publishing Company, 1973), pp. 224–7. See also Leor Halevi's study on mourning, *Muhammad's Grave: Death Rites and the Making of Islamic Society* (New York: Columbia University Press, 2007), esp. chapters four and five.
25. Hidayet Hosain, 'Translation of *Ash-Shama'il* of Tirmizi', *Islamic Culture* 8 (July 1934), p. 381.
26. Yūsuf Ibn ʿAbd al-Hādī, *Kitāb al-ḍabṭ wa'l-tabyīn li-dhawī al-ʿilal wa'l-ʿāhāt min al-muḥaddithīn*, Al-Asad Library, Damascus, Syria, MS 3216, fos 157a–168a, AH 889 or 890/1484 or 1485 CE. Copies of this manuscript can be found in three Saudi libraries: the Imam Muhammad b. Saʿud Islamic University Library in Riyadh, the Library of the Kaʿaba in Mecca and the Islamic University of Medina Library.
27. Waḍī Allāh b. Muḥammad ʿAbbās, 'Al-ʿillah', in Aḥmad b. Ḥanbal, *Kitāb al-ʿilal wa-maʿrifat al-rijāl*, ed. Waḍī Allāh b. Muḥammad ʿAbbās (Riyadh: Dār al-khānī, 2001), pp. 39–44.
28. Malti-Douglas, '*Mentalités*', p. 218.
29. al-Khiyamī, 'Jamāl al-Dīn', pp. 775–809; Al-Shaṭṭī, *Mukhtaṣar*, p. 77; Malti-Douglas, 'Yûsuf', pp. 25, 27; Muḥammad Khālid al-Kharsah, 'Tarjamat al-muʾallif', in idem (ed.), *Nujūm al-masā takshuf maʿānī al-rasā li'l-ṣāliḥāt min al-nisāʾ* (Damascus: Maktabat al-bayrūtī, 1990), p. 22.
30. Ibn ʿAbd al-Hādī, *Kitāb al-ḍabṭ*, fos 165a, 167b.
31. Ibid., fos 161b, 163a.

32. Al-Khaṭīb al-Baghdādī (d. 463/1072), *Kitāb mūḍiḥ awhām al-jam^c wa'l-tafrīq* (Hyderabad: Maṭba^cat al-^cuthmāniyya, 1959), 1:7.
33. Muḥammad b. 'Abd Allāh Ibn Ḥumayd, *Al-Suḥub al-wābila 'alá ḍarā'iḥ al-ḥanābila* (Rain Clouds Over Ḥanbalī Tombs) (s.l.: Maktabat al-Imām Aḥmad, 1989), p. 1,007. In *Al-Ḍaw*ʾ, 8:184, al-Sakhāwī indicated that he died after 870/1465.
34. Ibn Ḥajar al-ᶜAsqalānī recorded Ibn al-Yūnāniyya's death date as AH 783. See his *Al-Durar al-kamina fī aᶜyān al-miʾat al-thāmina* (Beirut: Dār al-Jīl, 1993), 4:56, no. 157. Ibn al-Yūnāniyya's death date is alternatively given as 793 in Ibn al-ᶜImād's *Shadharāt al-dhahab*, and in this same biographical entry it is recorded that he assumed his judgeship in Baalbek in 789.
35. Malti-Douglas, '*Mentalités*', p. 224.
36. Ibn Ṭūlūn, *Mufākahat, al-khillān fī ḥawādith al-zamān* (Banter among Friends on the Events of the Time) (Beirut: Dār al-kutub al-ᶜilmiyya, 1998), p. 214.
37. Ibn Ṭūlūn, *Mufākahat* [1964], 2:31. The results of this survey have not been recovered today, but the transition from Mamluk to Ottoman rule was certainly chaotic and disruptive. Nine days after the census was taken, Ibn Ṭūlūn attests that armed soldiers forced him from his home and destroyed his books. See Ibn Ṭūlūn, *Mufākahat* [1964], 2:34.
38. Muhammad Adnan Bakhit, 'The Christian Population of the Province of Damascus in the Sixteenth Century', in Benjamin Braude and Bernard Lewis (eds), *Christians and Jews in the Ottoman Empire: The Functioning of a Plural Society* (New York: Holmes and Meier Publishers, 1982), p. 20; Bakhit, *The Ottoman Province of Damascus in the Sixteenth Century* (Beirut: Librairie du Liban, 1982), p. 49; Wolf-Dieter Hütteroth and Kamal Abdulfattah, *Historical Geography of Palestine, Transjordan and Southern Syria in the Late Sixteenth Century* (Erlangen: Palm und Enke, 1977), pp. 37–8.
39. Rispler-Chaim, *Disability*, p. 38.
40. Malti-Douglas, '*Mentalités*', p. 211.

5

Public Insults and Undoing Shame: Censoring the Blighted Body

One can read any 10th/16th- or 11th/17th-century biography of the famous Meccan historian Jār Allāh Ibn Fahd (891–954/1486–1547) and find no mention of his biographical compilation *Al-Nukat al-ẓirāf fī man ubtuliya bi'l-ᶜāhāt min al-ashrāf* (Charming Anecdotes about Honourable People Who Were Afflicted with *ᶜĀhāt*), a book that caused quite a commotion when it was completed in Rajab 948/October or November 1541.[1] The curious silence surrounding *al-Nukat al-ẓirāf* may stem from a consensus on the book's insignificance, or from peer discretion about a book that brought much dishonour to its author and his family's legacy, or even from an unawareness that the book existed, since this first version was destroyed rather quickly after publication. In this suppressed work, Jār Allāh had named some of his noble Meccan contemporaries as disabled, and a group of men named as frontally bald (*ṣulᶜān*) were scandalised to have been identified in connection with their physical defects.

In early modern Ottoman Arab societies, 'biographical entries were written within a social setting marked by rivalries, enmity, and alliances, and were thus charged with "political" significance. Many a quarrel between notable households had its roots in unfavourable mentions in, or exclusions from, biographical works.'[2] The politicised nature of early modern biographies was certainly not lost on Jār Allāh, who on 12 Rabīᶜ II 944/17 September 1537, just four years before the publication of his *Al-Nukat al-ẓirāf*, had appended a note to a manuscript of al-Suyūṭī's biographical dictionary *Dhayl ṭabaqāt al-ḥuffāẓ* in which he complained that the author had 'left out a group of relevant people, among whom is his teacher and my great-grandfather . . . Taqī al-Dīn Muḥammad b. Fahd al-Hāshimī al-Makkī'. Surely, Jār Allāh understood that al-Suyūṭī had quietly, but forcefully, integrated an insult against his great-grandfather into his biographical compilation, and noted that he had rectified this omission by including an entry for his great-grandfather in his own biographical compilation *Tuḥfat al-ayqāẓ*.[3] However, the frontally bald Meccan men who were so offended by their inclusion in *Al-Nukat al-ẓirāf* did not respond with the same scholarly quietude as did Jār Allāh. They mobilised quickly to register their displeasure by accusing Jār Allāh and his family of sundry illnesses and disabilities and by seeking the opinion of Aḥmad b. Muḥammad b. Ḥajar al-Haytamī (909–74/1504–67), a prominent Meccan jurist, about the lawfulness of the book.

Ibn Ḥajar's Fatwa on Slandering the Impaired Body

Ibn Ḥajar al-Haytamī, a cross-eyed *mufti* who incidentally was not named in this book, had only settled in Mecca in 940/1533, at the age of 31, eight years before this affair. His early schooling took place at the Azhar mosque in Cairo, where he mainly studied under Zakariyyāʾ al-Anṣārī (d. 926/1520). He excelled in his study of Islamic and Arabic subjects; and, before reaching the age of 20, he was thus entrusted with teaching others in these fields. By the time he was approached by the group of aggrieved disabled men, he was only 39 years old but had acquired a substantial reputation as a skilled thinker of the Shāfiʿī school who engaged publicly and frequently in scholarly debates.[4]

Ibn Ḥajar received the unnamed petitioner's question soon after publication of the book, and summarised the inquiry as follows:

> A question is asked about a man who wrote a book named *Al-Nukat al-ẓirāf fī man ubtuliya bi'l-ʿāhāt min al-ashrāf*. In this book, the author mentioned a group of men living today, about whom he said, 'So-and-so is bald from illness (*aqraʿ*), and so-and-so has a receding hairline (*aṣlaʿ*), and so-and-so is lame, and so-and-so is leprous, and so-and-so is blind'. He devoted a chapter to each type [of defect], and then went on to mention a group of the Prophet's companions as having receding hairlines (*ṣalaʿ*) and things like that. [The author] asserted to [me] his claim that this work is an admonition (*mawʿiẓa*), and the purpose of this book is nothing more than this. So, is this a form of the forbidden backbiting (*al-ghība al-muḥarrama*)? If not, does Islamic law allow mentioning something like this? Also, what connects the book's author to objections about the book? Is it or is it not obligatory to cut up this book because of the damage suffered by its existence and spread?[5]

The fatwa's solicitor obviously found *Al-Nukat al-ẓirāf* to be a troubling and transgressive book and Jār Allāh's authorial motive unseemly and opaque, if not outright illegal. The solicitor's suspicions were not to be taken lightly, as jurists frequently classified slander as one of Islam's gravest sins, alongside murder and polytheism. One of the earliest Qur'anic revelations augured badly for malicious gossip, proclaiming 'Woe to every slanderer, defamer!' In another verse, *ghība* is made tantamount to cannibalism. 'Spy not, nor let some of you backbite others.

Does one of you like to eat the flesh of his dead brother? You abhor it!'[6] Slandering someone compromises that person's public self, and by extension his or her family. A suspected slanderer like Jār Allāh was also compromised publicly and would have found his family members and their legacies of moral rectitude and intellectual rigour implicated in this affair. The Fahd family claimed Alid descent through Muḥammad b. al-Ḥanafiyya, imbuing them with exclusive, prestigious blood ties to Mecca. As such, they had maintained distinguished positions in Meccan social and scholarly circles since the 8th/14th century. In each generation, a single man emerged as the family's representative scholar, and the role was passed from father to son. The four eminent Fahd scholars were: Taqī al-Dīn Muḥammad b. Fahd al-Makkī (787–871/1385–1466), Najm al-Dīn Muḥammad b. Fahd al-Makkī (812–85/1409–80), ᶜIzz al-Dīn ᶜUmar b. Fahd al-Makkī (850–923/1447–1517) and Muḥibb al-Dīn Jār Allāh Muḥammad b. Fahd al-Makkī (891–954/1486–1547).[7]

Yet, in spite of the weight of Jār Allāh b. Fahd's personal and familial reputation, Ibn Ḥajar al-Haytamī issued a scathing fatwa condemning the book's personal revelations as vicious backbiting and rejecting the author's claim that the work served as an admonition. His response to the submitted question began:

> Yes, what has been said is a form of the forbidden backbiting, because the Islamic community has agreed upon it, and the Prophet has designated it as something that one would hate to have mentioned about oneself, regardless of whether it was about one's body (like being tall, bleary-eyed, one-eyed, bald due to an ailment [*aqra*ᶜ], black, yellow), one's name, one's character, one's deeds (like eating a lot), one's clothes (like having wide sleeves), one's child, one's wife, one's slave, one's riding animal or one's home (like its being cramped). *Ghība* is the same if it is uttered with the tongue or communicated in writing, since the pen works just like the tongue, or through gestures. Al-Nawawī [d. 676/1277] said that there is no difference [among these various modes of expressing *ghība*]. Al-Ghazālī [d. 505/1111] agreed, but added that the heart can commit *ghība*. What they have said has been said by others.[8]

Relying on Prophetic tradition (*sunna*) and community consensus (*ijma*ᶜ), Ibn Ḥajar concluded that *ghība* was subjectively determined and could be committed against people's bodies, personal qualities, actions, household members and possessions. The definition is wide-ranging, possibly making this one of the easier major sins to commit. In societies where men and women of all social strata commonly had nicknames based on physical and mental impairments, how does one avoid stumbling thoughtlessly into slander?[9] The subject was sufficiently relevant and sensitive to have been treated by al-Nawawī in his advice manual, where he delineated the boundary between acceptable and unacceptable usages of nicknames related to impairment.

> Allah said: 'Do not call each other by nicknames'. [Q 49: 11]. Scholars agree on the impermissibility of bestowing on someone a hated nickname, unless it is an actual description of him, such as the bleary-eyed, the one balding on the sides of his head (*al-ajlaḥ*), the blind, the lame, the squint-eyed, the leprous, the broken-skulled, the jaundiced, the hunchback, the deaf, the blue-eyed (*al-azraq*), the snub-nosed, the one with ectropion, the broken-toothed, the amputee, the ill, the paralytic and the one-handed, or if said nickname describes his father or mother. Scholars also agree on the permissibility of mentioning [a hated nickname] for the purpose of identifying someone to a person who only knows him through his physical defect.[10]

In the absence of any Qur'anic verse or prophetic tradition excusing any form of slander, Sunni theologians came to agree that *ghība* was permissible in six cases, as Ibn Ḥajar sought to explain:

> In Islamic law, an exception is made for what is said about the defects of other people if done with good intentions, which can only take place in six situations: redressing grievances (*taẓallum*), eliminating wrongdoing (*isti*ᶜ*āna* ᶜ*alá taghyīr al-munkar*), asking for a legal opinion (*istiftā*ᵓ), warning Muslims of evil (*taḥdhīr min al-sharr*), communicating about a known fault (*tajāhur bi'l-fisq*), and the sixth is for identifying someone whose nickname describes a visible physical defect, such as 'the lame' or 'the bleary-eyed'. Scholars used to do that for identification purposes, and so it was not hated if one learned it after becoming well known for it. Thereafter, mentioning [a physical defect] was permissible without an implication of deficiency, even if one could do without [mentioning] it. It is established knowledge that slander is only permitted in these six circumstances and no others. Still, [Ibn Fahd] has opposed these categories by adding to these a seventh, which is general advice (*al-naṣīḥa al-*ᶜ*āmma*), as in [mentioning] the deficiencies of hadith-narrators (*jarḥ al-ruwāh*), although this approaches the category of warning (*al-taḥdhīr*).[11]

As seen in the previous chapter, Ibn ᶜAbd al-Hādī's *Kitāb al-ḍabṭ* constituted an Islamically acceptable treatise about hadith-narrators and transmitters with physical blights, because his mention of people's deficiencies was necessary to warn Muslims against disreputable and unreliable narrators. Jār Allāh, however, appeared not to have linked the bodies he described to any discernible threat to the Muslim community, so his work did not fall under the licit category of warning.

> Verily, what this author has done is forbidden slander, because he mentioned defects of others without good intentions, as defined in Islamic law. This book did not fall under any of the six aforementioned categories, not even

> the last. This last condition is not applicable here because this author did not restrict himself to well-known faults that one's friends would have known and to not mentioning what could only be known from reading his book. As such, this book is, by consensus opinion, forbidden. His claim that he intended the mention of those *ᶜāhāt* as an admonition is absurd, since no one has ever said that one of the rationales for slander is mentioning people's defects in order to warn others about said defects. Still, even if he had mentioned that this is one of the permissible reasons for slander, what is right would be known.[12]

Jār Allāh violated moral codes governing respectability of the bodies of living men who were honoured in their communities and possessed local social capital. With his pen, Jār Allāh was able to loosen and unravel scholars' turbans, exposing them on the page in ways these men would never have done in their daily public lives. The association of turbanlessness with intimacy is elegantly portrayed in an ink-and-watercolour painting from the Indian Deccan depicting a scholar in an intimate teaching moment with his royal pupil, which would be in keeping with the Deccani painters' interest in depicting members of the ruling classes in private moments.[13] Intimacy is conveyed through various postures: the scholar's extended hand towards his student, his half-rising on his left leg and the figures' two heads inclined towards each other. The mentor has also removed his turban and set it on the ground, exposing his balding pate, suggesting that this scene does not depict a moment of public presentation. We know little of views of baldness in the Indian Deccan. A pre-5th-century Pali text describes a debate between the Buddha and a Brahmin, who castigated the former as a bald-shaven man (*muṇḍaka*). Baldness here was associated with exile, as people had their heads shaven before being forcibly removed from communities.[14] The Hoysaḷa king Nṛpa Kāma, who reigned from 1022 to 1027 in the Indian Deccan, was described as bald in an inscription, though the term does not seem to have been used derogatorily.[15] Of course, baldness may have had different connotations in the 16th- and 17th-century Muslim Deccan, but removing the turban in the presence of another signalled true intimacy. Ghaly has speculated that Jār Allāh probably took advantage of intimate moments in the baths or of sacred moments before prayer to learn of someone else's baldness. The Ḥanbalī and Shāfiᶜī rites permit washing the turban or washing the forehead without removing the turban, but the Mālikī and Ḥanafī schools require men to remove their turbans and wash their bare heads.[16] Catching a glimpse of someone's unturbaned head is not itself sinful; but, in Ibn Ḥajar's eyes, Jār Allāh's indiscreet revelations condemned him and his book.

Figure 5.1 'Young Prince and Mentor Sitting in Landscape'. (Source: Metropolitan Museum of Art, 13.228.10.2, Indian Deccan, c. 1600. Image copyright © The Metropolitan Museum of Art/Art Resource, New York.)

Historicising Male Baldness

Partial or total baldness resulting from shaving the head, ageing or disease had multiple significations in 9th/15th- and 10th/16th-century Cairo, Damascus and Mecca, especially in the realms of Islamic ritual and identity, crime and punishment and health and ageing. A bald-shaven head (*rāʾis ḥalīq*) can only result through conscious human action. Being a purposeful act, it had a wider range of meanings than uncontrollable hair loss through age or illness. Islamic law recommends that the heads of Muslim infants be shorn and the weight of the hair in silver or gold be distributed as alms. Adult men often shaved their heads after completing the pilgrimage to Mecca. Head-shaving could also have non-ritualistic associations. Some medieval Sufis also positioned their bodies as the primary site of expressing antinomian piety, often embracing devotional practices that rejected societal norms. An extreme diet, drunkenness, a vow of chastity, public nudity, matted hair and even a shaven head could mark a man as a Sufi.[17] In the realm of law, a judge could order humiliating discretionary punishments, such as shaving an offender's head or blackening his face with ashes.[18]

Spontaneous baldness that arises when the body sheds hair, and not when hair is deliberately removed, was also understood with tremendous nuance. There are in classical Arabic several types of natural hair loss: *jalḥ*, *nazaᶜ*, *quzᶜ*, *kawsaj*, *ṣalᶜ* and *qaraᶜ*. *Jalḥ* signifies balding on the sides of the head; *nazaᶜ* is baldness on either side of the forehead; *quzᶜ* is hair on one's head that it is so thin it is only visible when it blows in the wind; *kawsaj* is thin-beardedness. The fatwa petitioner asked about Ibn Fahd's discussion of people with *ṣalᶜ* and *qaraᶜ*, and Ibn Ḥajar only discussed those two types of hair loss, so I will define them with greater precision. *Ṣalᶜ* was probably a well-known condition for Sunni and Shiᶜi Muslims, as caliphs ᶜUmar, ᶜUthmān and ᶜAlī were commonly described as *ṣulᶜān*.[19] It was probably these caliphal associations that led one author to designate three traits of power: frontal baldness, a wide belly and slowness to anger.[20] In the dictionary *Ṣiḥāḥ al-lughah*, al-Jawharī (d. 393/1003) defined *ṣalᶜ* as frontal baldness or a receding hairline and *ṣulᶜa* as a frontally balding pate.[21] The littérateur al-Tawḥīdī (d. 414/1023) defined various types of baldness in his encyclopaedia as follows: 'If the hair has fallen from the front of the head, then the person is *ajlaḥ*. If more than that has fallen out, then he is *aṣlaᶜ*. If the hair of the temples falls out, then he is *anzaᶜ*.'[22] Al-Tawḥīdī's definitions of *jalḥ* and *ṣulᶜ* differ from those provided by the lexicographers and, as we shall see, by the medical specialists, which may derive from their intended uses. Al-Tawḥīdī wrote that 'these terms should make things easier for the expository writer . . . They are useful', suggesting that these topoi were understood by popular audiences in these particular ways.[23] However, Ibn al-Athīr (d. 630/1233), in his own dictionary, stated that the word *ṣullaᶜ* means 'land on which no plants grow' and derives from *ṣalᶜ al-rāʾis*, or the loss of hair from the head.[24] Ibn Manẓūr (d. 711/1311 or 1312) confirmed that *ṣalᶜ* is a pattern of baldness that begins at the hairline and progresses towards the back of the head.[25]

Medical literature on the subject nuanced these definitions even further. The Persian physician ᶜAlī b. Sahl Rabbān al-Ṭabarī (d. c. 256/870) defined *ṣalᶜ* as 'the dryness of the roots of the hair and the absence of nourishment to it [the hair]', noting that there was no cure for this condition. However, he suggested that 'frontal baldness may come from over-wearing turbans, which depletes moisture from the roots of the hair and dries them out. Perhaps it also comes from sexual intercourse because the brain is cold and moist, and sexual intercourse increases its coldness.' He then cited Hippocrates's claim that *ṣalᶜ* does not afflict castrated males, boys or menstruating women, because they all retain the moist qualities of their heads.[26] The physician Ibn Sīnā (d. 428/1037) designated *ṣalᶜ* as a baldness arising from dry humours. As such, the excess cold and moist humours in castrated males and women would prevent the onset of *ṣalᶜ*. He also identified hereditary factors, like the size of one's hair follicles, that affect susceptibility to *ṣalᶜ*, attributing the lower rate of *ṣalᶜ* among Ethiopians to their tight hair follicles that resist shedding. Though he offered no cure for *ṣalᶜ*, Ibn Sīnā did warn that awareness of preventative measures, like foregoing the constant wearing of heavy turbans, could delay its onset.[27] Further, he differentiated *ṣalᶜ*, a baldness that arises from predisposing factors, from *qaraᶜ*, *dāʾ al-thaᶜlab* (ophiasis, lit. 'fox disease') and *dāʾ al-ḥayya* (alopecia, lit. 'snake disease'), which all result from ailments. The physician Ibn Hindū (d. 410/1019) defined each disease thus:

> *dāʾ al-thaᶜlab* (alopecia, lit., fox disease): This is loss of hair due to extraneous purulent fluids that collect at the roots of hair and, because of their sharpness and acidity, they prevent the hair from growing. It is known as 'fox disease' because it often afflicts foxes.
>
> *dāʾ al-ḥayya* (ophiasis, lit., snake disease): This is similar to the above because both share the same cause. However, the snake disease looks different, for the part of the head which is afflicted looks like a snake that has shed its skin. The condition is also known as *qaraᶜ*.
>
> *ṣalᶜ* (baldness): Receding hair resulting from the loss of hair-nourishing fluid.[28]

All in all, *ṣalᶜ* seems to designate natural hair loss in adult males, whereas *qaraᶜ* is hair loss associated with afflictions and disease. Al-Jawharī defined *qaraᶜ* as baldness resulting from illness and *qurᶜa* as a head bald from illness.[29] Both Ibn al-Athīr and Ibn Manẓūr defined *qaraᶜ* as total hair loss resulting from illness and noted that people say the snake 'is called *aqraᶜ* because venom flows into its head and accumulates there until the skin of its head is shed'.[30] Al-Damīrī (d. 808/1405 or 1406) defined '*al-aqraᶜ* [as] someone with a hairless head that is white from poison'. Just as it was believed that an excess of internal poison caused a snake to shed its skin, so too was it thought that the poison of subdermal 'purulent fluids' weakened the roots of human hair and made it fall out. In fact, this link between snake venom and the causal agent of *qaraᶜ* is borne out in medieval recipes for the theriac (*diryāq*, alt. *tiryāq*), an antidote to snake venom, that also claimed efficacy against *dāᵓ al-ḥayya* and *dāᵓ al-thaᶜlab*.[31] Other medieval compilers and authors recorded treatments for *qaraᶜ*. Al-Ṭabarī recommended boiling walnuts, a Yemeni plant (*warsiyyā*) and *shān* in water until they formed an oily paste, then smearing said paste on one's head.[32]

Perceptions of Baldness

A prophetic parable related by Abu Hurayra reveals much about social attitudes to *qaraᶜ*. In this parable, three poor men – a leper, a man bald from illness (*al-aqraᶜ*) and a blind man – are approached in turn by an angel who offers to grant each man one wish. The leper asks for 'a good complexion and a good skin, and to be rid of what drives people from me'. The bald man requests 'good hair and to be cured of this disease, for the people feel repulsion for me', and the blind man wants 'to have back my sight and to be able to see people'. The angel granted all of their wishes and gave each of them a pregnant animal, so they could all become wealthy in livestock. Returning some time later to each one in the form of his previous illness, the disguised angel asks each man to spare him an animal from his vast herd. The bald and leprous men refuse, so they are then restored to their former poor, disabled selves. Only the blind man agrees to gift the angel with an animal, earning the angel's praise for his generosity. In this story, *qaraᶜ* is classified, alongside leprosy and blindness, as a physical impairment,[33] but only *qaraᶜ* and leprosy socially disable a person for their repellent, unaesthetic associations. Though blindness was certainly not a desired condition, the blind man in this parable is imbued with the clearest moral vision.[34]

Baldness was also featured in *ᶜāhāt*-themed lists and prose dating from as early as the 3rd/9th century. Al-Jāḥiẓ included a chapter on *al-ṣulᶜ* and *al-qurᶜ* and another on *al-quzᶜān* and *al-qurᶜān* in his *Kitāb al-burṣān*, which was written sometime before 237/851; and Ibn Qutayba listed the names of honourable men who were *ṣulᶜān* in his *Kitāb al-maᶜārif*.[35] Al-Thaᶜālibī identified ᶜUmar, ᶜUthmān, ᶜAlī, Marwān and ᶜUmar b. ᶜAbd al-ᶜAzīz as *ṣulᶜān* in his *Laṭāʾif al-maᶜārif*.[36] Ibn al-Jawzī and Ibn Rusta both named ᶜUtba b. Abī Sufyān, as well as caliphs ᶜUmar, ᶜAlī, ᶜUthmān and Marwān, as *ṣulᶜān*.[37] Historically, *ṣalᶜ* seems to have been associated with eminent Sunni leadership.

Essentially, both *ṣalᶜ* and *qaraᶜ* could afflict men of advanced age, but only *qaraᶜ* could also come about from an ailment. *Qaraᶜ* marked one's body as compromised and diseased. For Mamluk and Ottoman Arab adult men, honour resided in the hair of one's head and face. Full beards signified male virility and power, and as such were central to adult Muslim men's gender identity and sense of honour; full heads of hair were markers of youth and/or sound health; and large turbans projected the prestige of intelligence. Leslie Peirce, through her close analysis of the Ottoman Turkish city of Aintab's court registers of 948/1541 (incidentally, the same year in which Jār Allāh published *al-Nukat al-ẓirāf*), revealed slander cases as elucidating historically contingent and local constructions of honour and shame. 'Zones of honor for the adult male', she concludes, '[were] therefore potential targets of insult.'[38] With the publication of *al-Nukat al-ẓirāf*, a community found its honour tested.

Returning to the Fatwa

Now that Ibn Ḥajar had argued for the illegality of Jār Allāh's work, he continued by discussing appropriate forms of repentance and punishment.

> If he insists on his contention, he should receive a grave disciplinary punishment. Ultimately, such conviction could drag him to a difficult situation. There is no admonition in that [book], as it results from the temptation of Satan and Satan's beautification of the ugly so that the ignorant fool finds it beautiful, thereby entering in the realm of the greatest known censure. 'Is he, then, to whom the evil of his conduct is made alluring, so that he looks upon it as good, (equal to one who is rightly guided)?' [Q 35: 8]. And if he had considered His exalted words 'If they had only referred it to the Messenger, or to those charged with authority among them, the proper investigators would have tested it from them' [Q 4: 83], then he would have referred the question to experts in Islamic law before writing the book and would have done what they ordered him to do, but keeping these difficult questions to himself may indicate depraved intentions and the triumph of zealotry for worthlessness. It is incumbent on

> this author to renounce this ugly style, which is a slanderous attack on the dignity of Muslims. He has no right to argue 'there are precedents for mentioning that' . . . For that reason we would ask [Ibn Fahd], 'Are there precedents for this ugly composition? Who has come before you in this [enterprise]? Is it someone whose words and deeds are emulated, like Aḥmad [ibn Ḥanbal], [Yaḥyá] Ibn Maᶜīn, Abū Zurᶜa al-Rāzī or their counterparts who came before or after them? Or is it some unimportant person to whose words and deeds no one pays attention?' If it is the first, then you must explain who it is. But if it is the second, then Allah will not care in which valley the two of you will waste away. In the time of the masters of our masters, it happened that a long fatwa came down about authors. Their question was: 'Is it only permissible for an author to mention defects if he is referring to a deficiency? [p. 83] What defect, other than one related to or resulting from deficiencies, is a religious good?' Mentioning defects is strongly forbidden and unlawful if it is about the learned classes and reciters of Qur'an, but in fact, for no one is there a justification for it, just as al-Qurṭūbī (d. 671/1272) has said, which is related as the consensus opinion.
>
> The proof of that is found in [al-Nawawī's] *Sharḥ al-muhadhdhab* [in a hadith related] from Ibn ᶜAbbās – May Allah be pleased with both of them: 'Whoever harms a jurist harms the Messenger of Allah, and whoever harms the Messenger of Allah harms Allah'. It follows that this author must think about this and repudiate this work by destroying it, and he must then repent to Allah for having gone too far in offending the dead and the living, especially the most important members of this community.[39]

Ghība threatens to undermine social networks in human communities. The 'jurist–Prophet–God' hierarchy places Jār Allāh outside the direct line of authority between man and God and positions the jurist Ibn Ḥajar's body and soul as coextensive and interchangeable with the essence of God, essentially eliminating any moral authority to which Jār Allāh had lain claim.

> Perhaps he should also consider whether the noble politeness of al-Shāfiᶜī succeeded with regard to Fāṭima al-Zahrāᵓ when he alluded to her name and did not announce it egregiously out of tact for her . . . 'The Messenger of Allah cut a noble woman, and he spoke about her, saying "If some woman (*fulāna*) had stolen from a noble woman, I would have cut off her hand"'. In [al-Shāfiᶜī's] version, *fulāna* was a tactful reference to Fāṭima, even though her father had originally mentioned her by her name. If this author had considered the noble politeness of al-Shāfiᶜī in this case, then he would have realised that the enormity of what he did will not be repaired in a lifetime, unless he repents and repudiates this work, hoping for the forgiveness of Allah. May it serve as a warning against insisting on believing that admonition is in this [work]. Truly, there is no admonition in this at all. What is the admonition in 'Such-and-such a deceased person was one-eyed, or such-and-such a living person is leprous,

or similar things that harm the living and the dead'? Even if we overlooked the truth and supposed that there is admonition, this admonition is accompanied by innumerable malicious acts. Who has made it lawful to give an assumed benefit precedence over a confirmed harm? Only someone ignorant about Qur'an, tradition (*sunna*) and community consensus would say that. If he said 'what was said about a Companion of the Prophet does not slander me, because a) I related it, and b) they do not hate it because they are not frivolous people', then we would say, 'Slander applies to you, by any calculation, because you imitated someone who is not imitated in this and because whoever related it did not follow your example. Rather, he followed another example that did not expose or damage those mentioned. As for you, you have followed an example that leads people to condemn it. You have been disparaging of the Companions and have given reason to disparage them. You will bear the burdens of the sins committed in this respect until Doomsday. As for your claim that they do not abhor that, this is an absurd claim because abhorring it is something related to innate disposition and has nothing to do with frivolity one way or another.' All in all, if this author repented and destroyed that work, there would be nothing more to say about this to anyone. Before that happens, his censure is a matter for a wise man, even if he is annoyed, obstinate and stubborn and has not submitted to experts in Islamic law and judges. May Allah support them and those appointed to this matter in their faith. May He divide oppressors and the disobedient with the sword of His justice. [Ibn Fahd's] refraining from [submitting to authority], as people see, is fitting until he shows them his repentance and the depravity of the ugly acts included in that book by destroying it. Otherwise, it is incumbent on them to seize and cut up this work, just as in al-Jalāl al-Suyūṭī's legal ruling about someone who had built a house that was destroyed for depravity [occurring within the home]. Al-Ghazālī and others have shown the same. A group [of jurists] from the remaining legal schools have also made statements about this. If you ask 'How did you come to a ruling of censure? Legal proof texts and experts from the legal schools are decisive on speaking about bodies and their defects', I would say, 'That [sin] belongs among the lesser ones, as most of the authors have said, but the aforementioned book includes a greater one, verily, one of the grave sins'. May Allah – praise and exalt Him – in his mercy and kindness forgive me and the author. Amen. Allah – praise and exalt Him – knows best.[40]

Ibn Ḥajar ordered two courses of action for the author – repentance and destruction of the book, and even a conditional one for the petitioners – seizing and cutting up the book if Ibn Fahd refused to destroy it himself. Ibn Fahd did not repent and did not tear up the book, but rather steadfastly maintained the legitimacy of his project. However, bolstered by Ibn Ḥajar's ruling, a group of bald men who had been mentioned in *al-Nukat al-ẓirāf* stormed Ibn Fahd's home on 5 Shaᶜbān 948/23 November 1541, just days after the book's publication, seized his book, tore up the pages and washed the paper fragments at a mosque. The ink ran from the pages, destroying Jār Allāh's work.[41] Purifying the fragments through ritual ablutions ensured that the unIslamic words would no longer damage the community. Book-burning was also practised: the Sunni caliph ᶜUthmān, after completing his definitive recension of the Qur'an, the version that circulates today, famously ordered the burning of all earlier versions. This command set the basis for future legal decisions about the handling and disposal of unIslamic texts. As Leor Halevi has noted, medieval Muslim '[j]urists had advocated erasing or burning the books of Christians, obtained as booty in the course of war, as a cautionary measure to prevent the dissemination of falsehood'.[42]

The Aftermath

Twenty days later, floodwaters entered Mecca and damaged the Kaᶜaba and the Holy Mosque, inspiring a poet named Saᶜd Allāh to write verses linking this major deluge to the minor deluge that wiped Jār Allāh's book clean:

> Jār Allāh's work was completely erased
> With drops on the fifth day of the month of Shaᶜbān.
> The flood destroyed it on the fifth, and twenty days later
> came annihilation. The building fell.
> This damage spread and in it there is
> A reminder for those who would love obscenities and turmoil.[43]

Convinced that recent events confirmed his narrative of pious suffering and the acceptability of his text, Ibn Fahd drafted a new version of *al-Nukat al-Ẓirāf* approximately two days after the flood entered the city.[44] Then he wrote a defence of it in 949/1542 entitled *Al-Nuṣra wa'l-isᶜāffī al-radd ᶜalá al-muntaqidīn li-muʾallifī al-Nukat al-ẓirāf* (Advocacy and Succour against the Critics of My Book *Charming Anecdotes*) that is unrecoverable.[45] At the same time, he dispatched letters soliciting fatwas to Shams al-Dīn Muḥammad b. Ṭūlūn (880/1473–953/1546), a Ḥanbalī *mufti* and historian in Damascus who was also his close friend, and to four Cairene judges – Abū al-Fayḍ b. ᶜAlī al-Sulamī al-Ḥanafī, Aḥmad b. al-Najjār al-Ḥanbalī, Nāṣir al-Laqānī al-Mālikī (who was, incidentally, one of Ibn Ḥajar's former teachers) and Aḥmad al-Bulqīnī al-Shāfiᶜī – representing each of the Sunni schools of law. The letter read:[46]

> What do you say – may God be pleased with you – of a student who read a book entitled *Mufīd al-ᶜulūm* by the well-known Ḥanafī scholar Abī Bakr Muḥammad b. Mūsá al-Khawarizmī? The student saw chapters on the physical

> defects (*ᶜilal*) of noble people. The author mentioned a group of the early and late prominent figures of this community who were recognised by that [their defects], with such [epithets as] 'The Lame Man', 'The Bald Man' (*al-aqraᶜ*), 'The Blind Man' and the like. Seeing this, the student composed a book on this issue using the same justification proposed by the author of the aforementioned book, namely, promoting admonition, learning and entertainment. Would this intention be legitimate when embarking upon such an act? Give us the fatwa, asking that God would make Paradise your reward![47]

By Jār Allāh's account, all of them responded that his work accorded with the tenets of Islam and could not be categorised as *ghība*. The Ḥanafī scholar of Cairo wrote back: 'Your intention was not ugly, since Ibn Qutayba set the precedent for mentioning people with such *ᶜāhāt* as leprosy, lameness, deafness, amputation, cross eyes, blue eyes, buck teeth, thin beard, frontal baldness, halitosis, one eye and blindness'. According to Jār Allāh, the other three Cairene scholars sent similar responses to this first one.[48]

The fifth scholar, Ibn Ṭūlūn, had known Jār Allāh for more than thirty years at this point. One modern scholar has placed Ibn Ṭūlūn and Jār Allāh's first meeting in Damascus in 922/1516–7, when Jār Allāh visited Damascus to tour the city and to study with scholars, but there is some possibility that they met even earlier in 920/1515, when Ibn Ṭūlūn made the pilgrimage to Mecca at the age of 40.[49] During this trip, Ibn Ṭūlūn studied hadith and *shamāʾil* with Jār Allāh's father ᶜIzz al-Dīn b. Fahd on 6 Dhū al-Ḥijja 920/21 January 1515 in a public gathering place (*dār al-nadwa*).[50] In any case, when they met in Damascus in 922/1516 or 1517, they were at different life stages. Ibn Ṭūlūn was married to his 'one and only wife' Karīmat al-ᶜAllāma bint al-Shaykh Ibrāhīm b. Muḥammad b. ᶜAwn al-Shāghūrī al-Ḥanafī (d. after 923/1517), the daughter of a prominent Damascene shaykh, sometime before 915/1509.[51] They had not had more children since the death of their five-year-old daughter Sitt al-ᶜUlamāʾ Khadīja in 920/1514.[52] Jār Allāh was unmarried, childless and ten years younger than his friend. Ibn Ṭūlūn worked hard to earn a reputation as a capable historian, whereas Jār Allāh essentially inherited his forefathers' status as scholars. In spite of their differences, they shared a commitment to producing scholarship, travelling around the Arab provinces and making contact with scholars, reading new books and composing original histories. Ibn Ṭūlūn integrated his friend into his social circles in Damascus, and Jār Allāh sought out his expert opinion on the reliability of certain hadith-transmitters.[53] His father ᶜIzz al-Dīn b. Fahd died on or just before Friday, 13 Jumādā II 923/3 July 1517, while Jār Allāh was in Damascus. He learned of his father's death when a funeral prayer was read at the Umayyad Mosque to honour ᶜIzz al-Dīn on this Friday.[54] Jār Allāh left Damascus for Mecca the following day, arriving at his family's home sometime later in the same month.[55] Indeed, by this time, Jār Allāh and Ibn Ṭūlūn regarded themselves as the unofficial historians of the Hijaz and Greater Syria respectively, exchanging private letters every year in which they reported the deaths of notables from their home regions.[56] At times, information that they traded as friends was also incorporated into their chronicles and biographical dictionaries intended for public consumption; but their more informal channels of knowledge-transmission signal what types of events they found personally important and also the place of friendship in late Mamluk–early Ottoman historical production in the Arab provinces.[57] Given their history of friendship, it comes as no surprise that Ibn Ṭūlūn, who in his writings frequently referred to Jār Allāh to as 'our brother', wrote a warmly supportive letter:

> Imam Shams al-Dīn Muḥammad b. Mufliḥ al-Ḥanbalī [d. 763/1361] said in the book *Al-Ādāb al-sharᶜiyya* [Legal Customs] that al-Qūṭī said about a people that *ghība* applies to religion and only applies to honour or physical characteristics when it is uttered to imply defect [of character]. In his book *al-Maᶜārif*, Imam Abū Muḥammad b. Qutayba worked along these lines, mentioning hemiplegia, lameness, leprosy and other such things. Furthermore, there were no complaints that people wrote works on this subject, for instance, al-Ṣalāḥ al-Ṣafadī in his *Al-Shuᶜūr bi-akhyār al-ᶜūr* and *Nakt al-himyān ᶜalá nukat al-ᶜumyān*. They did not intend defect, but rather intended it, as cautious scholars have previously, as knowledge and inclusiveness (*iḥāṭa*) of the nobles whom these [physical conditions] had befallen and as a respectful message for posterity and as an admonition.[58]

Although Ibn Ṭūlūn owned the original copy of Ibn ᶜAbd al-Hādī's *Kitāb al-ḍabṭ*, a biographical dictionary of hadith specialists with *ᶜāhāt*, he neither referenced it as an acceptable critique of persons with *ᶜāhāt* nor mentioned it as an example of a literary genre that aligns *ᶜāhāt* with questionable moral qualities.[59] Even though Ibn Ṭūlūn supported the concept of the book, the uproar surrounding practices of *ghība* made him cautious about his own writings. As a postscript to this letter, Ibn Ṭūlūn admitted that he had been composing a commentary called *Taᶜjīl al-bishāra li-man ṣabara ᶜalá dhahāb al-baṣar* (Accelerating the Good Omen for Those Who Were Patient upon Losing Their Eyesight) but was now sufficiently intimidated by the turn of events in Mecca to leave out the name of a writer (*aḥad min al-udabāʾ*) whose sight was failing.[60] In spite of his language about including accomplished disabled people in histories of nobility, Ibn Ṭūlūn's impulse is checked by considerations of their desire to be so named. This brief addendum is rather telling, as it demonstrates an awareness that Ibn Qutayba's and al-Ṣafadī's books may have been seen as acceptable because they only mentioned deceased figures. (This same explanation may apply to Ibn ᶜAbd al-Hādī's *Kitāb al-ḍabṭ*, which only mentioned hadith specialists with *ᶜāhāt* who had lived between the 1st/7th and 3rd/9th centuries.) Even if Islamic law does allow one to mention a living person's physical defects under certain circumstances, 10th/16th-century social mores and taboos deemed it beyond the pale of decency.[61] Religious justifications simply had to be sought to defend these social codes.

Ibn Ṭūlūn's anxieties about naming the writer with failing sight may also have something to do with his reclusive tendencies at this point of his life. At the time of his exchange of letters with Jār Allāh, Ibn Ṭūlūn was a widower who had seen all three of his children predecease him. (Al-Ghazzī's biography of Ibn Ṭūlūn discreetly informs readers that 'when he died, he had no children and no wife'. In fact, the prevailing consensus among modern scholars is that Ibn Ṭūlūn was a 'committed bachelor' who died 'without issue'.)[62] As mentioned earlier, his daughter Sitt al-ᶜUlamāᵓ Khadīja (Rabīᶜ II 915–Dhū al-Qaᶜda 920/July 1509–December 1514), who in her short life had actually received an *ijāza* from al-Sirāj al-Ṣayrafī, died of the plague. When Ottoman forces conquered Syria, Ibn Ṭūlūn and his family were displaced from their Ṣāliḥiyya home, forcing them to relocate to al-Mizza, a village three miles southwest of al-Ṣāliḥiyya. While in exile, his wife and his children ᶜĀᵓisha and ᶜUthmān died, leaving him alone in this new place, prompting him to leave al-Mizza and to take up residence in al-Yūnusiyya, a Sufi lodge in Damascus. ᶜUthmān b. al-Shams b. Ṭūlūn died on 9 Dhū al-Qaᶜda 938/13 June 1532 at the age of seven. In addition to having read a portion of the Qur'an, learned many texts and received authorisation from several scholars to transmit texts, 'his father honoured him'.[63] ᶜĀᵓisha, who was also called Maryam, died on 13 Rabīᶜ I 943/30 August 1536, just ten days shy of her 17th birthday. In her lifetime, she had sat at the feet of many teachers and had received numerous certificates of transmission.[64] After the death of his nuclear family, Ibn Ṭūlūn withdrew from public life and eventually died a recluse.

Ibn Ṭūlūn's reluctance to name this particular writer probably influenced Jār Allāh's subsequent drafts of *al-Nukat al-ẓirāf*. While he was in Barābir Valley, near Mecca, in late Jumādā I 950/August 1543, Jār Allāh completed a third, expanded version of his work that was retitled *Al-Nukat al-ẓirāf fī mawᶜiẓa bi-dhawī l-ᶜāhāt min al-ashrāf* (Charming Anecdotes: An Admonition Regarding Honourable People with Physical Blights) to emphasise its admonitory aspects.[65] He organised this new fifty-nine-folio treatise somewhat differently from the original version and also from earlier examples of Arabic literature about physically blighted people. After the title page (fo. 1a) and incipit (1b–2a) comes a foreword (2a–3b) that surveys such precedents in the field of *ʿāhāt* literature as al-Khawarizmī's *Mufīd al-ʿulūm*, Ibn Qutayba's *Maʿārif*, al-Sakhāwī's *Al-Iʿlān bi'l-tawbīkh*, al-Ṣafadī's *Nakt al-himyān ʿalá nukat al-ʿumyān* and *Al-Shuʿūr bi'l-ʿūr*, al-Jāḥiẓ' *Kitāb al-ʿurjān* and Ibn al-Athīr al-Jazarī's *Kitāb al-lubāb*. In this section, Jār Allāh aligned his project with the works of al-Khawarizmī, al-Jāḥiẓ and al-Ṣafadī, claiming to have mimicked al-Khawarizmī's technique of listing names of people with particular blights, al-Jāḥiẓ's humorous assembly of anecdotes about his contemporaries and al-Ṣafadī's biographical dictionary of deceased luminaries. Following this segment is a lengthy introduction (3b–16a) that comprises two sections. In the first (3b–9a), the author surveyed Islamic discourses about *dhawī l-ʿāhāt*, citing al-Qasṭallānī, Ibn al-ʿImād, al-Sakhāwī, Imām al-Shāfiʿī, Ibn Ḥajar al-ʿAsqalānī, al-Nawawī, al-Mawardī and others, and in the second he vigorously defended his 948/1541 version of *al-Nukat al-ẓirāf* (9a–16a). Chapter 1, titled 'Concerning those with *ʿāhāt* and examples of honourable men among them', includes discussions of al-Khawarizmī's three chapters about people with *ʿāhāt* (16a–17a) and biographical entries culled verbatim from earlier sources on the prophets Yaʿqūb (17a–b) and Shuʿayb (18a), Abū Quḥāfah, the father of Abū Bakr (18b–19a), Abū Sufyān (19a–b), Ibn ʿAbbās (19b–21a), ʿItbān (21a), ʿAmr b. Qays b. Umm Maktūm (21b), Muḥarrama (21b–22a), al-Bukhārī (22a–b), al-Tirmidhī (22b), Abū l-Qāsim b. Fīrruh al-Shāṭibī al-Ḍarīr (22b), Abū l-ʿAlāʾ al-Maʿarrī (23a), Abū Zayd ʿAbd al-Raḥmān b. ʿAbdallāh al-Shahilī (23a), Abū ʿAbdallāh Muḥammad b. Aḥmad al-Andalusī al-Mālikī al-Aʿmá al-Naḥwī (23a–b), Aḥmad b. Yūsuf al-Raʿīnī al-Ḍarīr (23b), Abū l-Ḥasan ʿAlī b. ʿAbdallāh al-Sanhūrī al-Azharī al-Ḍarīr (23b), Abbasid family members (24a), Zakariyyāʾ al-Anṣarī (24a), a long list of blind and one-eyed scholars (24b–26b), hadith about diseased and disabled people, especially the Prophet's miraculous cures of the ill (27a–35b), and Companions of the Prophet (35b–38a).[66] Chapter 2 (38b–53b) focused on 'physical conditions like having one eye, cross eyes, frontal baldness (*ṣalʿ*), lameness, leprosy and a number of *ʿāhāt* and illnesses'. In the manuscript's explicit (*khātimat al-kitāb)* (54a–59a), the author described the rewards that accrue to the ill and disabled, summarised his main points, detailed his method of composition and lambasted the detractors who had destroyed his first version.

In this new version, Jār Allāh showed enough sensitivity to the criticism he received to remove most of his contemporaries' names, though he again named himself as having a receding hairline, identified one Ayyūb al-Makkī as disabled in a marginal note and identified his critic Ibn Ḥajar al-Haytamī as cross-eyed (*aḥwal*).[67] Otherwise, his references to living people were more circumspect. As for the bald men who destroyed his book, he only described them as profligate Meccans who were important in the community, adding that, though he had named them as *ṣul*ᶜ*ān* (m. sing. *aṣla*ᶜ) in the first version of the book, they were in truth *qur*ᶜ*ān* (m. sing. *aqra*ᶜ).[68] If the bald men were in fact profligates (*fujjār al-*ᶜ*aṣr*), why would Jār Allāh have included them in a book about honourable people? Was his original authorial motive more in line with that of Ibn ᶜAbd al-Hādī, who correlated 'defective bodies' with defective moralities in his *Kitāb al-Ḍabṭ*? The bulk of the first version of *al-Nukat al-ẓirāf* consisted of chapters dedicated to individual ᶜ*āhāt*, and in each chapter living people were named. Following these chapters, a group of Companions who had had ᶜ*āhāt* were mentioned, because they were an irreproachable group who represented a golden age of Islam. Although the discrepancy between the pious reputations of the disabled Companions and the impious ones of the disabled Meccan men would have been obvious to a contemporary Meccan, Jār Allāh could naively claim that he would never insult a Companion, so the entire book must be a praise book.

He seems not to have anticipated the fierce opposition, because he was ill-prepared for Ibn Ḥajar's challenge to name a literary precedent for *al-Nukat al-ẓirāf* and to prove that he had not committed *ghība*. Jār Allāh, in his own letter soliciting a fatwa, was only able to name al-Khawarizmī's *Mufīd al-*ᶜ*ulūm* as a literary precedent and did not directly ask the five legal experts about backbiting. In response, the Cairene judge Abū al-Fayḍ b. ᶜAlī al-Sulamī al-Ḥanafī only cited Ibn Qutayba's work as a sound precedent. Ibn Ṭūlūn also named Ibn Qutayba and added al-Ṣafadī's works on blind and one-eyed Muslims for good measure. When he rewrote the book, Jār Allāh referenced these and other works in the book's introduction, but his rebuttal of the charges of slander was remarkably weak. Although claiming that one of the six exceptions to *ghība* did fit his case, he never did specify which one, only avowing that 'When I wrote of *dhawī l-*ᶜ*āhāt*, I did not have any defect (*naqīṣa*) in mind. On the contrary, I wanted to identify these people, console them and present a light admonition.' It is unclear whom Jār Allāh intended to admonish, though past literary works, such as those penned by al-Ḥijāzī and al-Badrī, identified the disabled as blameless and their taunters as unprincipled aggressors. Additionally, the contemporary Meccan poet Shihāb al-Dīn b. al-ᶜUlayf (d. 926/1520) composed a similarly constructed poem about a man who defends his lame friend from gossipmongers who 'regaled [him] with the defects of a person with an *ᶜāha*', concluding that 'his situation proves that there is no objection in being lame'.[69] Perhaps Jār Allāh assumed that his readers would understand that a work praising *ahl al-ᶜāhāt* necessarily positions itself in opposition to detractors of disabled people. In any case, after this statement, he appealed to the deeds of the caliph ᶜUmar, who had declared that '*ghība* of bodies is not something forbidden'. In addition, the Prophet Muḥammad referred to people as 'black and short' and 'thin-bearded', so many eminent Muslim men have identified people by their physical differences. What is more, Jār Allāh claimed that his text could not have been written with malicious intent since he had named himself as frontally bald, his maternal grandfather as lame, and a number of his teachers as blind.[70] In the last folios of the book, Jār Allāh offers a bright summary of his project: 'All of the afflicted provide us beautiful examples of seeking merit and honour . . . I intended this work as true admonition and pure entertainment, so that it may serve as an admonishment to those who admonish and as entertainment to students.'[71]

Ibn Ḥajar's challenge for Jār Allāh to name a literary precedent for his work and to defend it against charges of slander, along with Jār Allāh's placement of his book within acceptable literary standards and his arguments for its moral appropriateness, may itself be a traditional response in literary controversies. Frédéric Lagrange has parsed Abū Ḥayyān al-Tawḥīdī's (d. 414/1023) introduction to *Akhlāq al-wazīrayn* (The Morality of the Two Viziers), a lengthy and scathing invective against two sitting Buyid princes, to reveal a particular strategy against criticisms of slander. Al-Tawḥīdī directed most of his attacks against one of the viziers, Ibn ᶜAbbād, for relishing both the active and passive roles in male–male anal intercourse. But, to lessen the outrage over such accusations, al-Tawḥīdī first classified his work as one of satire 'to situate himself in a certain literary continuity, even though his work could be seen as the founding of a new genre. Every creation at the heart of the *adab* has to be camouflaged through its location in a pre-existing literary movement, a tradition through which one could award oneself predecessors, thereby guaranteeing for oneself a sort of generic *isnad*.'[72] In the second part of al-Tawḥīdī's defence, he argued that one of the six exceptions to *ghība* applied in his case, specifically the legal compulsion to expose the moral failings of a political leader.

With far less artfulness and confidence, Jār Allāh deployed a similar two-pronged defence that turned on establishing a generic precedent and finding a moral justification. Instead of satire, Jār Allāh claimed admonition and entertainment as his genres of choice, though he seemed to have been unaware of several important works of *ahl al-ᶜāhāt* literature, including most of the texts cited in this book's introduction. He was possibly uninterested in understanding the history of this genre because he was only appropriating it to legitimise his insults against his contemporaries. If his attempt to situate his book in a literary tradition felt thin, then his religious justification reads even more weakly. Unlike al-Tawḥīdī, who cited a moral imperative to protect Muslims from evil, which is one of the six exceptions to *ghība*, as justification for his book, Jār Allāh just said that one of the known exceptions did, indeed, apply to his case, though he never specified which one. Jār Allāh's unpreparedness for the backlash against his book demonstrates a grave misreading of this cultural moment that did not end when his book was destroyed. By rewriting the text, he believed that an audience existed for his work; but the reception of the revised *al-Nukat al-ẓirāf* seems to have been rather muted, as early modern sources are altogether silent about the book. (Seven months after Jār Allāh had completed this revised version, Ibn Ṭūlūn made the pilgrimage to Mecca, but there is no evidence that he read the book or was given a copy of it.[73])

So, what do we know of the reception? For one, Jār Allāh's autograph manuscript is the only known extant copy, suggesting that later generations did not know of this work or, if they did, did not deem it worthy of copying. Secondly, none of Jār Allāh's biographers mentioned this book. In any case, the manuscript's title page bears the name of three works – Jār Allāh's *al-Nukat al-ẓirāf*, Majd al-Dīn al-Fayrūzabādī's (d. 817/1414) *Safar al-suʿāda* and al-Mundhirī's (d. 656/1258) *Arbiʿūn ḥadīth* – all written in what appears to be Jār Allāh's own hand. His reasons for collating his book with these two short collections of hadith remain obscure, but it is possible that he wanted to ensure its survival by attaching it to religious texts that people would have been loath to discard or destroy, or that he used the compilation as a didactic text, for he continued to receive students even after this incident. Although none of his sons became historians, meaning that the Ibn Fahd legacy as Meccan historians died with Jār Allāh, other family members recognised and benefited from his social position and knowledge. His relative Taqī al-Dīn b. Ḥazan b. Fahd (d. 987/1580) was his student and grew up to become a respected jurist.[74] In 953/1546, the Aleppan historian Ibn al-Ḥanbalī (d. 971/1563) came to Mecca to study with Jār Allāh, who died in Mecca in 954/1547. Some years later, in his *Durr al-ḥabab fī taʾrīkh aʿyān ḥalab*, a biographical dictionary of Aleppan notables, Ibn al-Ḥanbalī explicitly declared a man's sexual preference for young men – and, in an echo of Jār Allāh's experiences, many of Ibn al-Ḥanbalī's peers felt that mentioning such a sexual preference was tantamount to *ghība*. Though murmurs of *ghība* were heard against him, no other adverse consequences ensued.[75]

Conclusion

The intersections of honour and the male body came to a forceful head in mid-10th/16th-century Mecca (and Aleppo), but the themes have permeated every chapter of this book. For al-Ḥijāzī, taking *balādhur* to improve his memory brought him honour and marked him as a dedicated student. It was only after the drug had caused boils to erupt all over his body that he was ostracised by his community and regarded with scepticism. He tried to shift public perception of the boils by depicting his ordeal as suffering in God's name. From this experience comes an effort to ascribe other positive values to blighted bodies. Many of his poems, as well as those compiled by his student al-Badrī, directly address the disbelief and shame of outsiders who found it difficult to believe that a person with blights could be found desirable. Al-Badrī arranged a selection of love poems about men with afflicted body parts into a quasi-narrative of love, pain, medical treatment, recovery and death, situating disease and blight, both temporary and permanent, as natural features of a virile man's life. In this era, disease and blightedness were prevalent enough to contribute to the diffusion of these themes in religious, literary and historical discourses and in the public consciousness of both native residents of Cairo, Damascus and Mecca and visitors to these cities. Ibn ᶜAbd al-Hādī aligned blighted hadith-transmitters with dishonourable faulty hadith.

This single theme of blightedness was sustained in public and private discourses over 150 years, filtered through different media: poetry, literary and historical prose, religious polemic, letters of friendship, moral consolation and biography. In these threads of conversations and narratives, we have seen just how distinct blights were differently valued in changing contexts. The textual traditions described in this book developed from close personal ties, scholarly friendship, shared travels and various writings on the theme of physical difference. Although this particular study has focused overwhelmingly on the body, this was certainly not the only subject that unified them, as Yossef Rapoport has found:

> Working women were the subject of at least three intriguing literary works composed during the second half of the fifteenth century. Ibn Ṭūlūn devoted a treatise to traditions about spinners, entitled *Qiṭf al-Zahrāt fīmā qīla fī al-Ghazzālāt* (Bunch of Flowers on the Sayings concerning Female Spinners). The Cairene litterateur Shihāb al-Dīn al-Ḥijāzī al-Ḥazrajī [sic] (d. 875/1471) composed a collection of epigrams directed to various types of women, including spinners, seamstresses and other women of professions. The Damascene Ibn al-Mibrad (d. 909/1503) collected an anthology of traditions and anecdotes about women, most of them in praise of women who work the spindle.[76]

That three of our writers expounded on not only the productive labour of women workers but also *ahl al-ᶜāhāt* perhaps speaks to their sensibility to individuals who did not share their social position and class. (Cairo Geniza documents confirm the division of manufacturing labour along gender lines. Women primarily carried out those tasks that could comfortably take place in the home, and men manufactured and sold goods in public spaces.) But then again, it may also signal a basic uniformity of literary tropes. Whatever the case may be, finding other converging interests within this group of writers makes their shared awareness of corporeal themes seem less like accidental convergences and more like a significant tradition of scholarly contact. It may also confirm the utility of Michael Chamberlain's call in his own study of networks of friendship and scholarship in Ayyubid and Mamluk Damascus for scholars to consider the strategic concerns and ethical zones of scholarly friendships. Unequal power relations between masters and disciples or teachers and students created situations of obligatory devotion, and the duties of pupils to teachers are well documented in Islamicate histories; but other, more freely exchanged bonds of friendship thrived in these contexts too, and here, researchers may be able to trace writing trends and literary influences that proliferated beyond conventional scholarly hierarchies and outside of institutional affiliations.

Notes

1. For Jār Allāh Ibn Fahd, see *EI*^{2}, s.v. 'Ibn Fahd', 3:760; al-Sakhawī, *Al-Ḍawʾ*, 3:52; al-ᶜAydarūsī, *Taʾrīkh nūr al-sāfir ᶜan akhbār al-qarn al-ᶜāshir* (Egypt: s.n., 1980–6), p. 241; al-Ghazzī, *Kawākib*, 2:131; Ibn al-ᶜImād, *Shadharāt*, 8:301; Muḥammad al-Ḥabīb al-Hīla, *Al-Taʾrīkh wa'l-muʾarrikhūn bi-Makka min al-qarn al-thālith al-hijrī ilá al-qarn al-thālith ᶜashar* (History and Historians of Mecca from the Third to the Thirteenth Hijri Century) (Mecca: Muʾassasat al-furqān li'l-turāth al-islāmī, 1994), pp. 195–213.
2. Khaled El-Rouayheb, *Before Homosexuality in the Arab-Islamic World, 1500–1800* (Chicago: University of Chicago Press, 2005), p. 50.
3. Muḥammad b. Aḥmad al-Dhahabī, Taqī al-Dīn Muḥammad al-Makkī b. Fahd and al-Suyūṭī, *Kitāb tadhkirat al-ḥuffāẓ* (Beirut: Dār al-kutub al-ᶜilmiyya, 1998), p. 382.
4. *EI*^{2}, s.v. 'Ibn Ḥadjar al-Haytamī, Abū 'l-ᶜAbbās b. Muḥammad b. Muḥammad b. ᶜAlī b. Ḥadjar, Shihāb al-Dīn, al-Haytamī al-Saᶜdī' (Leiden: E. J. Brill, 1960–), 3:776–8.
5. Aḥmad b. Muḥammad Ibn Ḥajar al-Haytamī, *Al-Fatāwá al-kubrá al-fiqhiyya* (Grand Juridical Fatwas) (Cairo: ᶜAbd al-Ḥamīd Aḥmad Ḥanafī, 1938), 4:82.

6. Qur'an 49: 12, 104: 1.
7. Of the Fahd scholars, Taqī al-Dīn b. Fahd had the farthest-reaching influence and acquired the most prestigious reputation as a historian. His chronicles about contemporary Mecca served as a core text upon which his descendants expanded. Najm al-Dīn b. Fahd wrote two major histories, *Al-Durr al-kamīn*, an extension of Taqī al-Dīn al-Fāsī's (d. 832/1428) Mecca-centred biographical dictionary *Al-ʿIqd al-thamīn fī taʾrīkh al-Balad al-Amīn* (The Precious Necklace: A History of the Honest Town) and *Itḥāf al-wará bi-akhbār Umm al-Qurá* (The Gifts of Mortals: Reports about Mecca), a history of Mecca from the time of the Prophet until months before the author's own death. ʿIzz al-Dīn b. Fahd's *Bulūgh al-qirá* (The Elegance of Hospitality) is a history of Mecca from 885/1480 to 922/1516. Jār Allāh b. Fahd's diaristic chronicle *Nayl al-muná* began in Dhū al-Ḥijja 923/December 1517 and terminated in Rajab 946/November 1539.
8. Ibn Ḥajar al-Haytamī, *Fatāwá*, 4:82. The parenthetical statements are Ibn Ḥajar's own asides in the text.
9. For anxieties in medieval Latin Christendom about the negative effect that nicknames based on physical impairments may have had on social interactions and integration, see Irina Metzler, 'Disability in the Middle Ages: Impairment at the Intersection of Historical Inquiry and Disability Studies', *History Compass* 9.1 (2011), p. 53; and Metzler, 'What's in a Name? Considering the Onomastics of Disability in the Middle Ages', in W. Turner and T. Pearman (eds), *Disabilities of Medieval Europe* (Lampeter: Edwin Mellen Press, forthcoming).
10. Al-Nawawī, *Kitāb al-adhkār* (The Book of What Is Said), ed. Muḥammad Fayyāḍ al-Barūrī (Damascus: Dar al-Mallāḥ, 1971), p. 250.
11. Ibn Ḥajar al-Haytamī, *Fatāwá*, 4:82.
12. Ibid., 4:82.
13. Marika Sardar, 'Islamic Art of the Deccan', in *Heilbrunn Timeline of Art History* (New York: The Metropolitan Museum of Art, 2000–) <http://www.metmuseum.org/toah/hd/decc/hd_decc.htm> (October 2003). Last accessed 17 November 2011.
14. Ananda K. Coomaraswamy, 'The Buddha's cūḍā, Hair, uṣṇīṣa, and Crown', *Journal of the Royal Asiatic Society of Great Britain and Ireland* 4 (October 1928), pp. 815–41; and Eisel Mazard, 'The Buddha Was Bald . . . But Is Everywhere Depicted with a Full Head of Hair', *New Mandala*, 30 December 2010. <http://asiapacific.anu.edu.au/newmandala/2010/12/30/the-buddha-was-bald/>. Last accessed 31 December 2010.
15. J. Duncan M. Derrett, *The Hoysaḷas: A Medieval Indian Royal Family* (Madras: Oxford University Press, 1957), p. 21; A. L. Basham, 'The Hoysaḷas: A Medieval Indian Royal Family', *BSOAS* 22.1/3 (1959), p. 167.
16. Ghaly, *Islam and Disability*, p. 96. The turban was such a key garment for scholarly identity that Jār Allāh's revelation may have registered as not only a violation of personal honour, but also of professional dignity. Certainly,

Jār Allāh and Ibn Ḥajar were aware of this association, having each written books about turbans. According to Albrecht Fuess, 'The ulama were apparently distinguished by the size of their turban (*ᶜimāmah*) and therefore as a class were named *arbāb al-ᶜamāʾim*, masters of the turbans. The wearing of turbans was not limited exclusively to the ulama, but for them it was much bigger, sometimes reaching abnormal sizes. The expression "to enlarge one's turban" became a synonym for showing off'. See his 'Sultans with Horns: The Political Significance of Headgear in the Mamluk Empire', *MSR* 12.2 (2008), pp. 74–5.

17. See Ahmet Karamustafa, *God's Unruly Friends: Dervish Groups in the Islamic Later Middle Period, 1200–1550* (Oxford: OneWorld, 2006); and Bashir, *Sufi Bodies*. Megan Reid has found many examples of men's antinomian piety in Ayyubid and Mamluk Egypt, but 'antinomian holy women seem not to have existed at all in medieval Islam'. See her 'Exemplars of Excess', p. 108.
18. Rudolph Peters, *Crime and Punishment in Islamic Law: Theory and Practice from the Sixteenth to the Twenty-First Century* (Cambridge: Cambridge University Press, 2005), pp. 34, 61. Of course, the association of bald-shaven heads with criminality predates the 10th/16th century. Al-Jāḥiẓ remarked that in the 3rd/9th century: 'For men, there was no harder or more odious punishment from the sultan than shaving the head and the beard'. *Kitāb al-burṣān*, p. 325.
19. Al-Thaᶜālibī, *Laṭāʾif*, p. 96. The editor/translator has added in a footnote: '[a]s with blindness, the frequency of baldness amongst the early Caliphs became regarded as a sign of nobility'.
20. Ibn Qutayba, *Kitāb ᶜuyūn al-akhbār*, 1:223.
21. Jār Allāh Ibn Fahd al-Makkī, *Al-Nukat*, fos 41a–b, citing Abū Naṣr al-Jawharī, *Ṣiḥāḥ al-lughah* (The Soundness of Language) (Beirut: Dār al-kutub al-ᶜilmiyya, 1999), 3:1,244, 1,262.
22. Al-Tawḥīdī, *Baṣāʾir*, 6:146.
23. Ibid., 6:147.
24. Jār Allāh Ibn Fahd al-Makkī, *Al-Nukat*, fo. 41b, citing Majd al-Dīn Ibn al-Athīr, *Nihāya fī al-gharīb al-ḥadīth wa'l-athar* (Beirut: Dār iḥyāʾ al-turāth al-ᶜarabī, 1985), 3:46.
25. Ibn Manẓūr, *Lisān*, p. 2,482.
26. Al-Ṭabarī, *Firdaws*, pp. 53, 136.
27. Ibn Sīnā, *Qānūn fī al-ṭibb*, in H. T. Bachour, *La Dermatologie chez les arabes* (Damascus, 1990), p. 267. Cited in Mourad Mokni, 'La peau et ses maladies d'après un traité de médecine tardif', Master's thesis, Université de Tunis, 2006, pp. 35–7.
28. Abū al-Faraj ᶜAlī b. al-Ḥusayn Ibn Hindū, *Miftāḥ al-ṭibb wa-minhāj al-ṭullāb*, trans. Aida Tibi, ed. Emilie Savage-Smith (Reading: Garnet Publishing, 2010), p. 70. Ophiasis is a form of alopecia, so one can also find translations of *dāʾ al-thaᶜlab* as simply 'alopecia'. Cf. Emilie Savage-Smith and

Peter Pormann, *Medieval Islamic Medicine* (Washington, DC: Georgetown University Press, 2007), p. 31; and Mokni, 'La peau', p. 35.

29. Al-Jawharī, *Ṣiḥāḥ*, 3:1,262.
30. Ibn al-Athīr, *Nihāya*, 4:44–5; Ibn Manẓūr, *Lisān*, p. 3,594.
31. *Kitāb al-diryāq*, Österreichische Nationalbibliothek, Vienna, MS A.F. 10, fos 11a, 15b; *Kitāb al-sumūm/Kitāb al-diryāq*, sold as Lot 21, Sotheby's, London, 25 April 2002, fo. 36a. Jaclynne Kerner has misconstrued these terms as 'the "drug" (i.e., poison) of the snake and the ?fox?'. See her 'Art in the Name of Science: Illustrated Manuscripts of the *Kitāb al-diryāq*', PhD dissertation, Institute of Fine Arts, New York University, 2004, p. 78. Similarly, Leigh Chipman's suggestion of a common cure for snakebite and *qara*ᶜ comes from misleading rubrication in a manuscript by alᶜAṭṭār al-Isrāʾīlī of the Mamluk pharmacological treatise *Minhāj al-dukkān* (Bibliotheca Alexandrina, Alexandria, Egypt). On fo. 197b, the copyist rubricised *luṭūkh al-ḥayyāt* (snake ointments), then listed the first ingredient as *ḥabb al-qar*ᶜ (pumpkin seed). On fo. 225b, *ḍimād al-ḥayyāt wa-ḥabb al-qar*ᶜ (snake poultice and pumpkin seed) – the poultice and the first ingredient – are rubricised. Chipman, in trying to make sense of this second rubric, translated it as a 'poultice for snakes and baldness?'. See her *The World of Pharmacy and Pharmacists in Mamlūk Cairo* (Leiden: E. J. Brill, 2010), p. 270.
32. Al-Ṭabarī, *Firdaws*, p. 135.
33. *Ṣaḥīḥ Bukhārī*, vol. 4, book 56, hadith 670; *Ṣaḥīḥ Muslim*, book 42, hadith 7,071. The English translations are taken from Salma Khadra Jayyusi (ed.), *Classical Arabic Stories: An Anthology* (New York: Columbia University Press, 2010), pp. 179–80. Baldness in the contemporary Middle East is treated as a cosmetic issue, not as a disease, and the medieval classification of baldness as disease is borne out by modern genetic studies. One team of scientists has found that baldness is an auto-immune disorder that has genetic 'commonalit[ies] with rheumatoid arthritis, type I diabetes and coeliac disease'. See Lynn Petukhova et al., 'Genome-wide association study in alopecia areata implicates both innate and adaptive immunity', *Nature* 466.1 (1 July 2010), p. 116. For an interview with lead author Angela Christiano, see Claudia Dreifus, 'Living and Studying Alopecia', *The New York Times*, 27 December 2010, p. D2.
34. Blindness occupied a special place in the Arabic lexicon and in the Muslim imagination. A. Fischer has argued that Muḥammad introduced to the Arab world a 'pious jargon', whose influence is particularly evident in the antiphrastic euphemism of *baṣīr* (sharp-sighted) for *a*ᶜ*má* (blind). See his 'Arab. *baṣīr* "scharfsichtig" per antiphrasin = "blind"', *ZDMG* 61 (1907), pp. 425–34.
35. Al-Jāḥiẓ, *Kitāb al-burṣān*, pp. 321–30; Ibn Qutayba, *Kitāb al-ma*ᶜ*ārif*, p. 196.
36. Al-Thaᶜālibī, *Kitāb laṭāʾif al-ma*ᶜ*arif*, ed. Pieter de Jong (Lugduni Batavorum: Brill, 1867), p. 69.

37. Ibn al-Jawzī, *Talqīḥ*, p. 448; Ibn Rusta, *Kitāb al-a^c^lāq*, p. 223.
38. Peirce, *Morality*, p. 195.
39. Ibn Ḥajar al-Haytamī, *Fatāwá*, 4:82–3.
40. Ibid., 4:83.
41. Jār Allāh Ibn Fahd al-Makkī, *Al-Nukat*, fos 15b, 59a.
42. Leor Halevi, 'Christian Impurity versus Economic Necessity: A Fifteenth-Century Fatwa on European Paper', *Speculum* 83 (2008), p. 934.
43. Jār Allāh Ibn Fahd al-Makkī, *Al-Nukat*, fo. 15b.
44. Ibid., fo. 59a.
45. Ibid., fo. 10b.
46. Ibid., fos 13b–14a.
47. I adapted this translation of Jār Allāh Ibn Fahd al-Makkī, *Al-Nukat*, fos 13a–b, from Ghaly, *Islam and Disability*, p. 101. In the introduction to *Mufīd al-^c^ulūm*, the author al-Qazwīnī, who has been misidentified as al-Khawarizmī, defined his work as 'entertainment for friends'.
48. Jār Allāh Ibn Fahd al-Makkī, *Al-Nukat*, fo. 13b.
49. Al-Hīla, *Al-Ta^ɔ^rīkh*, p. 196; Muḥammad b. Ibrāhīm Ibn al-Ḥanbalī, *Durr al-ḥabab fī ta^ɔ^rīkh a^c^yān ḥalab* (The Pearls of the Beloved: The History of the Notables of Aleppo), ed. Maḥmūd Aḥmad al-Fākhūrī and Yaḥyá Zakariyya ^c^Abāra (Damascus: Wizārat al-thaqāfa, 1972), 1:434.
50. Ibn Ṭūlūn's five-year-old daughter Khadīja had died in the previous month. Ibn al-Mullā al-Ḥaṣkafī, *Mut^c^at*, 1:429; Ibn Ṭūlūn, *I'lām al-wará bi-man wulliya nā^ɔ^iban min al-atrāk bi-dimashq al-shām al-kubrá* (Damascus: Wizārat al-thaqāfa wa'l-irshād al-qawmī, 1964), p. 208; Ibn al-^c^Imād, *Shadharāt*, 10:146.
51. For biographical details on Ibn Ṭūlūn's father-in-law Burhān al-Dīn Ibrāhīm b. Muḥammad b. ^c^Awn al-Shāghūrī al-Ḥanafī (d. 916/1511), see Ibn al-Mullā al-Ḥaṣkafī, *Mut^c^at*, 1:282–3, 2:661; al-Sakhāwī, *Al-Ḍaw^ɔ^*, 1:146–7; Ibn al-^c^Imād, *Shadharāt*, 8:73; and al-Ghazzī, *Kawākib*, 1:13, 260–1; 2:174. He also taught Ibn Ṭūlūn and awarded him an *ijāza* in *iftā^ɔ^* (the deliverance of formal legal opinions) on 29 Rabī^c^ II 911/29 August 1505. See Ibn Ṭūlūn, *Al-Fulk al-mashḥūn fī aḥwāl Muḥammad b. Ṭūlūn*, ed. Muḥammad Khayr Ramaḍān Yūsuf (Beirut: Dār Ibn Ḥazm, 1996), p. 52.
52. Ibn Ṭūlūn, *Mufākahat*, 2:61.
53. Ibn Ṭūlūn, *Al-Rasā'il al-ta'rīkhiyya* (Historical Letters) (Damascus: Maṭba^c^at al-Turqī, 1929), 2:2–4; Ibn Ṭūlūn, *Mufākahat* [1964], 2:6–10, 14.
54. Modern biographers of ^c^Izz al-Dīn have listed his death year as 921/1515, because Ibn Ṭūlūn wrote in *I^c^lām al-wará* about meeting him in Mecca at this time. Before the publication of *Mufākahat al-khillān*, the *I^c^lām* passage was widely accepted as the latest record of ^c^Izz al-Dīn being seen alive.
55. Ibn Ṭūlūn, *Mufākahat* [1964], 2:63.
56. Al-Suyūṭī, *Dhayl ṭabaqāt al-ḥuffāẓ* (Beirut: Dār iḥyā al-turāth al-^c^arabī, 1980), p. 383; Al-Ghazzī, *Kawākib*, 1:67; 2:117, 158.
57. For instance, Jār Allāh wrote to Ibn Ṭūlūn about Muḥammad b. ^c^Irāq's

death and burial in Medina, and his subsequent disinterment and reburial in Mecca in Ṣafar 933/1526 (Al-Ghazzī, *Kawākib*, 1:67); and Jār Allāh Ibn Fahd related this same event in his chronicle of Mecca (*Kitāb nayl al-muná bi-dhayl bulūgh al-qirá li-takmilat itḥāf al-wará: taʾrīkh makka al-mukarrama min sana 922H ilá 946H*, ed. Muḥammad al-Ḥabīb al-Hīla (Riyadh: Muʾassassat al-furqān li'l-turāth al-islāmī, 2000), 1:388–90.

58. Jār Allāh Ibn Fahd al-Makkī, *Al-Nukat*, fo. 14b.
59. He must have acquired it from one of Ibn ʿAbd al-Hādī's children after 922/1516, when he rebuilt his library after Ottoman troops had destroyed his original library.
60. Jār Allāh Ibn Fahd al-Makkī, *Al-Nukat*, fo. 14b. I know of no extant copy of this work.
61. Highlighting the professional incompetence of one's contemporaries did not imply sin. A line of an anonymous untitled manuscript penned in Mecca in Jumādā I 950/1543 reads: 'Our shaykh, the learned memoriser of the Qur'an, Shams al-Dīn al-Sakhāwī reported in his book *Al-Dhayl al-ṭāhir* that Shaykh Shihāb al-Dīn Aḥmad b. Naṣrallāh [d. 844/1440, also known as Muḥibb al-Dīn b. Naṣrallāh al-Baghdādī al-Ḥanbalī] described the defects (*masāwī*) of some of the judges of his time'. (See Staatsbibliothek zu Berlin, Berlin, Germany, MS Ahlwardt 8418, AH 950/1543 CE, fo. 63b.) Although *Al-Dhayl al-ṭāhir* is not extant, other works indicate that Ibn Naṣrallāh, who incidentally was one-eyed, criticised fellow judges of Cairo for their professional ineptitude. See al-Sakhāwī, *Dhayl ʿalá rafʿ al-iṣr*, ed. Jawdah Hilāl and Muḥammad Maḥmūd Ṣubḥ (Cairo: Al-Hayʾah al-miṣriyya al-ʿāmma li'l-kitāb, 2000), p. 116.
62. Al-Ghazzī, *Kawākib*, 2:54; Stephan Conermann, 'Ibn Ṭūlūn (d. 955/1548): Life and Works', *MSR* 8.1 (2004), p. 120; *EI*^{2}, s.v. 'Ibn Ṭūlūn', 3:957.
63. Ibn Mullā al-Ḥaṣkafī, *Mutʿat*, 1:27, 492. On p. 27, ʿUthmān's death date is given as 19 Dhū al-Qaʿada, whereas on p. 492 it is noted as 9 Dhū al-Qaʿada. Since Ibn al-Mullā al-Ḥaṣkafī's text preserves the only currently known biographical notice about ʿUthmān, the precise date of his death remains uncertain without recourse to the copy of *Mutʿat al-adhhān* in the Staatsbibliothek zu Berlin, MS no. 9888.
64. Ibid., 2:870, 876–7.
65. Jār Allāh Ibn Fahd al-Makkī, *Al-Nukat*, fo. 59a. The sole surviving manuscript is Jār Allāh's autograph copy, which is currently housed in the Chester Beatty Library, Dublin, Ireland, MS 3838, AH 950/1543 CE. For a description of the manuscript, see Arthur J. Arberry, *The Chester Beatty Library: A Handlist of the Arabic Manuscripts* (Dublin: Hodges Figgis & Co. Ltd, 1949), 4:26; al-Hīla, *Taʾrīkh*, pp. 208–9.
66. Jār Allāh's autograph notes that begin in the left margin on fo. 24a and snake clockwise across the upper margins of fos 24a and 23b, down the right margin of fo. 23b and across the bottom margins of fos 23b and 24a name more individuals with *ʿāhāt*.

67. Jār Allāh Ibn Fahd al-Makkī, *Al-Nukat*, fos 2a, 15a. Though not a contemporary, Ibn Fahd also named someone who had special significance to his family. In the margion of fo. 2a, he mentioned Muḥammad b. Aḥmad b. al-Raḍī Ibrāhīm Abū al-Yumn al-Ṭabarī (d. 809/1406), a preacher at Mecca's Holy Mosque who had taught hadith to Taqī al-Dīn b. Fahd. On him, see al-Fāsī, *Al-ᶜIqd al-thamīn fī taʾrīkh al-balad al-amīn*, ed. Muḥammad Ḥāmid al-Fiqī (Beirut: Muʾassassat al-risāla, 1986), 1:282–5, 8:113; al-Sakhāwī, *al-Ḍawʾ*, 6:287–8; Ibn Ḥajar al-ᶜAsqalānī, *Inbāʾ* [1998], 2:373.
68. Ibid., fos 15a, 42a.
69. Ibn al-ᶜUlayf al-Makkī, Shihāb al-Dīn Aḥmad b. al-Ḥusayn, *Al-Dīwān*, Kongelige Bibliothek, Copenhagen, Denmark, MS Cod. Arab. 244, fo. 20a. Cf. Qur'an 48: 17.
70. Ibid., fo. 13a.
71. Ibid., fo. 58b.
72. Lagrange, 'Obscenity', p. 175.
73. Al-Ghazzī, *Kawākib*, 1:131.
74. Al-Shillī, *Kitāb al-sanāʾ*, p. 567; Abū al-Khayr, *Al-Mukhtaṣar*, p. 150.
75. El-Rouayheb, *Before Homosexuality*, p. 50.
76. Yossef Rapoport, *Marriage, Money and Divorce in Medieval Islamic Society* (Cambridge: Cambridge University Press, 1999), p. 49. As a note, al-Ḥijāzī's epigrams on spinners appear in his Al-Kunnas *al-jawārī*, the same collection containing verses on physically marked women.

Bibliography

Unpublished Primary Sources

Anonymous. Untitled. Staatsbibliothek zu Berlin. Berlin, Germany. MS Ahlwardt 8418. AH 950/CE 1543.

al-ᶜAṭṭār al-Isrāʾīlī, Abū Naṣr. *Kitāb minhāj al-dukkān wa-dustūr al-aᶜyān fī aᶜmāl wa-tarkīb al-adawiyya al-nāfiᶜa li'l-abdān*. Bibliotheca Alexandrina. Alexandria, Egypt. MS 5146. AH 1279/1862 CE.

al-Badrī Taqī al-Dīn. *Ghurrat al-ṣabāḥ fī waṣf al-wujūh al-ṣibāḥ*. British Library. London, England. MS 1423 (add. 23,445). 875/1471.

al-Ḥijāzī al-Khazrajī, Shihāb al-Dīn Aḥmad b. Muḥammad. *Nawādir al-akhbār wa-ẓarāʾif al-ashᶜār*. Panjab University Library, India.

al-Ḥijāzī al-Khazrajī, Shihāb al-Dīn Aḥmad b. Muḥammad. *Nayl al-rāʾid fī al-nīl al-zāʾid*. Bankipore Public Library. Bankipore, India. MS 1069.

Ibn ᶜAbd al-Hādī, Yūsuf. *Kitāb al-ḍabṭ wa'l-tabyīn li-dhawī al-ᶜilal wa'l-ᶜāhāt min al-muḥaddithīn*. Al-Asad Library. Damascus, Syria. MS 3216. Folios 157a–168a. AH 889 or 890/1484 or 1485 CE.

Ibn Fahd al-Hāshimī al-Makkī, Muḥibb al-Dīn Jār Allāh. *Al-Nukat al-ẓirāf fī al-mawʾiẓa bi dhawī al-ᶜāhāt min al-ashrāf*. Chester Beatty Library. Dublin, Ireland, MS 3838. 950/1543.

Ibn Ṭūlūn, Shams al-Dīn Muḥammad. *Kitāb al-arbaᶜīn ᶜan arbaᶜīn shaykhan*. Al-Asad Library. Damascus, Syria. MS 958.

Ibn al-ᶜUlayf al-Makkī, Shihāb al-Dīn Aḥmad b. al-Ḥusayn. *Al-Dīwān*. Kongelige Bibliothek. Copenhagen, Denmark. MS Cod. Arab. 244.

Kitāb al-diryāq. Österreichische Nationalbibliothek. Vienna, Austria. MS A.F. 10.

Kitāb al-sumūm/Kitāb al-diryāq. Sold to a private collector at Sotheby's as Lot 21 on 25 April 2002. London, England. 622/1225.

Published Primary Sources

al-ᶜAṭṭār al-Isrāʾīlī, Abū Naṣr. *Kitāb minhāj al-dukkān wa-dustūr al-aᶜyān fī aᶜmāl wa-tarkīb al-adawiyya al-nāfiᶜa li'l-abdān*, ed. by Ḥasan Zaghla. Frankfurt: Maᶜhad Taʾrīkh al-Ulūm al-ᶜArabiyya wa'l-Islāmīyah fī iṭār Jāmiᶜat Frānkfūrt, 1997.

al-ᶜAydarūsī, ᶜAbd al-Qādir b. Shaykh b. ᶜAbd Allāh. *Taʾrīkh nūr al-sāfir ᶜan akhbār al-qarn al-ᶜāshir*. Egypt: s.n., 1980–6.

al-ʿAynī Badr al-Dīn Maḥmūd. *ʿIqd al-jumān fī taʾrīkh ahl al-zamān*, ed. Muḥammad Muḥammad Amīn. 4 vols. Cairo: Hayʾat al-miṣriyya al-ʿāmma li'l-kitāb, 1987.

al-Badrī, Taqī al-Dīn. *Al-Durr al-maṣūn, al-musammá bi-Siḥr al-ʿuyūn*. 2 vols, ed. by Sayyid Ṣiddīq ʿAbd al-Fattāḥ. Cairo: Dār al-shaʿb, 1998.

al-Badrī, Taqī al-Dīn. *Nuzhat al-anām fī maḥāsin al-shām*. Cairo: Al-Maṭbaʿat al-salafiyya, 1922–3.

al-Badrī, Taqī al-Dīn. *Description de Damas*. 2 vols, ed. and trans. H. Sauvaire. Paris: Imprimente Nationale, 1896 (trans. of fos 49a–93a of MS ARAB 2253.2, housed at Bibliothèque Nationale de Paris, France).

al-Bayhaqī, Abū Bakr. *Manāqib al-Shāfiʿī*. 2 vols, ed. al-Sayyid Aḥmad Saqr. Cairo: Dār al-turāth, 1971.

al-Biqāʿī, Burhān al-Dīn Ibrāhīm. *ʿInwān al-zamān bi-tarājim al-shuyūkh wa'l-aqrān*. 4 vols, ed. Ḥasan Ḥabashī. Cairo: Dār al-kutub wa'l-wathāʾiq al-qawmiyya, 2001.

al-Biqāʿī, Burhān al-Dīn Ibrāhīm. *Iẓhār al-ʿaṣr li-asrār ahl al-ʿaṣr: taʾrīkh al-Biqāʿī*. 3 vols, ed. Muḥammad Sālim b. Shadīd al-ʿAwfī. Giza: Hajar li'l-ṭibāʿa wa'l-nashr wa'l-tawzī, 1992–.

al-Biqāʿī, Burhān al-Dīn Ibrāhīm. *Naẓm al-durar fī tanāsub al-āyāt wa-suwar*. 7 vols. Hyderabad: Maṭbaʿa majlis dāʾirat al-maʿārif al-ʿuthmāniyya, 2006.

al-Biqāʿī, Burhān al-Dīn Ibrāhīm. *ʿUnwān al-ʿunwān bi-tajrīd asmāʾ al-shuyūkh wa-baʿḍ al-talāmidha wa'l-aqrān*. Beirut: Dār al-kitāb al-ʿarabī, 2002.

al-Bukhārī, Muḥammad b. Ismāʾīl. *Ṣaḥīḥ al-Bukhārī: The Translation of the Meanings of Ṣaḥīḥ al-Bukhārī*. 9 vols, trans. Muḥammad Muḥsin Khān. Beirut: Dār al-ʿarabiyya, 1985.

Burton, Richard F. (trans.) *The Book of the Thousand Nights and a Night: A Plain and Literal Translation of the Arabian Nights Entertainment*. 10 vols. London: The Burton Club, 1900.

al-Dhahabī, Muḥammad b. Aḥmad. *Kitāb tadhkirat al-ḥuffāẓ*. 4 vols. Hyderabad: Maṭbāʿa dāʾirat al-maʿārif al-niẓāmiyya, 1914–15.

al-Dhahabī, Muḥammad b. Aḥmad, Taqī al-Dīn Muḥammad b. Fahd al-Makkī and al-Suyūṭī. *Kitāb tadhkirat al-ḥuffāẓ*. Beirut: Dār al-kutub al-ʿilmiyya, 1998.

al-Fāsī, Taqī al-Dīn Muḥammad b. Aḥmad. *Al-ʿIqd al-thamīn fī taʾrīkh al-balad al-amīn*. 8 vols, ed. Muḥammad Ḥāmid al-Fiqī. Beirut: Muʾassassat al-risāla, 1986.

al-Fīrūzābādī. *Al-Qamūs al-muḥīṭ*. Cairo: s.n., 1855.

al-Ghassānī, Abū Muḥammad al-Qāsim. *Ḥadīqat al-azhār fī māhiyyat al-ʿushb wa'l-ʿaqqār*, ed. Muḥammad al-ʿArabī al-Khaṭṭābī. Beirut: Dār al-gharb al-islāmī, 1985.

al-Ghazzī, Najm al-Dīn. *Kawākib al-sāʾira bi-aʿyān al-miʾah al-ʿashira*. 3 vols, ed. Jibrāʾil Sulaymān Jabbūr. Beirut: Al-Maṭbaʿat al-amīrikāniyya, 1945.

al-Ḥijāzī al-Khazrajī, Shihāb al-Dīn Aḥmad b. Muḥammad. *Al-Kunnas al-jawārī fī al-ḥisān min al-jawārī, wa-bi-dhaylihi, Jannat al-wuldān fī al-ḥisān min al-ghilmān*, ed. Rajāb ʿAkkāwī. Beirut: Dār al-ḥarf al-ʿarabī, 1998.

Hosain, Hidayet. 'Translation of *Ash-Shamaʾil* of Tirmizi'. *Islamic Culture* 7 (July 1933): 395–421.

Hosain, Hidayet. 'Translation of *Ash-Shamaʾil* of Tirmizi'. *Islamic Culture* 8 (July 1934): 364–86.

Ibn Abī Uṣaybiʿa. *Kitāb ʿuyūn al-anbāʾ fī ṭabaqāt al-aṭibbaʾ*, ed. Umruʾ al-Qays b. al-Ṭaḥḥān. Egypt: Maṭbaʿat al-wahbiyya, 1882.

Ibn al-Aḥmar al-Naṣrī, Ismāʿīl b. Yūsuf. *Nathīr farāʾid al-jumān fī Naẓm fuḥūl al-zamān*. Beirut: Dār al-thaqāfa li'l-ṭibāʿa wa'l-nashr wa'l-tawzīʿ, 1967.

Ibn al-Athīr, Majd al-Dīn. *Nihāya fī al-gharīb al-ḥadīth wa'l-athar.* 5 vols. Beirut: Dār iḥyāʾ al-turāth al-ʿarabī, 1985.

Ibn Bashkuwāl. *Kitāb al-ṣilah fī taʾrīkh aʾimmat al-andalus wa-ʿulamāʾihim wa-muḥaddithīhim wa-fuqahāʾihim wa-udabāʾihim.* 2 vols, ed. Francisco Codera y Zaidin. Madrid: Rojas, 1882.

Ibn al-Bayṭār. *Kitāb al-jāmiʿ li-mufradāt al-adwiyya wa'l-aghdhiyya.* 4 vols in 2. Beirut: Dār al-Madīna, s.d.

Ibn Fahd al-Hāshimī al-Makkī, Muḥibb al-Dīn Jār Allāh. *Kitāb nayl al-muná bi-dhayl bulūgh al-qirá li-takmilat itḥāf al-wará: taʾrīkh makka al-mukarrama min sana 922H ilá 946H.* 2 vols, ed. Muḥammad al-Ḥabīb al-Hīla. Riyadh: Muʾassasat al-furqān li'l-turāth al-islāmī, 2000.

Ibn Fahd al-Hāshimī al-Makkī, Taqī al-Dīn. *Laḥẓ al-alḥāẓ bi-dhayl ṭabaqāt al-ḥuffāẓ*. Beirut: Dār iḥyāʾ al-turāth al-ʿarabī, s.d.

Ibn Fahd al-Hāshimī al-Makkī, ʿUmar. *Muʿjam al-shuyūkh*, ed. Muḥammad al-Zāhī. Riyadh: Manshūrāt Dār al-Yamāma li'l-baḥth wa'l-tarjama wa'l-nashr, 1982.

Ibn al-Furāt, Muḥammad b. ʿAbd al-Raḥīm. *Taʾrīkh Ibn al-Furāt*. 4 vols (vols 9, 10, 14 and 17). Basra: Maṭbaʿa ḥaddād, 1967.

Ibn Ḥabīb, Muḥammad. *Kitāb al-muḥabbar*, ed. Ilse Lichtenstadter. Beirut: Manshūrāt al-maktab al-tijārī li'l-ṭibāʿa wa'l-nashr, 1942.

Ibn Ḥabīb, Muḥammad. *Kitāb al-munammaq fī akhbār Quraysh*, ed. Khvurshid Aḥmad Fariq. Beirut: ʿAlam al-kitāb, 1985.

Ibn Ḥabīb al-Ḥalabī, Badr al-Dīn al-Ḥasan. *Al-Najm al-thāqib fī ashraf al-manāqib*, ed. Muṣṭafā Muḥammad Ḥusayn al-Dhahabī. Cairo: Dār al-Ḥadīth, 1996.

Ibn Ḥajar al-ʿAsqalānī, Aḥmad b. ʿAlī. *Dīwān Shaykh al-Islām Ibn Ḥajar al-ʿAsqalānī*, ed. Firdaws Nūr ʿAlī Ḥusayn. Cairo: Dār al-faḍīla, 2000.

Ibn Ḥajar al-ʿAsqalānī, Aḥmad b. ʿAlī. *Al-Durar al-kamina fī aʿyān al-miʾat al-thāmina.* 5 vols. Beirut: Dār al-Jīl, 1993.

Ibn Ḥajar al-ʿAsqalānī, Aḥmad b. ʿAlī. *Inbāʾ al-ghumr bi-anbāʾ al-ʿumr*. 3 vols, ed. Ḥasan al-Ḥabashī. Cairo: s.n., 1969–72.

Ibn Ḥajar al-Haytamī, Aḥmad b. Muḥammad. *Al-Fatāwá al-kubrá al-fiqhiyya.* 4 vols. Cairo: ʿAbd al-Ḥamīd Aḥmad Ḥanafī, 1938.

Ibn al-Ḥanbalī, Muḥammad b. Ibrāhīm. *Baḥr al-ʿawwām fīmā aṣāba fīhi al-ʿawāmm*. Cairo: Dār al-thaqāfat al-ʿarabiyya, 1990.

Ibn al-Ḥanbalī, Muḥammad b. Ibrāhīm. *Durr al-ḥabab fī taʾrīkh aʿyān ḥalab*. 2

vols, ed. Maḥmūd Aḥmad al-Fākhūrī and Yaḥyá Zakariyya ᶜAbāra. Damascus: Wizārat al-thaqāfa, 1972.
Ibn al-Ḥimṣī, Shihāb al-Dīn Aḥmad. *Ḥawādith al-zamān wa-wafayyāt al-shuyūkh wa'l-aqrān.* 3 vols, ed. ᶜUmar ᶜAbd al-Salām Tadmurī. Ṣaydā/Beirut: Al-Maktabat al-ᶜaṣriyya, 1999.
Ibn Hindū, Abū al-Faraj ᶜAlī b. al-Ḥusayn. *Miftāḥ al-ṭibb wa-minhāj al-ṭullāb*, trans. Aida Tibi, ed. Emilie Savage-Smith. Reading: Garnet Publishing, 2010.
Ibn Hishām. *The Life of Muḥammad: A Translation of Isḥāq's Sīrat Rasūl Allāh*, trans. A. Guillaume. Lahore and Karachi: Oxford University Press, 1967.
Ibn Hishām al-Lakhmī. *Madkhal ilá taqwīm al-lisān wa-taᶜlīm al-bayān*, ed. Maᵓmūn b. Muḥyī al-Dīn al-Jannān. Beirut: Dār al-kutub al-ᶜilmiyya, 1995.
Ibn al-ᶜImād, ᶜAbd al-Ḥayy b. Aḥmad. *Shadharāt al-dhahab fī akhbār man dhahab.* 10 vols. Damascus/Beirut: Dār Ibn Kathīr, 1986–.
Ibn Iyās, Muḥammad b. Aḥmad al-Ḥanafī. *Badāᵓiᶜ al-zuhūr fī waqāᵓīᶜ al-duhūr.* 16 vols, ed. Muḥammad Muṣṭafá. Cairo: s.n., 1960.
Ibn al-Jawzī, ᶜAbd al-Raḥmān. *Talqīḥ fuhūm ahl al-athar fī ᶜuyūn al-taᵓrīkh wa'l-siyar.* Cairo: Maktabat al-ādāb, 1975.
Ibn Khalīl b. Shāhīn al-Ẓāhirī al-Ḥanafī, Zayn al-Dīn ᶜAbd al-Bāsit. *Nayl al-amal fī dhayl al-duwal.* 9 vols, ed. ᶜUmar ᶜAbd al-Salām Tadmurī. Ṣaydā/Beirut: Al-Maktabat al-ᶜaṣriyya, 2002.
Ibn Khallikān, *Wafayāt al-aᶜyān wa-anbāᵓ abnāᵓ al-zamān.* 8 vols, ed. Iḥsān ᶜAbbās. Beirut: Dār ṣādir, 1968–77.
Ibn Kinnān, Muḥammad b. ᶜĪsá. *Al-Murūj al-sundusiyya al-fasīḥa fī talkhīs Taᵓrīkh al-Ṣāliḥiyya*, ed. Muḥammad Aḥmad Dahmān. Damascus: Maṭbaᶜa al-taraqī, 1947.
Ibn Manẓūr, Muḥammad b. Mukarram. *Lisān al-ᶜarab.* 15 vols. Beirut: Dār ṣādir, 1956.
Ibn al-Mullā al-Ḥaṣkafī. *Mutᶜat al-adhhān min al-Tammatuᶜ bi'l-iqrān bayna tarājim al-shuyūkh wa'l-aqrān* [= extracts from Ibn Ṭūlūn's *Al-Tammatuᶜ bi'l-iqrān bayna tarājim al-shuyūkh wa'l-aqrān*]. 2 vols, ed. Ṣalāḥ al-Dīn Khalīl al-Shaybānī al-Mawṣilī. Beirut: Dār ṣādir, 1999.
Ibn Qayyim al-Jawziyya. *Medicine of the Prophet*, trans. Penelope Johnstone. Cambridge: Islamic Texts Society, 1998.
Ibn al-Qiftī, Jamāl al-Dīn. *Inbāh al-ruwāh ᶜalá anbāh al-nuḥāh.* 4 vols, ed. Muḥammad Abū al-Faḍl. Cairo: Dār al-kutub al-miṣriyya, 1950.
Ibn Qutayba. *Ādab al-kātib*, ed. M. Grünert. Leiden: E. J. Brill, 1900.
Ibn Qutayba. *Kitāb al-maᶜārif.* Cairo: s.n., 1882.
Ibn Qutayba. *Kitāb al-maᶜārif*, ed. Tarwat ᶜUkāsha. Cairo: Dār al-maᶜārif, 1969.
Ibn Qutayba. *Kitāb ᶜuyūn al-akhbār.* 4 vols. Cairo: Dār al-kutub al-miṣriyya, 1925–30.
Ibn Rajab, ᶜAbd al-Raḥmān b. Aḥmad. *Al-Dhayl ᶜalá ṭabaqāt al-ḥanābila.* 2 vols, ed. Muḥammad Ḥamīd al-Faqī. Cairo: Maṭbaᶜat al-sunna al-muḥammadiyya, 1952–3.

Ibn Rusta, Aḥmad b. ᶜUmar. *Kitāb al-aᶜlāq al-nafīsa*, ed. M. J. de Goeje. Leiden: E. J. Brill, 1891.

Ibn Taghrībirdī. *Ḥawādith al-duhūr fī madá al-ayyām wa'l-shuhūr*. 2 vols. Cairo: Lajnat iḥyāᵓ al-turāth al-islāmī, 1990.

Ibn Taghrībirdī. *Al-Nujūm al-ẓāhira fī mulūk miṣr wa'l-qāhira*. 16 vols. Cairo: s.n., 1929.

Ibn Ṭūlūn, Shams al-Dīn Muḥammad. *Al-Fulk al-mashḥūn fī aḥwāl Muḥammad b. Ṭūlūn*, ed. Muḥammad Khayr Ramaḍān Yūsuf. Beirut: Dār Ibn Ḥazm, 1996.

Ibn Ṭūlūn, Shams al-Dīn Muḥammad. *Iᶜlām al-wará bi-man wulliya nāᵓiban min al-atrāk bi-dimashq al-shām al-kubrá*. Damascus: Wizārat al-thaqāfa wa'l-irshād al-qawmī, 1964.

Ibn Ṭūlūn, Shams al-Dīn Muḥammad. *Mufākahat al-khillān fī ḥawādith al-zamān: taᵓrīkh Miṣr wa'l-Shām*. 2 vols, ed. Muḥammad Muṣṭafá. Cairo: Al-Muᵓassassat al-miṣriyya al-ᶜāmmah li'l-taᵓlīf wa'l-tarjama wa'l-ṭibāᶜ wa'l-nashr, 1964.

Ibn Ṭūlūn, Shams al-Dīn Muḥammad. *Mufākahat al-khillān fī ḥawādith al-zamān: taᵓrīkh Miṣr wa'l-Shām*. Beirut: Dār al-kutub al-ᶜilmlyya, 1998.

Ibn Ṭūlūn, Shams al-Dīn Muḥammad. *Al-Qalāᵓid al-jawhariyya fī taᵓrīkh al-Ṣāliḥiyya*. 2 vols, ed. Muḥammad Aḥmad Dahmān. Damascus: s.n., 1949–56.

Ibn Ṭūlūn, Shams al-Dīn Muḥammad. *Al-Rasāᵓil al-taᵓrīkhiyya*. 4 vols. Damascus: Maṭbaᶜat al-Turqī, 1929.

Ibn al-Ukhuwwa. *The Maᶜālim al-Qurba fī Aḥkām al-Ḥisba of Ḍiyaᵓ al-Dīn Muḥammad ibn Muḥammad al-Qurashī al-Shāfiᶜī, known as Ibn al-Ukhuwwa*, ed. and trans. Reuben Levy. London: Luzac & Co., 1938.

Ibn Waḥshiyya. *Medieval Arabic Toxicology: The Book of Poisons of Ibn Waḥshiyya and Its Relation to Early Indian and Greek Texts*, trans. Martin Levey. Philadelphia: American Philosophical Society, 1966.

al-Ibshīhī, Shihāb al-Dīn Muḥammad b. Aḥmad. *Mustaṭraf fī kull fann mustaẓraf*, ed. Muṣṭafá Muḥammad al-Dhahabī. Cairo: Dār al-ḥadīth, 2000.

al-ᶜĪyāḍ b. Mūsā, Qāḍī. *Al-Shifāᵓ bi-taᶜrīf ḥuqūq al-Muṣṭafá*. 2 vols, ed. Alī Muḥammad al-Bajāwī. Cairo: Maṭbaᶜat ᶜīsa al-bābī al-ḥalabī, 1977.

al-Jāḥiẓ, Abū ᶜUthmān. *Al-Bayān wa'l-tabyīn*. 4 vols, ed. ᶜAbd al-Salām Muḥammad Hārūn. Cairo: Maktabat al-khānjī, 1968.

al-Jāḥiẓ, Abū ᶜUthmān. *Kitāb al-burṣān wa'l-'urjān wa'l-'umyān wa'l-ḥūlān*, ed. Muḥammad Mursī al-Khawlī. Cairo/Beirut: s.n., 1972.

al-Jāḥiẓ, Abū ᶜUthmān. *Kitāb al-burṣān wa'l-'urjān wa'l-'umyān wa'l-ḥūlān,* ed. ᶜAbd al-Salām Muḥammad Hārūn. Beirut: Dār al-jīl, 1990.

al-Jarīrī, Muᶜāfá b. Zakariyyā. *Al-Jalīs al-ṣāliḥ al-kāfī wa'l-anīs al-nāṣiḥ al-shāfī*. 4 vols, ed. Muḥammad Mursī Khawlī. Beirut: ᶜĀlam al-kutub, 1987.

al-Jawbarī, ᶜAbd al-Raḥmān. *Mukhtār kashf al-asrār wa-hatk al-astār*. Beirut: Dār taḍmūn, 1992.

al-Jawharī, Abū Naṣr. *Ṣiḥāḥ al-lughah*. 7 vols. Beirut: Dār al-kutub al-ᶜilmiyya, 1999.

al-Khaṭīb al-Baghdādī. *Kitāb mūḍiḥ awhām al-jamᶜ wa'l-tafrīq*. 2 vols. Hyderabad: Maṭbaᶜat al-ᶜuthmāniyya, 1959.

al-Khawārizmī, Jamāl al-Dīn (misattributed). *Kitāb mufīd al-ᶜulūm wa-mubīd al-humūm*, ed. ᶜAbdallāh b. Ibrāhīm al-Anṣārī. Ṣaydā and Beirut: Manshūrat al-maktabat al-ᶜaṣriyya, 1980.

al-Manṣūrī al-Dawādar, Rukn al-Dīn Baybars. *Zubdat al-fikra fī taᵓrīkh al-hijra*, ed. Donald S. Richards. Beirut: Al-Sharikat al-muttaḥida li'l-tawzīᶜ, 1998.

al-Maqqarī, Aḥmad b. Muḥammad. *Al-Nafḥ al-ṭīb min ghuṣn al-andalus al-raṭīb*. 8 vols, ed. Iḥsan ᶜAbbās. Beirut: Dār ṣādir, 1968.

al-Maqrīzī, Taqī al-Dīn Aḥmad. *Kitāb al-khiṭaṭ al-maqrīziyya*. 3 vols. Cairo: s.n., 1959.

al-Maqrīzī, Taqī al-Dīn Aḥmad. *Kitāb al-sulūk li-maᶜrifat duwal al-mulūk*. 4 vols, ed. Muḥammad Muṣṭafá Ziyāda and Saᶜīd ᶜAbd al-Fattāḥ al-ᶜAshūr. Cairo: Lajnat al-taᵓlīf wa'l-tarjama wa'l-nashr, 1934, repr. in 1956.

al-Nawawī. *Kitāb al-adhkār*, ed. Muḥammad Fayyāḍ al-Barūrī. Damascus: Dar al-Mallāḥ, 1971.

al-Nuᶜaymī, ᶜAbd al-Qādir b. Muḥammad. *Al-Dāris fī taᵓrīkh al-madāris*. 2 vols. Damascus: Maṭbaᶜat al-taraqī, 1948.

al-Nuwayrī, Shihāb al-Dīn Aḥmad b. ᶜAbd al-Wahhāb. *Nihāyat al-arab fī funūn al-adab*. 33 vols. Cairo: Maṭbaᶜat dār al-kutub al-miṣriyya, 1923.

al-Qasṭallānī, Aḥmad b. Muḥammad. *Al-Mawāhib al-laduniyya bi'l-minaḥ al-muḥammadiyya*. 4 vols, ed. Ṣāliḥ Aḥmad al-Shāmī. Beirut: Al-Maktab al-islāmī, 1991.

al-Qurṭubī, Muḥammad b. Aḥmad. *Al-Jāmiᶜ li-aḥkām al-Qurᵓān*. 20 vols. Cairo: Dār al-kitāb al-ᶜarabī li-ṭibāᶜa wa-nashr, 1967.

al-Rāfiᶜī, ᶜAbd al-Karīm. *Al-Tadwīn fī akhbār qazwīn*. 4 vols, ed. ᶜAzizallāh al-ᶜAṭāradī. Beirut: Dar al-kutub al-ᶜilmiyya, 1987.

al-Rāzī, Fakhr al-Dīn. *Manāqib al-Shāfiᶜī*. Egypt: Al-Maktabat al-ᶜalāmiyya, 1862.

al-Rāzī, Ibn Abī Ḥātim. *Ādāb al-Shāfiᶜī*, ed. ᶜAbd al-Ghānī ᶜAbd al-Khāliq. Beirut: Dār al-kutub al-ᶜilmiyya, 1953.

al-Ṣafadī, Khalīl b. Aybak. *Faḍḍ al-khitām ᶜan al-tawriyya wa'l-istikhdām*, ed. al-Muḥammadī ᶜAbd al-ᶜAzīz al-Ḥinnāwī. Cairo: s.n., 1979.

al-Ṣafadī, Khalīl b. Aybak. *Al-Ḥusn al-ṣarīḥ fī miᵓat malīḥ*, ed. Aḥmad Fawzī Hayb. Damascus: Dār Saᶜd al-Dīn, 2003.

al-Sakhāwī, Muḥammad b. ᶜAbd al-Raḥmān. *Al-Ḍawᵓ al-lāmiᶜ li-ahl al-qarn al-tāsiᶜ*. 12 vols. Beirut: Dār maktabat al-hayāt, 1966.

al-Sakhāwī, Muḥammad b. ᶜAbd al-Raḥmān. *Dhayl ᶜalá rafᶜ al-iṣr*, ed. Jawdah Hilāl and Muḥammad Maḥmūd Ṣubḥ. Cairo: Al-Hayᵓah al-miṣriyya al-ᶜāmma li'l-kitāb, 2000.

al-Sakhāwī, Muḥammad b. ᶜAbd al-Raḥmān. *Al-Dhayl al-tām ᶜalá Duwal al-islām li'l-Dhahabī*. 3 vols, ed. Ḥasan Ismāᵓīl Marwa. Beirut: Dār Ibn al-ᶜImād, 1992–.

al-Sakhāwī, Muḥammad b. ᶜAbd al-Raḥmān. *Al-Jawāhir wa'l-durar fī tarjama Shaykh al-Islām Ibn Ḥajar*. 3 vols. Beirut: Dār Ibn Ḥazm, 1999.

al-Sakhāwī, Muḥammad b. ᶜAbd al-Raḥmān. *Kitāb al-tibr al-masbūk fī tawārīkh al-mulūk*. Cairo: Maktabat al-kulliyāt al-azhariyya, 1972.

al-Sakhāwī, Muḥammad b. ᶜAbd al-Raḥmān. *Al-Maqāṣid al-ḥasana fī bayān kathīr min al-aḥādīth al-mushtahirat al-alsinah*. Egypt: Maktabat al-khānijī, 1956.

al-Sakhāwī, Muḥammad b. ᶜAbd al-Raḥmān. *Wajīz al-kalām fī al-Dhayl ᶜalá Duwal al-islām*. 4 vols, ed. Bashār Maᶜrūf, Aḥmad al-Khaṭīmī and ᶜIṣām Fāris al-Ḥarastānī. Beirut: Muᵓassassat al-risāla, 1995.

Sarī al-Raffā, Abū al-Ḥasan b. Aḥmad. *Al-Muḥibb wa'l-maḥbūb wa'l-mashmūm wa'l-mashrūb*. 4 vols, ed. Miṣbāḥ Ghalāwinjī. Damascus: Majmaᶜ al-lughat al-'arabiyya, 1986.

al-Ṣayrafī, ᶜAlī b. Dāwūd. *Inbāᵓ al-haṣr bi-anbāᵓ al-ᶜaṣr*, ed. Ḥasan Ḥabashī. Cairo: Dār al-fikr al-ᶜarabī, 1970.

al-Ṣayrafī, ᶜAlī b. Dāwūd. *Nuzhat al-nufūs wa'l-abdān fī tawārīkh al-zamān*. 4 vols, ed. Ḥasan Ḥabashī. Cairo: Wizārat al-thaqāfa, markaz taḥqīq al-turāth, 1970–94.

al-Shāfiᶜī, Muḥammad b. Idrīs. *Dīwān al-Imām al-Shāfiᶜī*, ed. Imīl Badīᶜ Yaᶜqūb. Beirut: Dār al-kitāb al-ᶜarabī, 1991.

al-Shillī, Muḥammad b. Abī Bakr. *Kitāb al-sanāᵓ al-bāhir bi-takmīl al-Nūr al-sāfir fī akhbār al-qarn al-ᶜāshir*, ed. Ibrāhīm b. Aḥmad al-Maqḥafī. Sanaa: Maktabat al-irshād, 2004.

al-Suyūṭī, Jalāl al-Dīn. *Dhayl ṭabaqāt al-ḥuffāẓ*. Beirut: Dār iḥyā al-turāth al-ᶜarabī, 1980.

al-Suyūṭī, Jalāl al-Dīn. *Naẓm al-ᶜiqyān fī aᶜyān al-aᶜyān*, ed. Philip K. Hitti. New York: Syrian-American Press, 1927.

al-Ṭabarī, ᶜAlī b. Sahl Rabbān. *Firdaws al-ḥikma fī al-ṭibb,* ed. Muḥammad Zubayr al-Ṣiddīqī. Berlin: Maṭbaᶜ Āftāb, 1928.

al-Tawḥīdī, Abū Ḥayyān. *Al-Baṣāᵓir wa'l-dhakhāᵓir*. 9 vols in 5, ed. Wadād al-Qāḍī. Beirut: Dār ṣādir, 1988.

al-Thaᶜālibī, ᶜAbd al-Malik. *The Laṭāᵓif al-maᶜarif of Thaᶜālibī: The Book of Curious and Entertaining Information*, trans. C. E. Bosworth. Edinburgh: Edinburgh University Press, 1968.

al-Thaᶜālibī, ᶜAbd al-Malik. *Kitāb laṭāᵓif al-maᶜarif*, ed. Pieter de Jong. Lugduni Batavorum: Brill, 1867.

al-Thaᶜālibī, ᶜAbd al-Raḥmān. *Al-Jawāhir al-ḥisān fī tafsīr al-Qurᵓān*. 5 vols, ed. ᶜAmmār al-Ṭālbanī. Algiers: Al-Muᵓassasat al-waṭaniyya li'l-kitāb, 1985.

al-Tirmidhī, Muḥammad b. ᶜĪsā. *Al-Shamāᵓil al-muḥammadiyya*, ed. Muḥammad ᶜAwwāma. Medina: s.n., 2001.

al-Zabīdī, Muḥammad Murtaḍā. *Tāj al-ᶜarūs min jawāhir al-qāmūs*. 10 vols. Jamāliyya, Egypt: Al-Maṭbaᶜat al-khariyya, 1888.

al-Zamakhsharī, Abū al-Qāsim Muḥammad b. ᶜUmar. *Rabīᶜ al-abrār fī nuṣūṣ al-akhbār*. 5 vols, ed. ^{c}Abd al-Amīr Mihnā. Beirut: Muʾassassat al-a^{c}lamī li'l-maṭbū^{c}āt, 1992.

Secondary Sources

^{c}Abbās, Waḍī Allāh b. Muḥammad. 'Al-^{c}illah', in Aḥmad b. Ḥanbal. *Kitāb al-^{c}ilal wa-ma^{c}rifat al-rijāl*, pp. 31–44, ed. Waḍī Allāh b. Muḥammad ^{c}Abbās. Riyadh: Dār al-khānī, 2001.

Abdelshafy, Ashraf. 'Imagination of the Blind'. *Banipal* 25 (Spring 2006): 105–6.

Abū al-Khayr, ^{c}Abd Allāh Murdād. *Al-Mukhtaṣar min kitāb nashr al-nūr wa'l-zahr fī tarājim afāḍil Makka*, ed. Muḥammad Sa^{c}īd al-^{c}Āmūdī and Aḥmad ^{c}Alī. Jiddah: ^{c}Ālam al-ma^{c}rifa, 1986.

Afshārī, Mihran and Mahdī Madāyanī, *Chahārdeh risāleh dar bābe futuvvate va aṣnaf.* Tehran: Chashmah, 2002.

Ahmed, Leila. 'Arab Culture and Writing Women's Bodies'. *Feminist Issues* 9.1 (1989): 41–55.

^{c}Akkāwī, Rajāb. '^{c}Amalnā fī risālatayn', in Shihāb al-Dīn al-Ḥijāzī. *Al-Kunnas al-jawārī fī al-ḥisān min al-jawārī, wa-bi-dhaylihi, Jannat al-wuldān fī al-ḥisān min al-ghilmān*, pp. 17–18, ed. Rajāb 'Akkāwī. Beirut: Dār al-ḥarf al-^{c}arabī, 1998.

Ali, Samer. *Arabic Literary Salons in the Islamic Middle Ages: Poetry, Public Performance, and the Presentation of the Past.* Notre Dame: University of Notre Dame Press, 2010.

Ali, Wijdan. 'From the Literal to the Spiritual: The Development of the Prophet Muḥammad's Portrayal from 13th-Century Ilkhanid Miniatures to 17th-Century Ottoman Art'. *Electronic Journal of Oriental Studies* 4 (2001): 1–24.

Amer, Sahar. 'Medieval Arab Lesbians and Lesbian-Like Women'. *Journal of the History of Sexuality* 18.2 (2009): 215–36.

Andrews, Walter and Mehmet Kalpaklı. *The Age of Beloveds: Love and the Beloved in Early-Modern Ottoman and European Culture and Society.* Durham: Duke University Press, 2005.

Arberry, Arthur J. *The Chester Beatty Library: A Handlist of the Arabic Manuscripts.* 8 vols. Dublin: Hodges Figgis & Co. Ltd, 1949.

Atıl, Esin. *Renaissance of Islam: Art of the Mamluks.* Washington, DC: Smithsonian Press, 1981.

Ayalon, David. 'The Muslim City and the Mamluk Military Aristocracy'. *Proceedings of the Israel Academy of Sciences and Humanities* 2 (1968): 311–29.

Ayalon, David. 'Discharges from Service, Banishments and Imprisonments in Mamlūk Society'. *Israel Oriental Studies* 2 (1972): 25–50.

Baer, Eva. *The Human Figure in Islamic Art: Inheritances and Islamic Transformations.* Costa Mesa, CA: Mazda Publishers, 2004.

Bailey, H. W. *Zoroastrian Problems in the Ninth-Century Books.* Oxford: Clarendon Press, 1943.

Baker, Naomi. *Plain Ugly: The Unattractive Body in Early Modern Culture.* Manchester and New York: Manchester University Press, 2010.

Bakhit, Muhammad Adnan. 'The Christian Population of the Province of Damascus in the Sixteenth Century', in *Christians and Jews in the Ottoman Empire: The Functioning of a Plural Society*, pp. 19–66, ed. Benjamin Braude and Bernard Lewis. New York: Holmes and Meier Publishers, 1982a.

Bakhit, Muhammad Adnan. *The Ottoman Province of Damascus in the Sixteenth Century.* Beirut: Librairie du Liban, 1982b.

Bakhtin, Mikhail. *Speech Genres*, ed. Carol Emerson and Michael Holquist. Austin: University of Texas Press, 1986.

Barbe-Gall, Françoise. *How to Read a Painting*. London: Francis Lincoln Ltd, 2010.

Barbier de Meynard, M. A.-C. 'Surnoms et sobriquets dans la littérature arabe'. *JA* 9 (March–April 1907): 173–244.

Barska, Anna. 'Ways of Understanding Body in the Maghreb'. *Hemispheres* 21 (2006): 17–29.

Bartlett, Jennifer, Sheila Black and Michael Northen (eds) *Beauty is a Verb: The New Poetry of Disability*. El Paso, TX: Cinco Puntos, 2011.

Basham, A. L. 'The Hoysaḷas: A Medieval Indian Royal Family', *BSOAS* 22.1/3 (1959): 165–7.

Bashir, Shahzad. 'Shah Isma'il and the Qizilbash: Cannibalism in the Religious History of Early Safavid Iran'. *History of Religions* 45.3 (2006): 234–56.

Bashir, Shahzad. *Sufi Bodies: Religion and Society in Medieval Islam.* New York: Columbia University Press, 2011.

Bauer, Thomas. *Liebe und Liebesdichtung in der arabischen Welt des 9. und 10. Jahrhunderts: eine literatur- und mentalitätsgeschichtliche Studie des arabischen Gazal.* Wiesbaden: Harrassowitz, 1998.

Bauer, Thomas. 'Literarische Anthologien der Mamlūkenzeit', in *Die Mamluken. Studien zu ihrer Geschichte und Kultur. Zum Gedenken an Ulrich Haarmann (1942–1999)*, pp. 71–122, ed. Stephan Conermann and Anja Pistor-Hatam. Schenefeld: EB-Verlag, 2003.

Bauer, Thomas. 'Ibn Ḥajar and the Arabic Ghazal of the Mamluk Age', in *Ghazal as World Literature*, 1, pp. 35–55, ed. Thomas Bauer and Angelika Neuwirth. Beirut: Ergon Verlag, 2005.

Bauer, Thomas. 'Mamluk Literature: Misunderstandings and New Approaches'. *MSR* 9.2 (2005b): 105–32.

Bazna, Maysaa S. and Tarek A. Hatab. 'Disability in the Qur'an: The Islamic Alternative to Defining, Viewing, and Relating to Disability'. *Journal of Religion, Disability and Health* 9.1 (2005): 5–27.

Behrens-Abouseif, Doris. *Beauty in Arabic Culture.* Princeton: Markus Wiener, 1999.

Berlekamp, Persis. 'From Iraq to Fars: Tracking Cultural Transformations in the 1322 Qazwīnī ʿAjāʾib Manuscript', in *Arab Painting: Text and Image in Illustrated Arabic Manuscripts*, ed. Anna Contadini. Leiden: Brill, 2010, pp. 73–91.

Bonebakker, Seeger A. *Some Early Definitions of the Tawriya and Ṣafadī's Fadd al-Xitam ᶜan at-Tawriya wa-l-Istixdam*. The Hague: Moulton & Co., 1966.

Borg, Alexander. 'Towards a History and Typology of Color Categorization in Colloquial Arabic', in *Anthropology of Color: Interdisciplinary Multilevel Modeling*, ed. Robert E. MacLaury, Galina V. Paramei and Don Dedrick. Amsterdam: John Benjamins Publishing, 2007, pp. 263–93.

Bos, Gerrit. 'Jewish Traditions on Strengthening Memory and Leone Modena's Evaluation'. *Jewish Studies Quarterly* (1995): 39–58.

Bos, Gerrit. '*Balādhur* (Marking-Nut): A Popular Medieval Drug for Strengthening Memory'. *BSOAS* 59.2 (1996): 229–36.

Bosworth, C. E. *The Mediaeval Islamic Underworld: The Banū Sāsān in Arabic Society and Literature*. 2 vols. Leiden: E. J. Brill, 1976.

Bouhdiba, Abdelwahab. *Sexuality in Islam*, trans. Alan Sheridan. London: Saqi Books, 1998.

Broadbridge, Anne. 'Academic Rivalry and the Patronage System in Fifteenth-Century Egypt: Al-ᶜAyni, Al-Maqrizi, and Ibn Hajar al-ᶜAsqalani'. *MSR* 3 (1999): 85–107.

Brockelmann, Carl. *Geschichte der arabischen Litteratur*. 2 vols. Leiden: E. J. Brill, 1943–.

Brockelmann, Carl. *Geschichte der arabischen Litteratur: Supplementband*. 3 vols. Leiden: E. J. Brill, 1943–.

al-Bustānī, Fuʾād Afrām (ed.). *Dāʾirat al-maᶜārif: qāmūs ᶜāmm li-kull fann wa-maṭlab*. 15 vols. Beirut: s.n., 1956.

Chamberlain, Michael. *Knowledge and Social Practice in Medieval Damascus*. New York: Cambridge University Press, 1994.

Chebel, Malek. *Le corps dans la tradition au Maghreb*. Paris: Presses Universitaires de France, 1984.

Chipman, Leigh. *The World of Pharmacy and Pharmacists in Mamlūk Cairo*. Leiden: E. J. Brill, 2010.

Conermann, Stephan. 'Ibn Ṭūlūn (d. 955/1548): Life and Works'. *MSR* 8.1 (2004): 115–39.

Coomaraswamy, Ananda K. 'The Buddha's cūḍā, Hair, uṣṇīṣa, and Crown'. *Journal of the Royal Asiatic Society of Great Britain and Ireland* 4 (October 1928): 815–41.

Cooperson, Michael. *Classical Arabic Biography: The Heirs of the Prophet in the Age of al-Maʾmūn*. New York: Cambridge University Press, 2000.

Coussonet, Patrice. 'Pour une lecture historique des "Mille et Une Nuits": Essai d'analyse du conte des deux vizirs égyptiens'. *Institut des Belles Lettres Arabes* (1985): 85–115.

Creswell, K. A. C. *The Muslim Architecture of Egypt*. 2 vols. New York: Hacker Art Books, 1979.

Derrett, J. Duncan M. *The Hoysaḷas: A Medieval Indian Royal Family*. Madras: Oxford University Press, 1957.

Dols, Michael. *The Black Death in the Middle East.* Princeton: Princeton University Press, 1977.
Dols, Michael. 'Leprosy in Medieval Arabic Medicine'. *Journal of the History of Medicine and Allied Sciences* 34.3 (July 1979): 314–33.
Dols, Michael. 'The Leper in Islamic Society'. *Speculum* 58.4 (October 1983): 891–916.
Dols, Michael. *Majnūn: The Madman in Medieval Islamic Society.* New York: Oxford University Press, 1992.
Dreifus, Claudia. 'Living and Studying Alopecia'. *The New York Times.* 27 December 2010, p. D2.
Elgood, C. 'On the Significance of al-Baras and al-Bahaq'. *Journal of the Proceedings of the Asiatic Society of Bengal* 27 (1931): 177–81.
El-Rouayheb, Khaled. *Before Homosexuality in the Arab-Islamic World, 1500–1800.* Chicago: University of Chicago Press, 2005.
Encyclopaedia of the Qur'an. 6 vols, ed. Jane Dammen McAuliffe. Leiden: E. J. Brill, 2001.
Encyclopedia of Women and Islamic Cultures. 3 vols, ed. Suad Joseph. Leiden: E. J. Brill, 2003.
Ettinghausen, Richard. *Arab Painting.* New York: Rizzoli, 1977.
Ferhat, Halima. *Le Maghreb aux XIIIème siècles: les siècles de la foi.* Casablanca: s.n., 1993.
Fernandes, Leonor. 'The Foundation of Baybars al-Jashankir: Its Waqf, History, and Architecture'. *Muqarnas* 4 (1987): 21–42.
Fernandes, Leonor. *The Evolution of a Sufi Institution in Mamluk Egypt: The Khanqah.* Berlin: K. Schwartz, 1988.
Ferry, Anne. *Tradition and the Individual Poem: An Inquiry into Anthologies.* Stanford: Stanford University Press, 2001.
Fischer, A. 'Arab. *baṣīr* "scharfsichtig" per antiphrasin = "blind"', *ZDMG* 61 (1907): 425–34.
Frembgen, J. W. 'Honour, Shame, and Bodily Mutilation: Cutting Off the Nose Among Tribal Societies in Pakistan'. *JRAS* 16 (2006): 243–60.
Frenkel, Yehoshu'a. 'Women in Late Mamluk Damascus in the Light of Audience Certificates (*Samāʿāt*)', in *Egypt and Syria in the Fatimid, Ayyubid and Mamluk Eras*, pp. 409–23, ed. Urbain Vermeulen and Jo van Steenbergen. Leuven: Peeters, 2006.
Friedmann, Yohanan. 'Finality of Prophethood in Sunnī Islām'. *JSAI* 7 (1986): 177–215.
Fuess, Albrecht. 'Sultans with Horns: The Political Significance of Headgear in the Mamluk Empire'. *MSR* 12.2 (2008): 71–94.
Ghaly, Mohammed. 'Islam en Handicap: theologische perspectieven'. *Theologisch Debat* 2.3 (2005): 20–3.
Ghaly, Mohammed. *Islam and Disability: Perspectives in Theory and Jurisprudence.* London and New York: Routledge, 2010.
Giladi, Avner. '"The Child Was Small . . . Not So the Grief for Him": Sources,

Structure, and Content of al-Sakhāwī's Consolation Treatise for Bereaved Parents'. *Poetics Today* 14.2 (1993): pp. 367–86.

Giladi, Avner. 'Islamic Consolation Treatises for Bereaved Parents: Some Bibliographical Notes'. *SI* 81 (1995): 197–202.

Goldziher, Ignaz. 'Muhammedanischer Aberglaube über Gedächtniskraft und Vergesslichkeit, mit Parallelen aus der jüdischen Litteratur', in *Festschrift zum siebzigsten Geburtstage A. Berliners*, pp. 131–55. Frankfurt am Main: J. Kauffmann, 1903.

Goldziher, Ignaz. *Muslim Studies*, ed. S. M. Stern, trans. S. M. Stern and C. R. Baker. Chicago: Aldine Publishing Company, 1973.

Grabar, Oleg and Mika Natif. 'The Story of Portraits of the Prophet Muḥammad'. *SI* 96 (2004): 19–38 + 4 plates.

Grafton, Anthony. *The Footnote: A Curious History*. Cambridge, MA: Harvard University Press, 1999.

Hafejee, A. et. al. 'Traditional Tattoo Treatment Trauma'. *British Journal of Dermatology* 153, suppl. 1 (2006): 62.

Hafsi, Bedhioufi. *Corps et traditions islamiques: divisions ontologiques et ritualités du corps*. Tunis: Noir sur Blanc, 2000.

Haj, Fareed. *Disability in Antiquity*. New York: Philosophical Library, 1970.

Haldane, Duncan. *Mamluk Painting*. Warminster: Aris and Phillips, 1978.

Halevi, Leor. *Muhammad's Grave: Death Rites and the Making of Islamic Society*. New York: Columbia University Press, 2007.

Halevi, Leor. 'Christian Impurity versus Economic Necessity: A Fifteenth-Century Fatwa on European Paper'. *Speculum* 83 (2008): 917–45.

Hamori, Andras and Thomas Bauer. 'Anthologies,' in *EI*^{3}, ed. Gudrun Krämer, Denis Matringe, John Nawas and Everett Rowson. Leiden: E. J. Brill, 2008. Brill Online. University of Michigan-Ann Arbor. <http://www.encislam.brill.nl.proxy.lib.umich.edu/subscriber/entry?entry=ei3_COM-0031>

Ḥawwā, Muḥammad b. Maḥmūd. *Ḥuqūq dhawī al-iḥtiyājāt al-khāṣṣah fī al-sharī^{c}at al-Islāmiyya*. Beirut: Dār Ibn Ḥazm li'l-ṭibā^{c}a wa'l-nashr wa'l-tawzī^{c}, 2010.

al-Hīla, Muḥammad al-Ḥabīb. *Al-Taʾrīkh wa'l-muʾarrikhūn bi-Makka min al-qarn al-thālith al-hijrī ilá al-qarn al-thālith ^{c}ashar: jam^{c} wa-^{c}arḍ wa-ta^{c}rīf*. Mecca: Muʾassasat al-furqān li'l-turāth al-islāmī, 1994.

Hillenbrand, Carole. 'Aspects of al-Ghazali's Views on Beauty', in *Gott ist schön und Er liebt die Schönheit: Festschrift für Annemarie Schimmel zum 7. April 1992*, pp. 249–65, ed. Alma Giese and J. Bürgel. Bern and New York: Peter Lang, 1994.

Hourani, Albert. *A History of the Arab Peoples*. Cambridge, MA: Harvard University Press, 1991.

Howell, Paul P. and John A. Allan. *The Nile: Sharing a Scarce Resource: A Historical and Technical Review of Water Management and of Economical and Legal Issues*. New York: Cambridge University Press, 1994.

Hunwick, John O. 'An Andalusian in Mali: A Contribution to the Biography of Abū Isḥāq al-Sāḥilī, c. 1290–1346'. *Paideuma* 36 (1990): 59–66.

Hütteroth, Wolf-Dieter and Kamal Abdulfattah. *Historical Geography of Palestine, Transjordan and Southern Syria in the Late Sixteenth Century*. Erlangen: Palm und Enke, 1977.

Ibn Ḥumayd, Muḥammad b. ᶜAbd Allāh. *Al-Suḥub al-wābila ᶜalá ḍarāʾiḥ al-ḥanābila*. s.l.: Maktabat al-Imām Aḥmad, 1989.

ᶜInānī, Muḥammad Zakariyya. *Al-Nuṣūṣ al-ṣiqilliyya min shiᶜr Ibn Qalāqis al-Iskandarī (567 AH) wa-āthārihi al-nathriyya*. Cairo: Dār al-maᶜārif, 1982.

Irwin, Robert. *The Arabian Nights: A Companion*. New York: Routledge, 1994.

Jacques, R. Kevin. 'The Other Rabīᶜ: Biographical Traditions and the Development of Early Shāfiᶜī Authority'. *Islamic Law and Society* 14.2 (2007): 143–79.

James, David. 'Arab Painting, 358 A.H./969 A.D.–1112 A.H./1700 A.D.'. *Mārg: A Magazine of the Arts* 29.3 (June 1976): 11–50.

al-Jammāl, Aḥmad Ṣādiq. *Al-Adab al-ᶜāmmī fī miṣr fī al-ᶜaṣr al-mamlūkī*. Cairo: Al-Dār al-qawmiyya, 1966.

Jarus, Owen. 'Long Pilgrimages Revealed in Ancient Sudan Art'. *Live Science*, 3 November 2011. <http://www.livescience.com/16854-sudan-yields-medieval-art-signs-long-pilgrimages.html>

Jayyusi, Salma Khadra (ed.). *Classical Arabic Stories: An Anthology*. New York: Columbia University Press, 2010.

Karamustafa, Ahmet. *God's Unruly Friends: Dervish Groups in the Islamic Later Middle Period, 1200–1550*. Oxford: OneWorld, 2006.

Kashani-Sabet, Firoozeh. 'The Historical Study of Disability in Modern Iran'. *Iranian Studies* 43.2 (2010): 167–95.

Kawash, Sabri Khalid. 'Ibn Ḥajar al-Asqalānī (1372–1449 A.D.): A Study of the Background, Education, and Career of a ᶜĀlim in Egypt'. PhD dissertation. Princeton University, 1969.

Kerner, Jaclynne. 'Art in the Name of Science: Illustrated Manuscripts of the *Kitāb al-diryāq*'. PhD dissertation. Institute of Fine Arts, New York University, 2004.

al-Kharsah, Muḥammad Khālid. 'Tarjamat al-muʾallif', in *Nujūm al-masā takshuf maᶜānī al-rasā li'l-ṣāliḥāt min al-nisāʾ*, pp. 14–23, ed. Muḥammad Khālid al-Kharsah. Damascus: Maktabat al-bayrūtī, 1990.

al-Khiyamī, Ṣalāḥ Muḥammad. 'Jamāl al-Dīn Yūsuf b. ᶜAbd al-Hādī al-Maqdisī al-Dimashqī, al-mutawaffa sanat 909 H: ḥayāt wa-āthāruhu l-makhṭūṭa wa'l-maṭbūᶜa'. *Majallat Maᶜhad al-Makhṭūṭāt al-ᶜArabiyya* 26.2 (1982): 775–809.

Khuri, Fuad. *The Body in Islamic Culture*. London: Saqi Books, 2001.

Kilito, Abdelfattah. *The Author and His Doubles: Essays on Classical Arabic Culture*, trans. Michael Cooperson. Syracuse: Syracuse University Press, 2001.

Kilpatrick, Hilary. 'Abū l-Farağ's Profile of Poets: A 4th/10th Century Essay at the History and Sociology of Arabic Literature'. *Arabica* 44.1 (1997): 94–128.

Kugle, Scott. 'The Heart of Ritual is the Body: Anatomy of an Islamic Devotional Manual of the Nineteenth Century'. *Journal of Ritual Studies* 17.1 (2003): 42–60.

Kugle, Scott. *Sufis and Saints' Bodies: Mysticism, Corporeality, and Sacred Power in Islam*. Chapel Hill: University of North Carolina Press, 2007.

Labbé, Theola. 'A Legacy Hidden in Plain Sight'. *Washington Post*. 11 January 2004, p. A01.

Lagrange, Frédéric. 'The Obscenity of the Vizier', in Kathryn Babayan and Afsaneh Najmabadi (eds), *Islamicate Sexualities: Translations Across Temporal Geographies of Desire*, pp. 161–203. Cambridge, MA: Harvard University Press, 2008.

Leder, Stefan. *Das Korpus al-Haiṯam ibn ᶜAdī (st. 207/822): Herkunft, Überlieferung, Gestalt früher Texte der aḫbār Literatur*. Frankfurt am Main: Klostermann, 1991.

Leder, Stefan. 'Charismatic Scripturalism: The Hanbali Maqdisis of Damascus'. *Der Islam* 74 (1997): 279–304.

Lozano Cámara, Indalecio. 'Un Fragmento del *Kitāb rāḥat al-arwāḥ fī l-ḥašīš wa-l-rāḥ*'. *Miscelanea de Estudios Arabes y Hebraicos* 38 (1989–90): 163–83.

Lozano Cámara, Indalecio. 'Un Nuevo Fragmento del *Kitāb rāḥat al-arwāḥ fī al-ḥašīš wa al-rāḥ* de Taqī al-Dīn al-Badrī'. *BEO* 49 (1997): 235–48.

Maghen, Ze'ev. *Virtues of the Flesh: Passion and Purity in Early Islamic Jurisprudence*. Leiden: E. J. Brill, 2005.

Mahdi, Muhsin. *The Thousand and One Nights*. Leiden: E. J. Brill, 1995.

Malti-Douglas, Fedwa. 'Yûsuf ibn ᶜAbd al-Hâdî and His Autograph of the *Wuqûᶜ al-Balâ bil-Bukhl wal-Bukhalâ*'. *BEO* 31 (1979): 17–50.

Malti-Douglas, Fedwa. '*Mentalités* and Marginality: Blindness and Mamluk Civilisation', in *The Islamic World from Classical to Modern Times: Essays in Honour of Bernard Lewis*, pp. 211–37, ed. C. Issawi, C. E. Bosworth, R. Savory and A. L. Udovitch. Princeton: Darwin Press, 1989.

Marmon, Shaun. 'Black Slaves in Mamlūk Narratives: Representations of Transgression'. *Al-Qanṭara* 28.2 (2007): 435–64.

Matar, Nabil. 'Confronting Decline in Early Modern Arabic Thought'. *Journal of Early Modern History* 9.1–2 (2005): 51–78.

Mazard, Eisel. 'The Buddha Was Bald . . . But Is Everywhere Depicted with a Full Head of Hair'. *New Mandala*. 30 December 2010. <http://asiapacific.anu.edu.au/newmandala/2010/12/30/the-buddha-was-bald/>

McGinn, Bernard. 'Portraying Antichrist in the Middle Ages', in Werner Verbeke, Daniel Verhelst and Andries Welkenhuysen (eds), *The Use and Abuse of Eschatology in the Middle Ages*, pp. 1–48. Leuven: Leuven University Press, 1988.

McRuer, Robert. *Crip Theory: Cultural Signs of Queerness and Disability*. New York: New York University Press, 2006.

Melchert, Christopher. *Ahmad ibn Hanbal.* Oxford: OneWorld Publications, 2006.

Meri, Josef and Jere L. Bacharach (eds). *Medieval Islamic Civilization: An Encyclopedia*, 1st edn. New York: Routledge, 2006.

Metzler, Irina. 'Disability in the Middle Ages: Impairment at the Intersection of Historical Inquiry and Disability Studies'. *History Compass* 9.1 (2011): 45–60.

Metzler, Irina. 'What's in a Name? Considering the Onomastics of Disability in the Middle Ages', in W. Turner and T. Pearman (eds), *Disabilities of Medieval Europe*. Lampeter: Edwin Mellen Press, forthcoming.

Miles, M. 'Signing in the Seraglio: Mutes, Dwarfs and Jestures at the Ottoman Court 1500–1700'. *Disability and Society* 15 (2000): 115–34.

Milstein, Rachel. *Miniature Painting in Ottoman Baghdad.* Costa Mesa, CA: Mazda Publishers, 1990.

Milstein, Rachel and Bilha Moor. 'Wonders of a Changing World: Late Illustrated *ʿAjāʾib* Manuscripts (Part I)'. *JSAI* 32 (2006): 1–48.

Mirzoeff, Nicholas. 'Framed: The Deaf in the Harem', in *Deviant Bodies: Critical Perspectives on Difference in Science and Popular Culture*, pp. 49–77, ed. Jennifer Terry and Jacqueline Urla. Bloomington: Indiana University Press, 1995.

Mitchell, Piers. 'Pre-Columbian Treponemal Disease from 14th-Century AD Safed, Israel, and Implications for the Medieval Eastern Mediterranean'. *American Journal of Physical Anthropology* 121.2 (2003): 117–24.

Miura, Toru. 'The Ṣāliḥiyya Quarter in the Suburbs of Damascus: Its Formation, Structure, and Transformation in the Ayyūbid and Mamlūk Periods'. *BEO* 47 (1995): 129–81.

Mokni, Mourad. 'La peau et ses maladies d'après un traité de médecine tardif'. Master's thesis. Université de Tunis, 2006.

Muṣṭafá, Shākir. *Madīna li'l-ʿilm: Āl Qudāma wa'l-Ṣāliḥiyya.* Damascus: Dār Ṭalās, 1997.

Nawas, John. 'A Profile of the *mawālī ʿulamāʾ*', in *Patronate and Patronage in Early and Classical Islam*, pp. 454–80, ed. Monique Bernards and John Nawas. Leiden: E. J. Brill, 2005.

Peirce, Leslie. *Morality Tales: Law and Gender in the Ottoman Court of Aintab.* Berkeley: University of California Press, 2003.

Pellat, Charles. 'Nouvel essai d'inventaire de l'oeuvre Ġahizienne'. *Arabica* 31 (1984): 117–64.

Peters, Rudolph. *Crime and Punishment in Islamic Law: Theory and Practice from the Sixteenth to the Twenty-First Century.* Cambridge: Cambridge University Press, 2005.

Petry, Carl F. *The Civilian Elite of Cairo in the Later Middle Ages.* Princeton: Princeton University Press, 1981.

Petukhova, Lynn et al. 'Genome-wide association study in alopecia areata implicates both innate and adaptive immunity'. *Nature* 466.1 (1 July 2010): 113–18.

Piamenta, Moshe. *A Dictionary of Post-classical Yemeni Arabic*. 2 vols. Leiden: E. J. Brill, 1990.
Popovic, Alexandre. *The Revolt of African Slaves in Iraq in the 3rd/9th Century*. Princeton: Markus Wiener, 1998.
Qayyum, Abdul. 'Al-Ḥijāzī, the Author of *Nawādir al-Akhbār*'. *Islamic Culture* 18 (July 1944): 254–68.
Rabbat, Nasser O. *The Citadel of Cairo: A New Interpretation of Royal Mamluk Architecture*. Leiden: E. J. Brill, 1995.
Raḥmānī, Aftab Aḥmad. *The Life and Works of Ibn Hajar al-Asqalani*. Bangladesh: Islamic Foundation Bangladesh, 2000.
Rapoport, Yossef. *Marriage, Money and Divorce in Medieval Islamic Society*. Cambridge: Cambridge University Press, 1999.
Reid, Megan. 'Exemplars of Excess: Devotional Piety in Medieval Islam, 1200–1450 CE'. PhD dissertation. Princeton University, 2005.
Rieu, Charles and W. Cureton (eds). *Catalogus codicum manuscriptorum orientalium qui in Museo Britannico asservantur Pars secunda, codices arabicos amplectens*. London: British Museum, 1846–71.
Rispler-Chaim, Vardit. *Disability in Islamic Law*. New York: Springer, 2006.
Robinson, Chase F. 'Neck-Sealing in Early Islam'. *JESHO* 48.3 (2005): 401–41.
Rosenthal, Franz. '"Blurbs" (*taqrîẓ*) from Fourteenth-Century Egypt'. *Oriens* 27 (1981): 177–96.
Rosenthal, Franz. *A History of Muslim Historiography*. Leiden: E. J. Brill, 1968.
Rosenthal, Franz. 'Male and Female: Described and Compared', in J. W. Wright and Everett K. Rowson (eds), *Homoeroticism in Classical Arabic Literature*, pp. 24–54, ed.. New York: Columbia University Press, 1997.
Rosenthal, Franz. *The Herb: Hashish versus Medieval Muslim Society*. Leiden: E. J. Brill, 1971.
Rowson, Everett. E-mail to the author. 9 November 2006.
Sabra, Adam. *Poverty and Charity in Medieval Islam: Mamluk Egypt, 1250–1517*. Cambridge: Cambridge University Press, 2000.
Sadan, Joseph. 'Kings and Craftsmen, a Pattern of Contrasts: On the History of a Medieval Arabic Humoristic Form (Part I)'. *SI* 56 (1982): 7–53.
Sadān, Yūsuf. *Al-Adab al-ᶜarabī al-hāzil wa-nawādir al-thuqalāᵓ: al-ᶜāhāt wa'l-masāwiᵓ al-insāniyya wa-makānatuhā fī al-adab al-rāqī*. ᶜAkkā: Maktabat wa-Maṭbaᶜat al-Sarūjī, 1983.
Sadān, Yūsuf. 'Risāla fī al-damāma li-Muḥammad b. Ḥamza al-Kūzliḥṣārī al-Īdīnī wa-mā sabaqahā min muwāqif al-udabāᵓ min al-ᶜāhāt wa'l-qabḥ'. *Al-Karmil* 9 (1988): 7–33.
Sanders, Paula. 'Gendering the Ungendered Body: Hermaphrodites in Medieval Islamic Law', in Nikki R. Keddie and Beth Baron (eds), *Women in Middle Eastern History: Shifting Boundaries in Sex and Gender*, pp. 74–98. New Haven: Yale University Press, 1991.
Sardar, Marika. 'Islamic Art of the Deccan', in *Heilbrunn Timeline of Art History*.

New York: The Metropolitan Museum of Art, 2000–. <http://www.metmuseum.org/toah/hd/decc/hd_decc.htm>

Savage-Smith, Emilie and Peter Pormann. *Medieval Islamic Medicine*, Washington, DC: Georgetown Univesity Press, 2007.

Savage-Smith, Emilie. 'Anatomical Illustration in Arabic Manuscripts', in *Arab Painting: Text and Image in Illustrated Arabic Manuscripts*, pp. 147–60, ed. Anna Contadini. Leiden: E. J. Brill, 2010.

Scalenghe, Sara. 'Being Different: Intersexuality, Blindness, Deafness, and Madness in Ottoman Syria'. PhD dissertation. Georgetown University, 2006.

Scalenghe, Sara. *The Body Different: Disability in the Middle East, 1500–1800*. Cambridge: Cambridge University Press, forthcoming.

Schimmel, Annemarie. *And Muhammad Is His Messenger: The Veneration of the Prophet in Islamic Piety*. Chapel Hill: University of North Carolina Press, 1985.

Schimmel, Annemarie. *Islamic Names*. Edinburgh: Edinburgh University Press, 1989.

Schöller, Marco. *The Living and the Dead in Islam: Studies in Arabic Epitaphs*. 2 vols. Wiesbaden: Harrassowitz, 2004.

Schweik, Susan. *The Ugly Laws: Disability in Public*. New York: New York University Press, 2009.

Shahin, Mamdouh M. A. *Hydrology and Water Resources of Africa*. New York: Springer, 2002.

Shamir, Orit and Alisa Baginski. 'Medieval Mediterranean Textiles, Basketry, and Cordage Newly Excavated in Israel', in *Towns and Material Culture in the Medieval Middle East*, pp. 136–57, ed. Yaacov Lev. Leiden: E. J. Brill, 2002.

Shani, Raya Y. 'Noah's Ark and the Ship of Faith in Persian Painting: From the Fourteenth to the Sixteenth-Century'. *JSAI* 27 (2002): 127–203.

al-Shaṭṭī, Muḥammad Jamīl. *Mukhtaṣar ṭabaqāt al-ḥanābila*. Damascus: Maṭbaᶜat al-taraqī, 1920.

Shoshan, Boaz. *Popular Culture in Medieval Cairo*. Cambridge: Cambridge University Press, 1993.

Shoshan, Boaz. 'The State and Madness in Medieval Islam'. *IJMES* 35 (2003): 329–40.

Shubayr, Muḥammad ᶜUthmān. *Al-Imām Yūsuf b. ᶜAbd al-Hādī al-Ḥanbalī wa-atharuhu fī al-fiqh al-Islāmī*. Amman: Dār al-furqān, 2001.

Siebers, Tobin. *The Mirror of Medusa*. Berkeley and Los Angeles: University of California Press, 1983.

Siebers, Tobin. *Disability Aesthetics*. Ann Arbor: University of Michigan Press, 2010.

Simmons, Ann M. 'Back to Africa, from Iraq'. *Los Angeles Times*. 14 January 2004, pp. A1, A14.

Smart, J. R. 'The Muwaššaḥāt of al-Šihāb al-Ḥijāzī', in Federico Corriente and Angel Sáenz-Badillos (eds), *Poesía estrófica; actas del Primer Congreso*

Internacional sobre Paralelos Romances (Madrid, diciembre de 1989), pp. 347–56. Madrid: Instituto de Cooperación con el Mundo Arabe, 1991.

Staffa, Susan Jane. *Conquest and Fusion: The Social Evolution of Cairo,* A.D. *642–1850*. Leiden: E. J. Brill, 1977.

Staph. 'Dell'anacardio', trans. Giuseppe Belluomini. *Annali di medicina omiopatica per la Sicilia* 4 (1838): 318–60.

Stephan, Stephan H. 'Lunacy in Palestinian Folklore'. *Journal of the Palestine Oriental Society* 5 (1925): 1–16.

Stierlin, Henri and Anne Stierlin. *Splendours of an Islamic World: Mamluk Art in Cairo, 1250–1517*. New York: Tauris Parke Books, 1997.

Ṭalas, Muḥammad Asᶜad. 'Muqaddima', in Yūsuf b. ᶜAbd al-Hādī, *Thimār al-maqāṣid fī dhikr al-masājid*, pp. 9–56, ed. Muḥammad Asᶜad Ṭalas. Beirut: s.n., 1943.

Tarawneh, Taha Thalji. *The Province of Damascus during the Second Mamluk Period (784/1382–922/1516)*. Jordan: Publications of the Deanship of Research and Graduate Studies, Muᵓtah University, 1994.

Tezcan, Baki. '*Dispelling the Darkness*: The Politics of "Race" in the Early Seventeenth-Century Ottoman Empire in the Light of the Life and Work of Mullah Ali'. *International Journal of Turkish Studies* 13.1 (2007): 85–95.

Tietze, Andreas. *Muṣṭafā ᶜĀlī's Description of Cairo of 1599: Text, Transliteration, Translation, Notes*. Vienna: Verlag der Österreichischen Akademie der Wissenschaften, 1975.

van Gelder, Geert Jan. 'Mirror for Princes or Vizor for Viziers: The Twelfth-Century Arabic Popular Encyclopedia *Mufīd al-ᶜulūm* and Its Relationship with the Anonymous Persian *Baḥr al-fawāᵓid*'. *BSOAS* 64.3 (2001): 313–38.

van Gelder, Geert Jan. 'Beautifying the Ugly and Uglifying the Beautiful: The Paradox in Classical Arabic Literature'. *Journal of Semitic Studies* 48.2 (2003): 321–51.

van Gelder, Geert Jan. 'Kitāb al-Burṣān: Al-Jāḥiẓ on Right- and Lefthandedness', In *Al-Jāḥiẓ: A Muslim Humanist for Our Time*, pp. 239–52, ed. Arnim Heinemann et al. Beirut: Orient-Institut/Würzburg: Ergon Verlag, 2009.

Vesely, Rudolf. 'Das Taqrīẓ in der arabischen Literatur', in *Die Mamluken. Studien zu ihrer Geschichte und Kultur. Zum Gedenken an Ulrich Haarmann (1942–1999)*, ed. Stephan Conermann and Anja Pistor-Hatam. Hamburg: EB Verlag, 2003, pp. 379–85.

Vrolijk, Arnoud. *Bringing a Laugh to a Scowling Face: a study and critical edition of the "Nuzhat al-nufūs wa-muḍhik al-ᶜabūs" by ᶜAlī Ibn Sūdūn al-Bashbughāwī (Cairo 810/1407 – Damascus 868/1464)*. Leiden: Research School CNWS, School of Asian, African, and Amerindian Studies, 1998.

Wetzstein, G. J. 'Aus einem briefe des Herrn Consul Wetzstein an Prof. Fleischer', *ZDMG* 23 (1869): 309–13.

Wetzstein, G. J. 'Touching the Penis in Islamic Law'. *History of Religions* 44.2 (2004): 89–119.

Wilfong, Terry. 'Reading the Disjointed Body in Coptic: From Physical Modification to Textual Fragmentation', in *Changing Bodies, Changing Meanings: Studies on the Human Body in Antiquity*, pp. 116–36, ed. Dominic Montserrat. London and New York: Routledge, 1998.

Zanello, Fabio. *Hashish e Islam: tradizione e consumo, visioni e prescrizioni nella poesia, nella letteratura e nelle leggi*. Rome: Cooper and Castelvecchi, 2003.

Zannad-Bouchrara, Traki. *Symboliques corporelles et espaces musulmans*. Tunis: Cèrès, 1984.

Ze'evi, Dror. *Producing Desire: Changing Sexual Discourse in the Ottoman Middle East, 1500–1900*. Berkeley: University of California Press, 2006.

Zilfi, Madeline. 'Review of *The Body in Islamic Culture*', *MESA Bulletin* 39.2 (2005): 206–7.

Index